STUDIES IN

AMERICAN LITERATURE

STUDIES IN AMERICAN LITERATURE

MALLIKARJUN PATIL

PUBLISHERS & DISTRIBUTORS (P) LTD

7/22, Ansari Road, Darya Ganj, New Delhi
Tel.: +91-11-4077 5252, 2327 3880
E-mail: orders@atlanticbooks.com
Web: www.atlanticbooks.com

Reprint 2025, 2018

Published by Atlantic Publishers & Distributors (P) Ltd.

Printed & bound in India by Atlantic Print Services

Preface

As one can understand, reading is a pleasure in a civilized world. It provides us both knowledge and joy, apart from academic benefits. As for English literature, it is a treasure house of knowledge—both worldly and the other-worldly. I have read vastly the American literature as some other areas of English literature. My studies in American literature are related to my vast experience gained in the course of my studies at graduation, postgraduation and at research levels and from guidance to M. Phil. and Ph.D. students. This is purely an academic pursuit. Of course, American literature has been my area of specialization these years. Besides, as a creative writer, I have immensely enjoyed American literature.

The present work *Studies in American Literature* is like an anthology on seminal works in American literature. This is the fruit of my study in the area for the last ten years. The book presents a chronological account of American literature right from the beginning to the present day. Most of the great writers have been discussed at length. It contains articles on Franklin's *Autobiography*, Emerson's *Essays*, Thoreau's treatise *Walden*, and the novels of Hawthorne, Stowe, Melville, Twain, James, Fitzgerald, Faulkner, Hemingway, Steinbeck, Bellow, Amy Tan and Morrison. There are articles on the poetry of Whitman, Dickinson, Frost, Stevens, Cummings, Hughes, Ginsberg and Plath. Papers on African-American writings have also been included. I have enjoyed reading great writers like Emerson, Thoreau, Whitman, Hemingway and others. The study is quite fruitful. I believe that the volume will help the teachers, readers and researchers alike.

Mallikarjun Patil

Contents

Introduction

Wherever there are people there is literature. Literature is a record of human experience. It is people's impression of life. People write it in the form of dairies, letters, pamphlets, essays, poems, plays and stories.

American literature began with the first English colonies in Virginia and New England. These colonists brought with them the literary wealth of their countries. Most of these Americans were the English migrants who began writing in the 16th century.

Colonial Times in America: The man sometimes called the first American writer was Capt. John Smith (1580-1631). He was an adventurer and he wrote *A True Relation of Virginia* (1608) in which he describes the new land of Virginia. His *General History of Virginia* (1624) depicts his life in that place. William Byrd (1674-1744) best describes life in Virginia in his *History of the Dividing Line* (1841) and *Secret Diary* (1840). The new people were planters and lived a church life, while many people particularly in the South kept in isolation, so Southern literature came quite later. Much writing was done in New England. William Bradford (1590-1657) and John Winthrop (1588-1649) were the governors of Massachusetts and they wrote early records about their life amidst the natives.

The Influence of Puritanism: The pilgrims in their ship "Mayflower" landed in Cape Cod in 1620. Puritanism dominated American literature for the next 300 years. These New England settlers were Protestants who purified the practices of the Church of England from the Roman Catholicism. Therefore, such people are known as Puritans. Another group known as Separatists was separating from the Church of England. Both groups worshipped God in their own ways.

The Puritans believed the Bible as God-manifestation. So Harvard College was set up in 1636 for educating the people. Religious feeling prompted people to write. Cotton Mother (1663-1728), the leading clergyman of Boston (in 1700), wrote 400 books including *Magnalia Christi Americana* (1702, *Christ's Great Achievements in America*). The clergymen asked people to keep diaries and journals. Samuel Sewall's (1652-1730) *The Diary* and *Selling of Joseph* (1700) are the earliest anti-slavery pamphlets in America. The Puritans did not encourage imaginative literature except a little poetry. The first book to be published in America was a psalm book (1640). Michael Wigglesworth's *The Day of Doom* was a memorable religious treatise. Edward Taylor's (1642-1729) poetry on Christian life was important. Jonathan Edward was the last Puritan. Puritanism lost its hold as worldliness and scientific temper grew. Yet Puritanism was lovely and of strong moral nature.

The Shaping of the New Nation: During the last 30 years of the 18th century, Americans began writing about their government. Benjamin Franklin (1706-90) contributed a lot to the cause of Americanism. He practised a simple life, embodying the "American idea". In his pamphlet *Common Sense*, the French man Michel Guillaume Crevecoeur (1735-1813) declared what an American is.

Thomas Paine: He argued in favour of declaring American independence in 1776. George Washington appreciated Paine. Thomas Jefferson (1743-1826) said "all men are created equal". Then the Americans formed a union and a Constitution. Poets like John Trumbull (1750-1831) and Joel Barlow (1754-1812) and novelists like Susanna Rowson (1762-1824) and Charles Brockden Brown (1771-1810) wrote novels in patriotic fervor. Philip Freneau (1752-1832) pleaded for a native literature and Noah Webster compiled American dictionary of English language saying that "every nation should have its own customs, habits and language".

Literature of the Early Republic: The early American writers modelled themselves upon English writers. For example, William Cullen Brynt (1794-1878) imitated William Wordsworth; Washington Irving followed the style of Addison and Steele and James Fenimore Cooper (1789-1851) that of Scott. Yet American writing differed in content, character and setting. H.H. Brackenridge's (1748-1816) *Modern Chivalry* is about frontier life. Brynt sang the beauty of New England; Irving's stories *The Legend of Sleepy Hallow* and *Rip Van Winkle* are memorable. Cooper's *Leather Stocking Tales* represents the new world life. The South is depicted in John Kennedy's (1795-1870) *Swallow Barn* and William Gilmore Simms's (1806-70) *The Yemassee*. This extends upto 1835.

The Flowering of American Literature: The mid-19th century saw the beginning of the great American literature. The period 1850-55 marked American renaissance. New England was the centre of American literature and Ralph Waldo Emerson (1803-82) its prominent writer.

Emerson and Thoreau: Emerson, a clergyman, lecturer and essayist, preached that man is a relic of God. He said "Trust Thyself" in *Self Reliance*. He said it made no difference what one's work is or where one lives. He lived in Concord and wrote stirring prose that inspired the nation. His neighbor Henry David Thoreau (1817-62) lived by Emerson's precepts. Thoreau's *Walden* is an experiment in living an independent life. His essay "Civil Disobedience" worked a miracle. Mahatma Gandhi was inspired by it.

Popular New England Poets: Conventional poets were Oliver Wendell Holmes (1809-94), James Russell Lowell (1819-91), Henry Wadsworth Longfellow (1807-82) and John Greenleaf Whittier (1807-92). Longfellow is known for his *A Psalm of Life* while Whittier's *Barbara Frietchie* is a ballad.

Poe and Hawthorne: Poe was a major Southern writer. He wrote of timeless places and people. His poems "The Raven" and "Ulalume" are haunting and his detective and psychological stories like "The Fall of the House of Usher" are noteworthy. He was a famous critic. Hawthorne (1804-64) wrote splendid novels like *The Scarlet Letter*.

Herman Melville (1819-91): Hawthorne's friend Melville was another important writer. His novels *Typee* (1846) and *Omoo* (1847) speak of South Sea. His *Moby Dick* (1851) is a masterpiece.

Whitman—Poet of the People: Whitman, a mid-19th century poet, was unique. His *Leaves of Grass* (1855) is distinct in form and content. It is the first great poetic work of America. His poems like "Song of Myself" are patriotic in tone. He was a spokesman for the Americans.

Transition to the Modern Age: The Civil War (1860s) was a harsh experience. Abraham Lincoln's (1809-65) "Gettysburg Address" is a moving account of it. Henry Timrod (1828-67) and Paul Hayne (1830-66) wrote of confederacy. Sidney Lanier's (1842-81) *The Song of the Chattahoochee* is unique. Emily Dickinson's (1830-86) poetry about death and immortality is as important as Whitman's. She is another great American poet.

Regional Prose after the Civil War: The post-war years suited prose. Bret Harte's (1836-1902) *The Luck of Roaring Camp* (1868), Joel Chandler Harris's (1848-1908) stories about Uncle Romus, George Cable's (1844-1925) fiction about Creoles and Edward Eggleton's (1837-1902) *Hoosier Schoolmaster* (1971) are interesting. Harriet Beecher Stowe (1811-96) is best known for her anti-slavery novel *Uncle Tom's Cabin* (1852). New England's life is depicted in the works of Sarah Orne Jewett (1849-1909) and Mary Wilkins Freeman (1852-1930). These stories represented the realistic life.

Three major novelists of the time were Mark Twain (1835-1910), a self-educated man; Henry James (1843-1916), a cosmopolitan writer and William Howells (1837-1920), a man in-between and a friend of both. Twain's *The Adventures of Tom Sawyer* (1876) and *The Adventures of Huckleberry Finn* (1884) are masterpieces. James wrote of the Americans in Europe. His *The American* (1877) and *The Ambassadors* (1903) deal with international theme. Howells was a champion of realism as seen in his *Dr. Breen's Practices* (1881).

The Birth of Nationalism: Twain, Howells and James were realists. They left their marks on certain aspects of life. Later writers after 1900 took care of it. Stephen Crane's (1871-1900) *The Red Badge of Courage* (1895) portrayed slum life. Frank Norris's (1870-1902) *The Octopus* (1901) depicted the violence of economic life. Theodore Dresser's (1871-1945) *Sister Carrie*

(1900) and *American Tragedy* (1925) describe man's commercial life. The 19th century closed the gay novels. Now political corruption, violent conflicts and loss of religious certitude gave way to tragic novels. Henry Adams' (1838-1918) *The Education of Henry Adams* speaks of this mood in America.

Modern American Literature: The 20th century American literature differs from that of the earlier American literature in so far that modern literature is complex and technically more sophisticated. It is varied in content, simple in language, realistic and individualistic in approach.

Poetry in the Middle West: In 1912 Harriet Monroe (1860-1936) founded *Poetry* magazine, which encouraged all the great poets later. It discovered poets like Lee Masters (1869-1950), Vachel Lindsay (1879-1931) and Carl Sandburg (1878-1967).

Poets of Modern New England: Edwin Arlington Robinson's (1869-1935) *Trsitram* (1927) and Robert Frost's (1874-1963) poems like "Birches" and "Mending Wall" are noteworthy. Frost was a passionate and provocative poet.

T.S. Eliot (1888-1965): Though he got British citizenship he wrote about American themes. He is known for his new poetic technique. His *Prufrock* is known for modern man's phobia. His *The Waste Land* (1922), for which he got Nobel Prize, is an epoch-making poem. Eliot reflected the disillusionment of modern times. E.E. Cummings (1894-1962), like Emily Dickinson, wrote a new kind of poetry. He satirized modern pettiness and emptiness. Hart Crane (1899-1932), Wallace Stevens (1879-1955), Marianne Moore (1887-1972), Edna Vincent Millay (1892-1950), Stephen Vincent Benet (1898-1943), Elinor Wylie (1885-1928) and Sarah Teasdale (1884-1933) wrote poetry of delicate perception. Ogden Nash (1902-71) and Phyllis McGinley (1905-78) are known for skillful verse.

Modern American Drama: Modern American Drama takes a realistic approach. American playwrights like Elmer Rice (1892-1967), Sidney Kingsley (b. 1906) show life as it is lived. George Kaufman (1889-1961) and Marc Connelly (1890-1980) use expressionistic techniques. Thornton Wilder's (1897-1975)

Our Town was experimental. Maxwell Anderson's (1888-1959) *Winterset*, T.S. Eliot's *Murder in the Cathedral* are poetic dramas.

Eugene O'Neill—Leading American Playwright: O'Neill (1888-1953) as an experimental playwright is great. His *The Emperor Jones* (1920) and *The Hairy Ape* (1922) are unique—one-character plays. His *Mourning Becomes Electra* enacts Aeschylus's tragedy of Oresteia.

Williams and Miller: Tennessee Williams (1911-83) portrayed a decadent Southland in *A Streetcar Named Desire* (1947) and *The Glass Menagerie* (1844). Arthur Miller's (1915-2004) *Death of a Salesman* (1949) reveals the loneliness of modern man. His *The Crucible* (1953) speaks of the unknown fear.

Modern American Fiction: It is the prose fiction which has been most admired in the 20th century. Modern American novelists are many, varied and great.

Historical Novelists: If James Fenimore Cooper was a pioneer of American historical novels, Harvey Allen (1889-1949) and Margaret Mitchell (1900-49) achieved other kind of success. Allen's *Anthony Adverse* (1933) and Mitchell's *Gone with the Wind* (1936) are bestsellers. Other such novelists are Walter Edmonds and A.B. Guthrie.

Regional Novelists: Willa Catcher's (1875-1947) *O Pioneers* (1913) and *My Antonia* (1918) are about Nebraska. The Norwegian born O.E. Rolvaag's (1876-1931) *Giants in the Earth* and Ruth Suckow's (1892-1960) *The Folks* (1934) are good. The Southern regional novels include Edith Wharton's (1862-1937) *The House of Mirth* (1905), Ellen Glasgow's (1874-1945) *Barren Ground* (1925), John Marquand's (1893-1960) *The Late George Apley* (1937) and Pearl S. Buck's (1892-1973) *The Good Earth*.

Novels Depicting Their Times: These include F. Scott Fitzgerald's (1896-1940) *This Side of Paradise* (1920) which discusses about the roaring forties and *The Great Gatsby* (1925); and Sinclair Lewis's (1885-1951) *Babbitt* (1922), a satire. John Steinbeck's (1902-68) *The Grapes of Wrath* (1939) is about farmers's hard life; John Dos Passos's (1896-1970) *U.S.A.* (1938), a trilogy, is about depression. Thomas Wolfe's (1900-38) novel *Look Homeward, Angel* (1929) is a masterpiece.

Hemingway and Faulkner: Ernest Hemingway (1899-1961) and William Faulkner represented modern life, giving importance to moral values. Hemingway thinks courage is a paramount virtue. He says one must achieve "grace under pressure". His *The Sun Also Rises* (1926) and *The Old Man and the Sea* (1952) are the best; and Faulkner's South novels include *The Sound and the Fury* (1929) and *Absalom, Absalom!* (1936).

The Modern Short Story: Poe defines American short story. Best story writers (who are also novelists) include Ring Lardner (1885-1933), Sherwood Anderson (1876-1941), Katherine Anne Porter (1894-1980), Irwin Shaw (1913-84), William Saroyan (1908-81), John O'Hara (1905-70), John Cheever (1912-82) and J.D. Salinger (b. 1919).

American Literature since the 1950's: The recent American literature varied both in structure and content.

Fiction: Recent fiction is varied. It is epical, historical, spy, war and science fiction. Even regional novels like James Clavell's (b. 1924) novels such as *King Rat* (1962) and *Tai-Pan* (1966) are set in the Far East. James Michener's (b. 1907) *Hawaii* (1959) and *Covenant* (1980) and Herman Wouk's (b. 1915) *Winds of War* (1971) are historical. Journalistic novels include Alex Haley's (b. 1921) *Roots* (1926), Truman Capote's (1924-84) *In Cold Blood* (1966), Norman Mailer's (1923) *Fire on the Moon* and Thomas Wolfe's (1930) *The Right Stud*. Experimental novels include Vladimir Nabokov's (1899-1977) *Lolita* (1955), Kurt Vonnegut's (b. 1922) *Slaughterhouse Five* (1969), Joseph Heller's (b. 1923) *Catch-22* (1961), a war novel, Thomas Pynchon's (b. 1937) *Gravity Rainbow* (1973) and John Barth's (b. 1930) *Giles Goat Boy* (1966). The last one is a mythic novel. Popular novels were largely about regionalism, ethnicity, social criticism and women's emancipation.

Regional writers from the South like Faulkner, Welty and Warren are well known. Larry McMurthy's (b. 1936) novel *Horseman, Pass By* (1961) is a personal fiction and William

Styron's (b. 1925) *Confessions of Nat Turner* (1967) is a meditation on history. Reynolds Price (b. 1933) and Flannery O'Conner (1925-64) have written on religion. John Cheever's *Bullet Part* (1969) and John Updike's *Babbit* are about suburbs.

The Black American Writers: They did well in fiction. Ralph Ellison's (b. 1914) *Invisible Man* (1952), James Baldwin's (b. 1924) *Another Country* and Toni Morrison's (b. 1931) *Song of Solomon* (1977) use elements of folklore.

Eminent Jewish Novelists: These include Saul Bellow (b. 1915), Isaac Bashevis Singer (b. 1904), Philip Roth (b. 1933) and Bernard Malamud (b. 1914). Bellow's *Herzog* (1964) and *Mr. Sammler's Planet* (1970) are about Jewish intellectuals; Singer's novels like *The Slave* (1962) and *Enemies, A Love Story* (1972) are moving portraits of Jewish life. Roth's *My Life as a Man* (1974) is autobiographical. Malamud's novels like *God's Grace* (1982) speak of religion and cultural life.

Feminist Literature: It flourished with difficulty. Mary McCarthy's (b. 1912) play *If As It Lays* (1970), Sadra Henchman's (b. 1936) *Endangered Species* (1977), Cynthia Buchanan's (b. 1937) *Maiden* (1972), Marilyn French's (b. 1929) *The Woman's Room* (1977), Erica Jong's (b. 1942), *Fear of Flying* (1974), Lois Gould's (b. 1938) *Final Analysis* (1974), Sue Kaufman's (1926-77) *Falling Bodies* (1974), Judith Rossner's (b. 1935) *Emmeline* (1980), Alix Shulman's (b. 1932) *Burying Questions* (1935), Gail Godwin's (b. 1937) *Violet Clay* (1978) and Mary Gordon's (b. 1949) *Final Payments* (1978) are good works.

Drama: The experimental drama of the 1960's reduced the gap between life and art. There were drama groups like La Mama Experimental Theatre Club (1961), The Company Theatre (1967) and The Negro Ensemble Company (1966), encouraging new playwrights like Sam Shepard (b. 1943), Lonne Elder (b. 1931), Megan Terry (b. 1932) and Lanford Wilson (b. 1937). Lorraine Hansberry's (1930-65) *Raison in the Sun* was a realistic success. Imamu Baraka's (b. 1934) *The Duplex* (1970) used common situations.

Great playwrights of 60's and 70's are Edward Albee and Sam Shepard. Albee's *Who's Afraid of Virginia Woolf* (1962) shows a couple's turbulent married life. He is the first American absurd playwright. Shepard's *The Buried Child* (1978) and *La Turista* (1966) show his realistic approach. David Rabe (b. 1940), David Mamet (b. 1947) and Neil Simon (b. 1927) were other playwrights.

Poetry: American poetry of the 1960's and 70's had many schools of thought. Poets like Allen Ginsberg (b. 1926, known for his *Planet News*) and Adrienne Rich (b. 1929, known for his *Diving into the Wreck*) believed that poetry could transform reality. Ginsberg was a protest poet. John Ashbery (b. 1927) thought we live in an absurd world. These poets experimented with the length of line, rhythm, diction and syntax, to create a direct expression of poetic experience. In the 1950's John Berryman (1914-72, known for his *Dream Songs*) and Robert Lowell (1917-77, known for his *Life Studies*) wrote personal poetry. Other confessional poets are Anne Sexton (1928-74), W.D. Snodgrass (b. 1926) and Sylvia Plath (1932-63).

1950's Black Mountain Poets included Denise Levertov (b. 1923), Robert Creeley (b. 1926), Robert Duncan (b. 1919) and Charles Olson (1910-70). For Levertov, a poem was a process of perceiving and feeling. For Robert Bly (b. 1926), a poem expressed what we are just beginning to think. He used images. Ashbery, Frank O'Hara (1926-66) and Kenneth Koch (b. 1925) were of the New York School, which emphasized the need for separation of reality from perception of it. James Merrill's (b. 1926) *The Book of Ephraim* (1976) is a complex long poem. A.R. Ammons's (b. 1926) poetry is naturalistic.

Benjamin Franklin's *Autobiography*

1

Benjamin Franklin (1706-96) was a great printer, scientist, statesman and writer. His *Autobiography*, in spite of its pragmatic nature, is perennially popular. It is a prize from the past. It is a kind of moral tract for the future. It is seen as a revolutionary document—an assertion of proletarian dignity and the tangible portrayal of a mind confident enough to news from government. Indeed, Franklin was then known as one of the wisest men of Europe. During his term (1765-75) as an agent in England Franklin was considered as the quintessential American. He was indeed a noble savage. His character indicated to Europeans just what the provinces could produce.

In 1771 when Franklin was the agent for Pennsylvania (for the second term), his friends heard the story of his life and asked him to commit it to papers. So Franklin wrote 65 pages bringing his life unto 1730 (Sections 1-7) and stopped it for many years. When American Revolution was over, American government sent him as its Commissioner to France and Franklin began Part II (Sections 8 and 9) in 1784 when he was 78. On return, he was president of Pennsylvania. He continued the *Autobiography* in 1788 and wrote Sections 10-12. He wrote the rest of it later before his death in 1790.

The publication history of Franklin's *Autobiography* as the Part I of it was pirated to France and England was mysterious. His two grandsons messed the affair depriving the public an authoritative version.

Franklin wrote his story with five reasons—(1) it may interest his son, (2) it may be a model for others, (3) it may relive his memoirs, (4) it may reminisce listeners, and (5) it may gratify Franklin's vanity. He first sketches a brief family history. His father came from Northampshire. He had three brothers. The family had the blacksmith business, making candles and soaps. His father Josiah Franklin said the boy Ben "Nothing is useful which is not honest" when he did some mischief. He was apprenticed to Uncle James, a printer. He wrote poetry and prose. He favored woman's education. At 16 he became a vegetarian and saved money for books. He wrote articles for his brother's *New England Courant*. Then Ben ran away to Philadelphia. William Bradford guided him to a printer. He decided to have his own printing business in Boston. There is a comic touch in Franklin's friendship with John Collins who migrated to Barbados. His Socratic approach to Governor Keith is another comic touch. When in England with Ralph, Franklin saved much money by sharing the room with him and by drinking water instead of beer.

Franklin, when in Philadelphia, did business in stores with Denham who with a legacy left him 'once more to the wide world'. He worked for Keimer's press and then had a hand in printing government money. All this work taught him practical knowledge. He became a 'through deist'.

After his return from England, Franklin started a club called 'Junto' for mutual help and improvement. He had his own paper. Franklin married Miss Read and set up his family in 1730. He also started a public library. This industry helped him wealth and distinction. Luckily his life was as much disposed to industry and frugality as himself. Franklin was a religious man. He believed in family life and religion. He felt merits are rewarded as wrongs are punished. He believed in God. He thought service to man is service to God. All this was the essentials of religion. This part of his autobiography is more moralistic as it is to instruct the public.

Franklin thought of perfecting himself. He felt bad habits lead man to bad acts. He devised 13 virtues as necessary or desirable for good life. These are temperance, silence, order, resolution, frugality, industry, sincerity, moderation, cleanliness, tranquility, chastity and humility. Franklin tried to master these virtues.

Part II of the *Autobiography* was written later. Franklin was a good planner and executer. He published his first *Almanac* in 1732 which sold well, advocating industry and frugality as the means to procuring wealth thereby securing virtues. His 1757 edition of it was special and it got published in France and England. He taught his brother James's son printing and he mourned for the death of his son these years.

Franklin, for the first time, became a clerk in the general assembly. Franklin found it that: "he that has once done you a kindness will be more obliged". He liked Whitefield's sermons. The first public affair on which Franklin concentrated was regulating the night watch. At this time, Franklin's printing business and his unrivalled newspaper were making him wealthier each day. Though otherwise satisfied Franklin found two deficiencies in Pennsylvania: it had no militia and no college. In 1743, he therefore drew up a proposal for an academy. This academy finally became the University of Pennsylvania. He also proposed a lottery to raise funds for a town battery complete with cannon. He served there as a common soldier. In 1742, Franklin had invented an improved stove which he refused to patent. He believed "That as we enjoy advantages from the inventions of others, we should be glad of an opportunity to serve others by an invention of ours."

As soon as Franklin disengaged himself from his business to perform his electrical experiments and philosophical studies, other people claimed his time. He became a council member and then alderman. He solved Indians 'rum problem'. He was instrumental in appointing street sweepers and street lights as in London's Globe then.

In 1753 having already served as comptroller for the American post office, Franklin was appointed along with William Hunter as postmaster general of the colonies. He had the further satisfaction of having honorary degrees from Harvard and Yale.

Franklin tried to ease the political situation between the colonials (the British) and the colonized (the Americans). But the former failed to understand his goodwill and plunged into a war that ended their rule in America.

Franklin's scientific reputation grew greatly. He enlightened people about his findings on lightening. He drew lightening from the clouds. This was recognized in Europe later and he was honored.

Woodrow Wilson writes, "The *Autobiography* is letters in business garb...addressing itself to the task, which in this country is every man's, of setting free the processes of growth, giving them facility and speed and efficacy."[1] Indeed, the *Autobiography* is a uniquely American book.

NOTE

1. Woodrow Wilson, Introduction to Franklin's *Autobiography*, Century Press, New York, 1901.

2 Ralph Waldo Emerson's Thoughts with Reference to *Self-Reliance*

Ralph Waldo Emerson was one of the earliest American writer-thinkers who spoke of man's overall progress. In fact, he meditated over man's self-progress. He said, "Fate helps those who help themselves". John Greenleaf Whittier once said of Emerson that he was "the one American who is sure of being remembered in a thousand years". Ralph Waldo Emerson was an American poet, lecturer and essayist. He was the leading member of the group of New England idealists known as transcendentalists. He spoke to his people of nineteenth century about new optimism that linked God, nature and man into a magnificent cosmos.

Emerson was born in Boston in 1803 as the third of six sons of William and Ruth Haskins Emerson. Emerson's father was a pastor of a Unitarian Church in Boston and also a chaplain to the state senate and an editor of the *Monthly Anthology*. Emerson's father died when he was young. So his mother Ruth and his aunt Mary Moody looked after the family. Emerson studied at Boston Latin School and graduated from Harvard College. He taught at school. He experimented with fiction and verse and read randomly in theology. Later he entered Harvard Divinity School. He completed his MA in 1826. Later he was elected to Phi Beta Kappa society.

Emerson met Ellen Tucker, a 17 year-old poet. They married in 1829 just after Emerson was ordained a pastor of the second church of Boston. He had been a Unitarian minister for three years at the Old North Church in Boston. The young couple were happy but both were ill. Ellen died of TB in 1831. At the same time, Emerson lost his interest in church preaching some of which he thought was irrelevant. In 1832, he went to Europe. Emerson travelled through Italy where he met the English writer Walter Landor and then went to Paris. In London, Emerson met the economist and philosopher John Stuart Mill. He befriended S.T. Coleridge. He stayed with William Wordsworth at Rydal Mount in Lake District. In Scotland, he met Thomas Carlyle, the great historian and social critic and laid the foundation of a lifelong friendship.

Emerson, after his return from Europe, began his career as a lecturer with an address in Boston. The lecture entitled *The Uses of Natural History* attempted to humanise science by explaining "the whole of nature as a metaphor or image of the human mind". Later he spoke on as diverse subjects as Italy, biography, English literature, the philosophy of history and human culture.

Emerson moved to Concord in Massachusetts and stayed with his step-grandfather Ezra Ripley. In 1835, he married Lydia Jackson of Plymouth. The couple moved to a house of their own in Concord, where they lived the rest of their lives. The Emerson house became a gathering place for a group of writers and conversationalists that included the Channings, Amos Bronson Alcott, Margaret Fuller, H.D. Thoreau and others. This group of writers made Concord "the Athens of America". Emerson's book *Nature* appeared in 1836. It contains his thoughts. It is his first definitive statement of his philosophical perspective and within this work may be found most of his best thoughts. The basic idea is that nature is God's idea made apparent to men. Not only does nature reveal truths; it disciplines men, rewarding, them when they go right and punishing them when they go wrong. His Phi Beta Kappa address in 1837 at Harvard on *American Scholar* was immediately popular. Emerson defined an American scholar as a 'man thinking'.

Since 1836 Emerson was a member of the Transcendental Club, which often met at his house and in 1840 he helped launch the magazine *Dial*. The *Dial* voiced the thoughts of American transcendentalists, apart from speaking about their experimental community life at Brook Farm. In 1841, Emerson published his first book of essays and essays such as *Self-Reliance* and *The Over-Soul* are world famous today. Emerson published his poems in 1847. Emerson lectured extensively in America and Europe. *English Traits* is his travel account of England. His works like *Conduct of Life* contain his fine philosophy. The Civil War troubled him though he supported anti-slavery movement and women's freedom movement. *Society and Solitude* (1870) and *Natural History of the Intellect* (1893) are his collections of lectures. Emerson was instrumental in establishing Concord School of Philosophy. Emerson died of pneumonia in Concord on April 27, 1882.

Emerson's world famous essay *Self-Reliance* begins grandly: "To believe your own thought, to believe that what is true for you in your private heart is true for all men,—that is genius.... Familiar as the voice of the mind is to each, the highest merit we ascribe to Moses, Plato and Milton is that they set at naught books and traditions, and spoke not what men but what they thought. A man should learn to detect and watch that gleam of light which flashes across his mind from within more than the luster of the firmament of bards and sages.... In every work of genius we recognize our own rejected thoughts: they come back to us with a certain alienated majesty.... There is a time in every man's education when he arrives at the conviction that envy is ignorance; that imitation is suicide; that he must take himself for better, for worse as his portion.... We but half express ourselves, and are ashamed of that divine idea which each of us represents.... A man is relieved and gay when he has put his heart into his work and done his best.... Trust thyself: every heart vibrates to that iron string. Accept the place the divine providence has found for you, the society of your contemporaries, the connection of events.... Infancy conforms to nobody: all conform to it.... Do not think the youth has no force, because he cannot speak to you and me. You court him: he does not court you. But the man is, as it were, clapped into jail by his consciousness. There is no Lethe for this.... These are the voices which we hear in solitude, but they grow faint and inaudible as we enter into the world. Society everywhere is in conspiracy against the manhood of every one of its members. Society is a joint-stock company, in which the members agree, for the better securing of his bread to each shareholder, to surrender the liberty and culture of the eater. The virtue in most respect is conformity. Self-reliance is its aversion. It loves not realities and creators, but names and customs.

Who so would be a man but be a nonconformist.... Nothing is at last sacred but the integrity of your own mind. Absolve you to yourself, and you shall have the suffrage of the world.... What have I to do with the sacredness of traditions, if I live wholly from within.... No law can be sacred to me but that of my nature. Good and bad are but names very readily transferable to that or this; the only right is what is after my constitution, the only wrong what is against it. A man is to carry himself in the presence of all opposition.... I ought to go upright and vital, and speak the rude truth in all ways. If malice and vanity wear the coat of philanthropy, shall that pass?...truth is handsomer than the affectation of love. Your goodness must have some edge to it,—else it is none. The doctrine of hatred must be preached as the counteraction of the doctrine of love when that pulses and whines. I shun father and mother and wife and brother, when my genius calls me.... Virtues are, in the popular estimate, rather the exception than the rule. There is the man and his virtues. Men do what is called a good action, as some piece of courage and charity.... Their virtues are penances. I do not wish to expiate, but to live. My life is for itself and not for a spectacle.... What I must do is all that concerns me, not what the people think.... It is easy in the world to live after the world's opinion; it is easy in solitude to live after our own; but the great man is he who in the midst of the crowd keeps with perfect sweetness the independence of solitude.... The objection to conforming to usages that have become dead to you is, that it scatters your force. It loses your time and blurs the impression of your character.... But do your work, and I shall know you. Do your work, and you shall reinforce yourself. A man must consider what a blindman's-buff is this game of conformity.... This conformity makes them not false in a few particulars, authors of a few lies, but false in all particulars. Their every truth is not quite true. Their two is not the real two, their four not the real four; so that every word they say chagrins us, and we know not where to begin to set them right.... For non-conformity the world whips you with its displeasure. And therefore a man must know how to estimate a sour face.... The other terror that scares us from self-trust is our consistency.... Suppose you should contradict yourself; what then?" Leave your theory, as Joseph his coat in the hand of the harlot, and flee. A foolish consistency is the hobgoblin of little minds, adored by little statesmen and philosophers and divines. With consistency a great soul has simply nothing to do. Speak what you think now in hard words, and tomorrow speak what tomorrow thinks in hard words again, though it contradict every thing you said today.—"Ah, so you shall be sure to be misunderstood."—Is it so bad, then, to be misunderstood? Pythagoras was misunderstood, and Socrates, and Jesus, and Luther, and Copernicus, and Galileo, and Newton, and every pure and wise spirit that ever took flesh. To be great is to be misunderstood.

Character teaches above our wills. Your genuine action will explain itself, and will explain your other genuine actions. Your conformity explains nothing. Act singly, and what you have already done singly will justify you now. Greatness appeals to the future. If I can be firm enough today to do right, and scorn eyes, I must have done so much right before as to defend me now. Be it how it will, do right now. Always scorn appearances, and you always may. The force of character is cumulative.... Honor is venerable to us because it is no ephemeris. It is always ancient virtue. We worship it today because it is not of today. We love it and pay homage, because it is not a trap for our love and homage, but is self-dependent, self-derived, and therefore of an old immaculate pedigree, even if shown in a young person.... I will stand here for humanity...that a true man belongs to no other time or place, but is the centre of things. Where he is, there is nature. He measures you, and all men, and all events. Ordinarily, every body in society reminds us of somewhat else, or of some other person. Character, reality, remind you of nothing else; it takes place of the whole creation. The man must be so much, that he must make all circumstances indifferent. Every true man is a cause, a country, and an age. A man Caesar is born, and for ages after we have a Roman Empire. Christ is born and millions of minds so grow and cleave to his genius, that he is confounded with virtue and the possible of man. An institution is the lengthened shadow of one man; as, Monachism of the Antonym; the Reformation, of Luther; Quakerism, of Fox; Methodism, of Wesley; Abolition, of Clarkson. Scipio, Milton called "the height of Rome"; and all history resolves itself very easily into the biography of a new stout and earnest persons.

Let a man then know his worth, and keep things under his feet. Our reading is mendicant and sycophantic. In history, our imagination plays us false. Kingdom and lordship, power and estate, are a gaudier vocabulary.... The world has been instructed by its kings, who have so magnetized the eyes of nations.... The magnetism which all original action exerts is explained when we inquire the reason of self-trust. The enquiry leads us to that source, at once the essence of genius, of virtue, and of life, which we call spontaneity or instinct. We denote this primary wisdom as intuition, while all later teachings are tuitions. The relations of the soul to the divine spirit are so pure, that it is profane to seek to interpose help. Man is timid and apologetic. He is no longer upright; he dares not say, 'I think I am', but quotes some saint or sage. He does not live in the present, but with reverted eye laments the past, or, heedless of the riches that surround him, stands on tiptoe to foresee the future. He cannot be happy and strong until he too lives with nature in the present, above time. We are like children who repeat by rote the sentences of grandmas and tutors. If we live truly, we shall see truly. It is as easy for the strong man to be strong, as it is for the weak to be weak. When we have new perception, we shall gladly disburden the memory of its hoarded treasures as old rubbish. When a man lives with God, his voice shall be as sweet as the murmur of the brook and the rustle of the corn.

Self-existence is the attribute of the supreme cause. Power is in nature the essential measure of right. Nature suffers nothing to remain in her kingdom which cannot help itself. Thus, all concentrates: let us not rove; let us sit at home with the cause. Bid the invaders take the shoes from off their feet, for God is here within. But now we are a mob. We must go alone. But your isolation must not be mechanical, but spiritual, that is, must be elevation. "What we love that we have, but by desire we bereave ourselves of the love. I must be myself. I cannot break myself any longer for you. If you can love me for what I am, we shall be the happier. If you are noble, I will love you; if you are not, I will not hurt you and myself by hypocritical attentions. Yes, but I cannot sell my liberty and my power, to save their sensibility. Besides, all persons have their moments of reason. The populace think that your rejection of popular standards is a rejection of all standard, and mere antinomianism; and the bold sensualist will use the name of philosophy to gild his crimes. Consider whether you have satisfied your relations to father, mother, cousin, neighbor, town, cat, and dog; whether any of these can upbraid you. But I may also neglect this reflex standard, and absolve me to myself. We are afraid of truth, afraid of fortune, afraid of death, and afraid of each other. Our age yields no great and perfect persons. We want men and women who shall renovate life and our social state. Our house-keeping is mendicant. We are parlor soldiers; we shun the rugged battle of fate where strength is born."

It is easy to see that a greater self-reliance must work a revolution in all the offices and relations of men; in their religion; in their education; in their pursuits; in their modes of living; in their association; in their property; in their speculative views.

Emerson says prayers are meant for self-purification but not to beg God for worldly gains. He says, "Prayer is the contemplation of the facts of life from the highest point of view." The secrets of fortune is joy in our hands. Welcome evermore to gods; and man is the self-helping man. For him all doors are flung wide. God loves him because men hated Him. As men's prayers are a disease of the will, so are their creeds a disease of the intellects. Secondly Emerson asks us not to travel. He says the soul is no traveler. The wise man stays at home. Traveling is a fool's paradise. Our houses are built with foreign goods. Our dependence on these foreign goods leads us to our slavish respect for numbers. Insists upon yourself; never imitate. Where is the master who could have taught Shakespeare? Shakespeare will never be made by the study of Shakespeare.

Abide in the simple and noble regions of thy life. Obey thy heart, and thou shall reproduce the foreworld again. Thirdly Emerson hates sophistication in life. He likes simplicity. He says the civilized man has built a coach, but has lost the use of his feet. For every stoic was a stoic; but in Christendom where is the Christian? The great genius returns to essential man. Society is a wave. The wave moves onward, but the water of which it is composed does not. The persons who make up a nation-today, next year die, and their experience with them." Emerson concludes the essay: "So use all that is called fortune.... Nothing can bring you peace but yourself. Nothing can bring you peace but the triumph of principles."

NOTE

All the textual references are from Emerson's *Self-Reliance.*

3

Nathaniel Hawthorne's *The Scarlet Letter*: A Chronicle of Puritan Life

American literature is as rich as British literature today. Ever since Emerson, Whitman and Dickinson wrote great works, American literature began shining greatly. As we know, the American transcendentalists Emerson, Thoreau and Hawthorne created a ripple in the peoples' taste for books in the mid-nineteenth century America. If Emerson enthralled his audience with his essays, Thoreau did it with his treatise on natural life in *The Walden*. Likewise, their great contemporary Nathaniel Hawthorne wrote everlasting works of fiction. Hawthorne's novels particularly *The Scarlet Letter, The House of the Seven Gables, The Blithdale Romance* and *The Marble Fawn* are classics. Besides, many of his minor novels and short stories established his reputation as a major American writer.

Hawthorne wrote his magnum opus *The Scarlet Letter* in 1849. It was published the same year. Immediately the critics as well as readers appreciated it as a lovely novel of human frailty and sorrow. The novel is written in twenty-four chapters. It is so interesting that the reader will not stop reading it until the end.

The introduction "The Custom-House" describes Hawthorne's life in brief. He says he served in a customhouse in his native town of Salem. There is a vivid description pertaining to several personnels working at the wharf. One information that engages our intellect is about the late Jonathan Pue, a surveyor of His Majesty's customs for the port of Salem. It is because of Pue's effort there lay a neglected package, carefully done in a piece of ancient yellow parchment. Hawthorne writes: "This envelope had the air of an official record of some period long past, when clerks engrossed their stiff and formal chorography on more substantial materials than at present. There was something about it that quickened an instinctive curiosity, and made me undo the faded red tape that tied up the package, with the sense that a treasure would here be brought to light."[1]

This rag of scarlet cloth was reduced to a rag. On a careful examination it assumed the shape of a letter. It was the capital letter A. The inside matter related to an affair of a bygone time. The details of it pertained to Hester Prynne, who appeared to have been rather a noteworthy personage in the view of ancestors. She had lived in the mid-seventieth century. It seems aged persons in the time of Pue remembered her as a very old but not descript woman, of a stately and solemn aspect. Mr. Pue had made this story out of a current talk. It had been her habit from an almost immemorial date to go about the country and help the needy and sick. Though she faced ignominy in the beginning she came to be revered as an angel later. Hawthorne's novel is about this selfsame heroine of the folk story heard across Boston for generations.

The first chapter "The Prison Door" depicts the story of Hester Prynne coming out of a jail after three months terms. She is taken to a scaffold in the market place of Boston, a new settlement by the seaboard in the 1650's. Hawthorne describes how Bostonians had gathered at the scaffold to have a look at Hester Prynne's prosecution. Chapter 2 "The Market Place" depicts Hester Prynne's trial for her adultery. It seems Hester Prynne who immigrated to America from England was waiting to receive her husband there shortly. But in the meanwhile she committed the crime of adultery. She had an affair with a man in church and had delivered a child. Now the governor of the province Bellingham, two ministers John Wilson and Arthur Dimmesdale, gather to prosecute her. In the next chapter "Recognition" the trial unfolds itself. The gentlemen of the jury ask her to confess the truth about the father of her child little Pearl:

> "Speak to the woman, my brother", said Mr. Wilson. "It is of moment to her soul, and, therefore, as the worshipful Governor says, momentous to thine own, in whose charge hers is. Exhort her to confess the truth!"

The Reverend Mr. Dimmesdale bent his head, in silent prayer, as it seemed and then came forward.

"Hester Prynne", said he, leaning over the balcony and looking down steadfastly into her eyes, "thou hearest what this good man says, and seest the accountability under which I labour. If thou feelest it to be for thy soul's peace, and that thy earthly punishment will thereby be made more effectual to salvation, I charge thee to speak out the name of thy fellow sinner and fellow-sufferer! Be not silent from any mistaken pity and tenderness for him; for, believe me, Hester, though he were to step down from a high place, and stand there beside thee, on thy pedestal of shame, yet better were it so than to hide a guilty heart through life. What can thy silence do for him, except it tempt him—yea, compel him, as it were—to add ignominy, that thereby thou mayest work out an open triumph over the evil within thee and the sorrow without. Take heed how thou deniest to him—who, perchance, hath, but wholesome, cup that is now presented to thy lips!"

"Woman, transgress not beyond the limits of Heaven's mercy!" cried the Reverend Mr. Wilson, more harshly than before. "That little babe hath been gifted with a voice, to second and confirm the counsel which thou hast heard. Speak out the name! That, and thy repentance may avail to take the scarlet letter off thy breast."

"Never", replied Hester Prynne, looking not at Mr Wilson, but into the deep and troubled eyes of the younger clergyman. "It is too deeply branded. Ye cannot take it off. And would that I might endure his agony as well as mine!"

"Speak, woman!" said another voice, coldly and sternly, proceeding from the crowd about the scaffold, "Speak; and give your child a father!" "I will not speak!", answered Hester, turning pale as death, but responding to this voice, which she too surely recognised. "And my child must seek a heavenly father; she shall never know an earthly one!" (pp. 83-85).

Thus, end the first scaffold scene in which Hester Prynne refuses to disclose the name of the man who fathered her child.

She decides to remain aloof in the interest of the man who committed the sin with her. Yet this was to upset her life long.

In the part "The Interview", Hester Prynne in jail for some more months is visited by Roger Chillingworth. Roger Chillingworth is Hester Prynne's (former) husband. He is a physician by profession. Both were of English stock and had recently immigrated to Germany. There from Hester Prynne had gone to Boston with the plan to receive her husband there a year later. Alas! Hester Prynne developed an affair with Arthur Dimmesdale and begot a child called Pearl. So there was a trial for her. Even Roger Chillingworth was an eyewitness of Hester Prynne's trial. Subsequently he meets her (in the guise of a doctor) to give Pearl some medicine. He voices his guilt and anger thus:

> "Hester", said he, "I ask not wherefore, nor how thou hast fallen into the pit, or say, rather, thou hast ascended to the pedestal of infamy on which I found thee. The reason is not far to seek. It was my folly, and thy weakness. I—a man of thought—the book-worm of great libraries—a man already in decay, having given best years to feed the hungry dream of knowledge—what had to do with youth and beauty like thine own?" (p. 91)

Roger Chillingworth asks her for her paramour's name which she declines to disclose. She replies, "Ask me not?" looking firmly into his face. She adds: "That thou shalt never know!" (p. 93). But he decides to find out the man and wreck his vengeance upon him. Before he could go he asks her neither to speak of his identity nor to speak of her relationship with him:

> "One thing, thou that wast my wife, I would enjoin upon thee", continued the scholar. "Thou hast kept the secret of thy paramour. Keep, likewise, mine! There are none in this land that know me. Breathe not to any human soul that thou didst ever call me husband! Here, on this wild outskirt of the earth, I shall pitch my tent; for, elsewhere a wanderer, and isolated from human interests, I find here a woman, a man, a child, amongst whom and myself there exist the closest ligaments. No matter whether of love or hate: no matter whether of right or wrong! Thou and thine,

Hester Prynne, belong to me. My home is where thou art and where he is. But betray me not!"

"Wherefore dost thou desire it?" inquired Hester, shrinking, she hardly knew why, from this secret bond. "Why not announce thyself openly, and cast me off at once?"

"It may be", he replied, "because I will not encounter the dishonour that besmirches the husband of a faithless woman. It may be for other reasons. Enough, it is my purpose to live and die unknown. Let, therefore, thy husband be to the world as one already dead, and of whom no tidings shall ever come. Recognise me not, by word, by sign, by look! Breathe not the secret, above all, to the man thou wottest of. Shouldst thou fail me in this, beware! His fame, his position, his life will be in my hands. Beware!"

"I will keep thy secret, as I have his", said Hester.

And she took the oath. (pp. 94-95)

Once her term of punishment was over Hester Prynne continued her normal life. She lived in a deserted hut. She lived like an untouchable. All the people tried to see her as if an alien. Hester did needle work and sold scarf-like things to different people including those in power. She earned some money for living. She used to help the sick and needy. Hawthorne says, "Lonely as was Hester's situation, and without a friend on earth who dared to show himself, she however, incurred no risk of want" (p. 100). In this manner she played her role in a Puritan society. Of course, she was strong enough to face the world and live herself. Yet the scarlet letter she wore made her perpetually a stranger to the people. All people looked at it without fail and branded her. In fact, "...the scarlet letter had endowed her with a new sense. She shuddered to believe, yet could not help believing, that it gave her a sympathetic knowledge of the hidden sin in other hearts. She was terror-stricken by the revelations that were thus made. What were they? Could they be other than the insidious whispers of the bad angel, who would fain have persuaded the struggling woman, as yet only half his victim, that the outward guise of purity was but a lie and that, if truth were everywhere to be shown, a scarlet letter would blaze on many a bosom besides Hester Prynne?... Sometimes the red infamy upon her breast would give a sympathetic throb, as she passed near a venerable minister or magistrate, the model of piety and justice, to whom age of antique reverence looked up, as to a mortal man in fellowship with angels"(pp. 106-07).

In the chapter "Pearl", Hawthorne writes about the little child Pearl. Hester Prynne called her "Pearl" not because she looked so precious but because she was so important as pearl for her life. Yet she seemed rather an airy spirit. Pearl is full of innocence and mystery. Like her mother Pearl was also a born outcaste. No other children liked her even when playing. So she used to play with sticks, papers, pebbles and the like. Of course, she stayed with Hester all the while. The mother liked the young one, for she remembered her the bliss of solitude. The two lived their life happily. A dialogue between the two evidences this:

"Child, what art thou?" cried the mother.

"Oh, I am your little Pearl!" answered the child.

But while she said it, Pearl laughed and began to dance up and down with the humoursome gesticulation of a little imp, whose next freak might be to fly up the chimney.

"Art thou my child, in very truth?" asked Hester.

Nor did she put the question altogether idly, but, for the moment, with a portion of genuine earnestness; for, "such was Pearl's wonderful intelligence, that her mother half doubted whether she were not acquainted with the secret spell of her existence and might not now reveal herself" (pp. 119-20).

One day Hester Prynne hears the rumour that the men in power including the ministers decided to take away her child and keep it under someone's custody, for they wanted the child grow in a Christian manner. Hester heard this with shock and surprise. So she decided to visit the Governor.

Once both Hester and Pearl go there, they encounter Bellingham and the two ministers talking about her. Even Roger Chillingworth is there. After an hour of waiting, she finds a chance to speak to them. The situation is critical for the wearer of scarlet letter:

Governor Bellingham stepped through the window into the hall, followed by his three guests.

"Hester Prynne", said he, fixing his naturally stern regard on the wearer of the scarlet letter, "there hath been much question concerning thee of late. The point hath been weightily discussed, whether we, that are of authority and influence, do well discharge our consciences by trusting an immoral soul, such as there is in yonder child, to the guidance of one who hath stumbled and fallen amid the pitfalls of this world. Speak thou, the child's own mother! Were it not, thinkest thou, for thy little one's temporal and eternal welfare that she be taken out of thy charge, and clad soberly, and disciplined strictly, and instructed in the truths of heaven and earth? What canst thou do for the child in this kind?"

"I can teach my little Pearl what I have learned from this!" answered Hester Prynne, laying her finger on the red token.

"Woman, it is thy badge of shame!" replied the stern magistrate. "It is because of the stain which that letter indicates that we would transfer thy child to other hands."

"Nevertheless", said the mother, calmly, though growing more pale, "this badge hath taught me—it daily teaches me—it is teaching me at the wiser moment—lessons whereof my child may be the wiser and better albeit they can profit nothing to myself"(p. 134).

The chapter "The Leech" is about Roger Chillingworth's harassing treatment of the minister Arthur Dimmesdale. Chillingworth bent up to find out who had an affair with his (former) wife, guesses it to be Arthur Dimmesdale. In fact, he befriends the other; both stay together, a common cook serving them under a single roof. Although the doctor stays in his room and the minister stays in his, both pass much of their time together. Roger Chillingworth plans again and again for understanding the other's inner mind. He detects him. He asks a volley of questions and analyses the same. In fact, he succeeds in his venture. He doubts the other and maltreats him. Hawthorne says, "In this manner, the mysterious old Roger Chillingworth became the medical adviser of the Reverend Mr Dimmesdale. As not only the disease interested the physician, but he was strongly moved to look into the character and qualities of the patient, these two men, so different in age came gradually to spend much time together" (p. 149). In the following chapter Hawthorne talks of the Leech's relations with his 'patient' Dimmesdale. The following scene discloses such a horror:

> ...old Roger Chillingworth, without any extraordinary precaution, came into the room. The physician advanced directly in front of his patient, laid his hand upon his bosom, and thrust aside the vestment, that hitherto had always covered it even from the professional eye.

Then, indeed, Mr Dimmesdale shuddered and slightly stirred. After a brief pause, the physician turned away.

But with what a wild look of wonder, joy and horror! With what a ghastly rapture, as it were, too mightily to be expressed only by the eye and features and therefore bursting forth through the whole ugliness of his figure and making itself even riotously manifest by the extravagant gestures with which he threw up his arms towards the ceiling and stamped his foot upon the floor! Had a man seen old Roger Chillingworth, at that moment of his ecstasy, he would have had no need to ask how Satan comforts himself, when a precious human soul is lost to heaven and won into his kingdom.

But what distinguished the physician's ecstasy from Satan's was the trait of wonder in it! (p. 167).

Thus, we find Roger Chillingworth haunting his patient. One night it so happens that Dimmesdale finds it very unbearable and likes to confess his sin the next day. Likewise he gets up and goes to the scaffold. He sits upon it as his desire for confession grows stronger. Meanwhile he shrieks. This he thinks may be heard across the settlement. In fact, it is heard nearby. Meanwhile, minister Wilson passes that way after he attended old Winthrop's death ceremony. Even Governor Bellingham awakes and will have a look outside. Afterwards Hester Prynne and Pearl appear there for a mysterious reason:

> "Pearl! Little Pearl!" cried he, after a moment's pause; then, suppressing his voice—"Hester! Hester Prynne! Are you there?"

"Yes; it is Hester Prynne!" she replied, in a tone of surprise; and the minister heard her footsteps approaching from the side-walk, along which she had been passing. "It is I, and my little Pearl."

"Whence come you, Hester?" asked the minister. "What sent you hither?"

"I have been watching at a death-bed", answered Hester Prynne, "at Governor Winthrop's death-bed, and have taken his measure for a robe, and am now going homeward to my dwelling".

"Come up hither, Hester, thou and Little Pearl", said the Reverend Mr Dimmesdale. "Ye have both been here before, but I was not with you. Come up hither once again, and we will stand all three together" (pp. 183-84).

The minister is all-eager for confession. But the peoples' all-loving faith in him has constrained him from doing so. Yet he wants to be with his woman Hester and his ill-begotten daughter Pearl. When the girl asks when he stays with them, he says he will be with them on the great judgement day. This is a fine scaffold scene in the middle of the novel.

Meanwhile we see Roger Chillingworth keeping a track of Dimmesdale. In fact, he observed his standing with Hester on the scaffold in that midnight. Hester takes an opportunity to see her former husband and tell him not to torture him any further. But Chillingworth denies of such a torture. She asserts: "Hast thou not tortured him enough? Has he not paid thee all?... Forgive, and leave his further retribution to the Power that claims it!" (pp. 207-09).

After this Hester meets Dimmesdale in a forest walk and cautions him against Chillingworth's ill will:

"Hester", said he, "hast thou found peace?"

She smiled drearily, looking down upon her bosom.

"Hast thou?" she asked.

"None—nothing but despair!" he answered. "What else could I look for, being what I am, and leading such a life as mine? Were I an atheist—a man devoid of conscience—a wretch with coarse and brutal instincts—I might have found peace long ere now. Nay, I never should have lost it! But, as matters tend with my soul, whatever of good capacity there originality was in me, all of God's gifts that were the choicest have become the ministers of spiritual torment. Hester, I am most miserable!" (p. 230). Now Hester tells him one great secret of her life in the past seven years. She tells him that Roger Chillingworth was her former husband. This shocks him. Of course, he forgives her later. She even asks him for elopement. Dimmesdale likes the idea though it appears wild.

However, Dimmesdale appears as if a fallen man. Hester tries her best to console him. She tells him:

> "Let us not look back.... The past is gone! Wherefore should we linger upon it now? See! With this symbol I undo it all, and make it as it had never been!" speaking so she even throws away the scarlet letter. But she wears it again. There is a fine talk and all the three—Dimmesdale, Hester and Pearl—involved in it.

Dimmesdale returns from his forest walk shortly. Now he is in a maze. He meets an elderly person of the parish, a woman and some street children. Some mariners confront him on the way. Still Dimmesdale is in his maze. He dreams of immigrating to England with Hester.

Later there is another festival day. This is known as New England Holiday. This day the governor is taken in a procession in the market place. There will be a function in a meeting hall. When the gathering is seen there Hester and her daughter attend it. Naturally all people look at them. Hester also finds her former husband. Meanwhile as she had told the captain of a ship which had just come from Spanish Main, he meets her. She knows him. He says he has booked three berths for her. That is to say Hester, Dimmesdale and Pearl were to go back to England by that ship. But the mariner says he has also booked a berth for Roger Chillingworth which fact shocks Hester. This makes her drop the plan of going there. Meanwhile Dimmesdale's electic sermon starts. Dimmesdale delivers a fine sermon that time. The same makes all the people wonder about the young minister's remarkable gifts of wisdom. But he is frail and weak as that of Hester. It is observed:

> While Hester stood in that magic circle of ignominy, where the cunning cruelty of her sentence seemed to have fixed her for ever, the admirable preacher was looking down from the sacred pulpit upon an audience whose very spirits had yielded to his control. The sainted minister in the church! The woman of the scarlet letter in the market place! What imagination would have been irreverent enough to surmise that the same scorching stigma was on them both! (p. 298).

An hour later the minister Dimmesdale walks out and steps up the scaffold to all people's surmise. He stumbles even. Then some people hold him. Now he calls Hester and speaks of his confession:

> "Hester Prynne", cried he, with a piercing earnestness, "in the name of Him, so terrible and so merciful, who gives me grace, at this last moment, to do what—for my own heavy sin and miserable agony—I withheld myself from doing seven years ago, come hither now, and twine thy strength about me! Thy strength, Hester; but let it be guided by the will which God hath granted me! This wretched and wronged old man is opposing it with all his might!—with all his own might, and the fiend's! come, Hester—come! Support me up yonder scaffold." (p. 305)

"For thee and Pearl, be it as God shall order", said the minister, "and God is merciful! Let me now do the will which He hath made plain before my sight. For, Hester, I am a dying man. So let me make haste to take my shame upon me!" (p. 306).

"Pearl kissed his lips. A spell was broken. The great scene of grief, in which the wild infant bore a part had developed all her sympathies; and as her tears fell upon her father's cheek, they were not the pledge that she would grow up amid human joy and sorrow, nor forever do battle with the world, but be a woman in it. Towards her mother, too, Pearl's errand as a messenger of anguish was fulfilled.

"Hester", said the clergyman, "farewell!"

"Shall we not meet again?" whispered she, bending her face down close to his. "Shall we not spend our immortal life together? Surely, surely, we have ransomed one another, with all this woe! Thou lookest far into eternity, with those bright dying eyes! Then tell me what thou seest!"

"Hush, Hester—hush!" said he, with tremulous solemnity. "The law we broke!—the sin here so awfully revealed!—let these alone be in thy thoughts! I fear! I fear! It may be, that, when we forgot our God—when we violated our reverence each for the other's soul—it was thenceforth vain to hope that we could meet hereafter, in an everlasting and pure reunion. God knows; and He is merciful! He hath proved his mercy, most of all, in my afflictions. By giving me this burning torture to bear upon my breast! By sending yonder dark and terrible old man, to keep the torture always at red-heat! By bringing me hither, to die this death of triumphant ignominy before the people! Had either of these agonies been wanting, I had been lost forever! Praised be His name! His will be done! Farewell!"

"That final word came forth with the minister's expiring breath. The multitude, silent till then, broke out in a strange, deep voice of awe and wonder, which could not as yet find utterance, save in this murmur that rolled so heavily after the departed spirit" (pp. 309-10).

Hawthorne's *The Scarlet Letter* is a great novel ever written in America. It is a great psychological novel. In the words of Spiller, "In his exposition of these complicated problems Hawthorne frankly employed fiction to study psychic case histories; in him, as already hinted, was a tough, cold streak, tempting him outside the personal relationships of his characters into indefatigable analyses of these specimens of moral experience. It is true that this semi scientific study sometimes chills the characters themselves, even in the richly human *Scarlet Letter*."[2]

NOTES

1. All the references of the text are taken from Nathaniel Hawthorne's *The Scarlet Letter*, Mladinska Knjiga, Ljubljana, 1966, p. 39.
2. Robert Spiller, *Literary History of the United States*, Amerind Publishing Co., New Delhi, 1963, p. 427.

H.D. Thoreau's *Walden*: A Way of Life

4

Only a few books in the world are most useful for mankind either for delight or for instruction. Such useful documents are rarely written. However a few such great classics of art, science and culture exist, they surely guide mankind towards nobility and greater consciousness. Henry David Thoreau's *Walden* is one of such great documents of the American literature. *Walden*, like Plato's *Republic* or Mahatma Gandhi's *Hind Swaraj* can guide the confused world. In fact, *Walden* is called a lay Bible. It advocates a simple life that is close to the life lived in woods. It is not for nothing, *Walden* is subtitled "Life in the Woods". *Walden* is the result of Thoreau's experiment with life; it is a recreation of his experiences; and it is his manual to the weary mankind. Henry Salt, one of Thoreau's early biographers writes of *Walden* in 1886: "It is incomparable alike in matter and style and deserves to be a sacred book in the library of every cultured and thoughtful man."[1] W.H. Hudson calls it: "the golden book in any century of books".[2] Thoreau's works *Walden* and *Civil Disobedience* influenced many a great men of mankind. *Walden* influenced Mahatma Gandhi and it made Leo Tolstoy read it. W.B. Yeats and Anton Tchekhov admired Thoreau. They said *Walden* is fresh and original.

Thoreau's *Walden* is a treatise in the line of Matthew Arnold's *Culture and Anarchy*. Not to speak of it bears a comparison with Sir Thomas Moor's *Utopia*. But one has to think of the substance of *Walden* in a philosophical way. Secondly *Walden* must be analyzed independently without referring to much of Thoreau's autobiography, because Thoreau's life is full of contradictions. We know Thoreau bore an eccentric nature. He had no ambitions. Emerson says he did not have any heroism in his character as such. He was timid and unsociable. Some critics speak of Thoreau's selfishness, perversity of thought and other peculiarities. R.L. Stevenson calls him a 'Skulker'. Henry James says Thoreau was a parochial representing a documented projection of his self. Critics speak of his 'morbid dislike of humanity'.

In the light of this *Walden* must be read independently as it is a social document about simple life—primitive but happy, isolated but harmonious, pure and noble. In the words of Martin Bickman, *Walden* is a "jeremiad calling for a retreat from the corruption of American society".[3] Definitely *Walden* advocates a life of simplicity, self-reliance and independence. Really it is a lay Bible.

Walden is an honest critique on American life criticizing its materialism. "It (*Walden*), then, is most thoroughly American in its heartbreaking awareness of the gap between American ideals and the immediate social and political realities betraying that ideal at every turn."[4] This statement can be evidenced. However *Walden* is loosely constructed into many chapters, each part highlights one or the other aspects of simple and free life. It is the uniquintessence of Thoreau's theory of human realities recorded over a period of nine years. Thoreau's views of life are categorized in different topics such as 'Economy', 'Life', 'Reading', 'Solitude', 'The Village', 'The Ponds', 'Higher Laws', etc.

Like all the great philosophers Henry David Thoreau believes happiness lies in simplicity, service and sacrifice. According to him, "the cost of the luxuries and many of the so-called comforts of life are not only not indispensable, but positive hindrances to the elevation of mankind. With respect to luxuries and comforts, the wisest have ever lived a more simple and meager life than the poor" (p. 14). Thoreau thinks life-comforts like food, clothing and shelter are essential. But in the name of these one should not indulge in any kind of atrocities. Like Wordsworth before and Gandhi after, one day Thoreau tired of the worldly ways, wished to live in the woods. So he went to Walden Pond or Walden-in-Pond and devoted much of his time for introspection. He made an experiment with primitive mode of life. That way he became a self-appointed rishi. He states, "My purpose in going to Walden Pond was not to live cheaply nor to live dearly there, but to transact some private business with the fewest obstacles" (pp. 19-20). Himself constructing his home, earning his living and cultivating his relationship with the woodland, animals and birds, Thoreau criticized the modern Americans' foolish imitation of Europe. His attack on superfluities is seen when he writes: "The head monkey at Paris puts on a traveler's cap and all the monkeys in America do the same" (p. 25). Like Emerson, Gandhi and Tolstoy, Thoreau values moral character. He says, "Bankruptcy and repudiation are the spring-boards from which much of our civilization vaults and turns its Somerset's.... This is the reason we are all poor in respect to a thousand savage comforts, though surrounded by luxuries" (p. 33). He quotes Chapman:

> The false society of men for earthly greatness
> All heavenly comforts rarify to air.

Maybe for this reason, the noble savages have gone; modern civilization has changed the old way of life; and 'men have become the tools of their tools'. Thoreau says, "We now no longer camp as for a night, but have settled down on earth and forgotten heaven" and as for our art, he says, "The best works of art are expression of man's struggle to free himself from this condition, but the effect of our art is merely to make this low state comfortable and that higher state to be forgotten" (p. 37). Known for his quality of self-reliance, Thoreau constructed his own house. He tells man should not resign the pleasures of construction to the carpenter alone. Nor should he permit others to think on his behalf. Like the 12th century Karnataka-Sharanas, Thoreau thinks salvation lies in duty and work. He says life is not an illusion, but a reality to be lived. He says,

> Heaven is under our feet
> As well as over our head

Thoreau's Walden Pond is a 'God's Drop' and an image of the universe. It is a place where one can live and die happily. Heaven will be there with the man if he remains good and does good. According to Thoreau, if we talk of heaven, it is like disgracing the earth. Indeed, Walden Pond becomes a metaphor for true life.

In Thoreau's view to live happily means one has to live his own life, his own self. For this man needs a good character, because character is lost, everything is lost. Thoreau says there is no odour so bad as that which arises from goodness tainted. His advice is to avoid the beginning of evil because, "The evil that we do lives after us" (p. 67).

Service to and sacrifice for others, should be practised for the sake of earning merit. But for this we need not become ascetics or follow a holy order. Sanyashyasram does not do any good. Besides, one should live freely and uncommitted.

Thoreau thinks reading is a means for polishing life. So for this we must read the classics which are the noblest recorded thoughts of man. He says reading is a noble exercise and "books must be read as deliberately and reservedly as they are written". Good books are the treasures of antiquity and the wealth of nations, fit for inheritance. One must read widely and acquaint with all types of knowledge. For this he asks us to establish more and more educational institutions. He states, "That is the uncommon school we want. Instead of nobleman, let us have noble villages of men. If it is necessary, omit one bridge over the river, go round a little there, and throw one arch at least over the darker gulf of ignorance which surrounds us" (p. 110). Thoreau knows the importance of solitude better. He says he had his own sun and moon and stars and a little world all to himself. "There can be", he says, "no very black melancholy to him who lives in the midst of Nature and has his senses still".

Thoreau, as a lover of nature advocates us a way of life amidst the biological surrounding. He records his experience at the Walden Pond. Life in the woods, he thinks, is simple and happy as the seasons bring man all necessities. Thoreau hates machine age and machines. He asks if we stay at home and mind our business, who will need machines? Why should we live with such hurry and waste of life? Like Gandhi, he thinks, railway as part of machinery will harm man's real business. He writes:

What's the railroad to me?

I never go to see
Where it ends.
It fills a few hollows,
And makes banks for the swallows.
It sets the sand a-blowing.
And the blackberries a-growing.
But I cross it like a cart-path in the woods.
I will not have any eyes put out and my
Ears spoiled by its smoke and steam and hissing". (p. 122)

Thoreau never felt lonely in Nature. He says, "In the midst of a gentle rain while these thoughts prevailed, I was suddenly sensible of such sweet and beneficent society in Nature" (p. 132). Every natural entity befriended him. Surely in company of birds, beasts and trees, he was no more alone than the weathercock or the North Star.

Thoreau lived happily. He followed husbandry. *Walden* gives an account of his mode of cultivation of many crops. In Thoreau's view agriculture is a sacred profession as it is everywhere held and followed. He says that if men were to live as simply as he then did, thieving and robbery would be unknown. Robberies take place because some people are very rich while others are very poor. Accordingly doing work is the only solution for social evils. Similarly Thoreau criticizes the evil aspects of governments. Like Gandhi, Thoreau opposes the state's poking its nose into an individual's affairs. Indeed, when he had been to a village and did not pay tax, he was imprisoned. O! it was there he wrote the world famous essay on Civil Disobedience which influenced Mahatma Gandhi later to start Satyagraha. He asks 'You who govern public affairs, what need have you to employ punishments?' Love virtues and the people will be virtuous. The virtues of a superior man are like the wind, the virtues of a common man are like the grass, when the wind passes over the grass, the grass bends" (p. 172).

Thoreau describes the beauty of ponds such as Walden Pond, which is surrounded by White Pond, Goose Pond, Fair Heaven Pond, Flint's Pond and others. A lake or pond is the landscape's beautiful feature. It is the earth's eye. Man is born and dead but Nature remains alive. Walden merits our admiration especially for its water, which is pure, blue in colour and it does not dry.

In the section "Higher Laws", the extent of Thoreau's concern for human beings and for the flora and fauna is displayed. Like Hardy, Thoreau says sporting with animals is unlawful. Nor should we eat meat? He writes: "The practical objection to animal food is its uncleanness; and, besides, when I had caught and cleaned and cooked and eaten my fish, they seemed not to have fed me essentially. It was insignificant and unnecessary, and cost more than it came to. A little bread or a few potatoes would have done as well, with less trouble and filth" (p. 214). So man must stop eating meat as ancient savages stopped eating off each other when they came into contact with more civilized people. Thoreau says we must avoid liquors too. According to him, intoxication destroys everything one day as the Grecian civilization succumbed to it. He says water is the best drink. One's body and mind must be as noble as a temple.

A striking thing about Thoreau is that he is much with the world of Nature. Surely he is studied as an ecologist today. To read about his association with as wonderful creatures as that of wasp, mice, ant, partridge, etc. is enlightening. His descriptions such as the 'Morning is the spring of the day' recollects Kalidas' observation of seasons. Evidently the author of *Walden* writes, "As every season seems best to us in its turn, so the coming in of spring is like the creation of cosmos out of chaos and the realization of the Golden Age" (p. 313). Winter animals commune with the poet Thoreau. The pond looks gorgeous. Self-introspection is necessary for one's progress. He writes, "It is not worth the while to go round the world to count the cats in Zanzibar" (p. 322). He says, 'Know thyself'. He questions us satirically "While England endeavours to cure the potato-rot, will not any endeavour to cure the brain-rot, which prevails so much more widely and fatally?" (p. 325). Accordingly everyone must mind his business—say what he has to say, meet his life however mean it is, cultivate poverty, be humble, lead a simple life. Thoreau thinks: "Money is not required to buy one necessary of the soul." He asks "Rather than love, than money, than fame, give me truth." He concludes that, "I learned this, at least, by my experiment, that if one advances confidently in the direction of his dreams, and endeavours to live the life which he has imagined, he will meet with a success unexpected in common hours" (p. 324). Thoreau writes, "Man has an unquestionable ability to elevate his life by a conscious endeavour." Lean Edel says, "Thoreau made his life a sylvan legend, that of man alone, in communion with nature."[5] Indeed, Thoreau is read everywhere.

NOTES

1. H.D. Thoreau, *The Critic,* 8, New Series (Dec. 3, 1887), 291, a reprinting from Temple Bar, 78 (Nov. 1886).
2. W.H. Hudson, *Birds in a Village* (Philadelphia: J.B. Lippincott Co., 1893), p. 190.
3. Martin Bickman, *Walden Volatile Truths* (New York: Twayne Publishers, 1992), p. 13.
4. *Ibid.,* p. 5.
5. Lean Edel, "H.D. Thoreau", *American Writers,* Vol. IV, General Editor, Leonard Unger (New York: Charles Scribner's Sons, 1974), p. 168.

5

Harriet Beecher Stowe's Depiction of "Life Among the Lowly" in *Uncle Tom's Cabin*

Harriet Beecher Stowe was born in Litchfield, Connecticut, as a daughter of Reverend Lyman Beecher of the local Congregational Church. Her father had thirteen children. Her father had married three times. All seven of her brothers became ministers later. In the family, most of the responsibility fell upon the eldest daughter Catherine who later became a writer and feminist. Stowe's childhood in Connecticut was intensively religious. There was to be more Jonathan Edwards than Walter Scotts in her. For a time, she attended the Hartford seminary, a progressive institution established by her sister Catherine. In 1832, her father, a minister of great renown, became the president of Lane Theological Seminary in Cincinnati, Ohio and the family moved to Cincinnati. It was here Harriet married Calvin Ellis Stowe, a professor of Biblical literature at Lane, at the seminary, in 1836. The couple had seven children. Mrs Stowe worked as a teacher in her sister's school. Her family was a poor one. So the poverty and necessity urged her to write. "I do it for the pay", she said. Mrs Stowe returned to New England in 1850 when her husband was offered a position as a professor of religion at Bowdon College in Brunswick, Maine. For the next eighteen years while raising a large family and publishing magazine articles she watched the dramatic escape of runaway slaves who crossed the nearby Ohio River. The border town of Cincinnati was alive with abolitionalist conflict and there Mrs Stowe took an active interest in community life. She came into contact with fugitive slaves and learned from friends and from personal visits what life was like for the African-Americans in the South. Harriet observed that, "The Carthaginian women in the last peril of their state cut off their hair for bow strings to give to the defenders of their country; and such peril and shame as now hangs over this country is worse than Roman slavery, and I hope every woman who can write will not be silent."[1] In 1850, the Fugitive Slave Law was passed and that same year, Harriet's sister-in-law urged the author to put her feelings about the evils of slavery from 1851 to 1852 in *The National Era*, an anti-slavery newspaper and as a book in 1852. This was her novel *Uncle Tom's Cabin*. More than 3,50,000 copies of the novel sold in one year. The increase in the literacy rate of America was another reason for the high sale of the new novel. As copyright laws were not so good the author lost a lot of profit for herself. An estimated one million copies of numerous pirate editions were sold in England and Stowe's novel swept across the European continent. There were thousands of editorials and reviews of the novel. It was an instant triumph. To this day, there is a subway stop in Berlin called "Onkel Toms Hutte". It is about the narration of the cruelties of slavery as seen through the eyes of Uncle Tom and Eliza. Since then the novel is translated into forty languages with a worldwide readership of millions. It is said although *Uncle Tom's Cabin* has never been a masterpiece, it is one of the most influential books of social criticism ever written. When asked to defend her fictionalized account, Stowe called her book, "a very inadequate representation of slavery", which is "too dreadful for the purpose of art". Mrs Stowe continued to write, publishing eleven other novels and numerous articles before her death at the age of eighty-five in Hartford Connecticut.

However, Harriet Beecher Stowe's *Uncle Tom's Cabin* is a great story about slavery. When she visited President Abraham Lincoln in the White House during the Civil War, it is said that he remarked her, "So you're the little woman who wrote the book that made this Great War!" Her novel was the most widely sold volume of the nineteenth century and while it did not start the war, "it focused national attention on the immorality and cruelty of slavery".[2] As Lionel Trilling said the novel has come down to us as a symbol of cringing submission and disgraceful self-abasement in a black, a fight. Henry James, as a boy, liked the novel as it offered a kind of entertainment. Down the times Americans remembered the character Uncle Tom even without reading it. The first screen version was released in 1909.

The novel *Uncle Tom's Cabin* earns a great name in the literary history of the world. Here Stowe does not just write about slavery. She writes that the so-called blacks are known for their simplicity, religiosity and sobriety. They are faithful and hardworking. She writes about the slave Tom because slavery offended her understanding of Christian doctrines. And slaves are closer to the spirit of Christ. In fact, she says the story came to her on its own. She claimed that Tom's death came to her as a vision in church and that she rushed home to begin the novel and that was unstoppable. She told that God wrote the novel and she was merely His instrument. She said: "God commanded her at the writing desk; God guarded her during interviews. Because the overwhelming majority of Stowe's readers at the time were white, Uncle Tom's martyrdom was a tremendous provocation."[3] Stowe had a lot of inspiration for writing the novel. She had a black girl servant who was actually a runaway. She heard the story of a runaway slave woman Eliza Buck. Stowe when in Maine helped a slave run away. Josiah Henson's autobiography which re-printed as *Uncle Tom's Story of His Life* in 1858 and for which she wrote a foreword inspired her amply. In fact, Hensons' life has similarity with Uncle Tom's. *The Slave*, or the Memoirs of Archie Moore (1836) was the first anti-slavery narrative. Sarah Hale's *Northwood*, or *Life North and South* (1827) was to inspire her for sure. Soon after her own novel nearly a dozen anti-slavery novels appeared in America. Of course, there were many pro-slavery novels. Some of such critics even criticized Stowe for her lack of understanding the Blacks. However, Darryl Pinckney thinks Stowe's book was so popular and it helped to break the prejudice of church people like herself against novel reading—and theatre going—as unworthy pursuits. Stowe wrote several works of this nature later. Her second novel *Dred*, or *A Tale of the Great Swamp* is a saga about a slave rebellion. Stowe's *Uncle Tom's Cabin* is a social meditation in world literature.

The novel has sixty-five chapters. It opens with a conversation between Arthur Shelby, a white estate owner in Kentucky and Mr Hale, a trader in slaves from the South. They are talking about slave trade. It appears Shelby is in debt and wants to sell some of his slaves. He decides to sell one Mr Tom and a child called Harry. Tom has a family too as Harry has its parents Eliza and George Harries. Why Tom, because he is a good worker. In Shelby's own words, "Tom is a good, steady, sensible, pious fellow. He got religion at a camp-meeting, four years ago; and I believe he really did get it. I've trusted him, since then, with everything I have—money, house, horses,—and let him come and go round the country; and I always found him true and square in everything"[4] (p. 6). Although Tom is needed for Shelby's running of business, he wants to sell him as he would fetch him a big amount. Or he has to sell all his numerous other slaves. The two will have some entertainment from Harry, that is Eliza's son. In fact, Shelby strikes the deal completely and Eliza overhears it. The same day she speaks of her fears to her Mistress and the latter avoids her fears saying that her child cannot be sold. In the evening of the day, Eliza's husband George visits her at the farm. George is a gentleman. He is a sort of genius. He is employed in another farm where he has been lent to a manufacturer as well. He has there invented a farming machine. But his real master is jealous of him. So he takes him back from the factory and assigns him some sort of bad work. George is harassed. So he tells his wife that to be born a Black is to be born in hell. He says, "I wish I had never been born myself and I wish I had never seen you and even the boy should have not been born. He says his life is a misery. So he tells her he will run away to Canada and will plan to buy her later. Master Shelby has several slaves. One of them is Tom living in a cabin. Aunt Chloe is his wife and he has children like Molly, Mose and Pete. The same day night Tom, George Shelby and others enjoy a dinner and make a family meeting. Uncle Tom is a sort of religious man and a patriarch. At this time, Shelby speaks to his wife about the disposal of Harry and Tom. Mrs Shelby does not like the idea. Still Shelby cannot help it. Eliza overhears this and runs away to Tom's cabin. There she tells them that she will go to Canada as a free slave.

The next day Haley comes to collect his slaves and does not find Harry. So he will have an encounter with Shelby. Finally Sam and Andy go with Haley in search of Eliza and her child. Eliza's strife is told to be miserable now. Stowe writes, "It is impossible to conceive of a human creature more wholly desolate and forlorn than Eliza, when she turned her footsteps from Uncle Tom's Cabin" (p. 56). She walks a long way. The child's burden is there. She gives Harry a few crumbs of bread. Harry feels unhappy when Eliza does not eat anything. Shortly weary and footsore Eliza enters a village by the Ohio river. The lands across the river appear like the Canaan of liberty. Now she stays at a tavern. Meanwhile, Haley, Andy and Sam arrive there in search of her. No sooner she spots them than she runs to the bank of the river Ohio. Stowe writes, "Eliza's was a desperate leap,—impossible to anything but madness and despair and Haley, Sam, and Andy instinctively cried out, and lifted up their hands as she did it" (p. 67). Haley and others looked her in surprise. Then as a man Mr Symmes guides her, she takes shelter in the house of Mr John Bird, while Haley contacts Tom Lokhar and Marks for catching her. Meanwhile, Sam and Andy go back home.

Mr Bird is a senator in Ohio state. He is a gentleman. His wife Mary Bird is an affectionate lady, known for her sympathy for slaves. When Eliza goes to their house, the couple are discoursing about the welfare of Negroes. Mary asks Mr Bird: "And what is the law? It doesn't forbid us to shelter these poor creatures a night, does it and to give 'em something comfortable to eat, and a few old clothes, and to send them quietly about their business?" (p. 87). But he argues that as a senator he cannot help just to approve a law in the interest of the white people in the state of Kentucky. Shortly, the Birds notice the presence of Eliza and her child and provide her shelter in a Christian manner. The discourse between the two parties is moving one:

> "You needn't be afraid of anything; we are friends here, poor woman! Tell me where you came from, and what you want", said she.

> "I came from Kentucky", said the woman.
>
> "When?" said Mr Bird, taking up the interrogatory.
>
> "To-night."
>
> "How did you come?"
>
> "I crossed on the ice."
>
> "Crossed on the ice!" said every one present.
>
> "Yes", said the woman, slowly, "I did. God helping me, I crossed on the ice; for they were behind me—right behind,—and there was no other way!" (p. 92)

Mr Bird is a man of law rather. So he does not want any problem from the side of Eliza's hunters. So he decides to send the stranger off. Stowe describes vividly his conducting of the woman and her child to a safe place.

Senator John Bird took Eliza to the farmhouse of 'Honest Old John Van Trompe'. Though it was night-time, the latter received her with sympathy and assurance. He said he had seven sons as strong as him to protect her against her hunters.

Be it as it may, Tom is sold. So on his departing day, his wife Chloe prepares him a fine breakfast. Chloe and her children know Tom will go to "That undiscovered country, from whose bourn/No traveller returns" (p. 106). Mrs Shelby bursts there sorrowfully. Soon Haley appears to catch his nigger. Tom rises up meekly to follow his new master and rises up his heavy box on his shoulder. As his master Shelby and his good-natured son George are not there, he asks his wife to convey his love for them. Stowe speaks of Mr Shelby's hard-heartedness. So, "Mr Shelby at this time was not at home. He had sold Tom under the spur of driving necessity, to get out of the power of a man whom he dreaded,—and his first feeling, after the consumption of the bargain, had been that of relief. But his wife's expostulations awoke his half-slumbering regrets and Tom's manly disinterestedness increased the unpleasantness of his feelings" (p. 109). Anyway, Tom leaves. Master George meets him later and offers him a silver dollar. There is an exchange of love and affection between the two. When he has to part company with his old master, Tom tells him: "Be a good mas'er, like yer creator in the days o' yer youth, Mas'er George" (p. 112).

Mr George, Eliza's husband too escapes from the clutches of his cruel master Harries. He meets his former master Wilson of the manufacturing unit at a hotel in Kentucky. When Wilson enquires George, now under the false name Henry Butler of Oakland, Shelby County, he says he is running away. Wilson, however, advises him not to do so as he is a Christian. Wilson says he is an American, so he should be a good citizen. For all his advice, George speaks of his background, slaves' condition of life in America and their rights: "My country again! Mr Wilson, you have a country but what country have I, or any one like me, born of slave mothers? What laws are there for us? We don't make them,—we don't consent to them,—we have nothing to do with them; all they do for us is to crush us, and keep us down. Haven't I heard your Fourth-of-July speeches? Don't you tell all, once a year, that governments derive their just power from the consent of the governed? Can't a fellow think, that hears such things? Can't he put this and that together, and see what it comes to?" (p. 122).

"D' you call these laws of my country? Sir, I haven't any country, any more than I have any father. But I'm going to have one. I don't want anything of your country, except to be let alone,—to go peaceably out of it; and when I get to Canada, where the laws own me and protect me, that shall be my country, and its laws I will obey. But if any man tries to stop me, let him take care, for I am desperate. I'll fight for my liberty to the last breath I breathe. You say your fathers did it; if it was right for them, it is right for me!" (p. 124).

Finally, George goes off.

Likewise, Haley and Tom jog away to an auctioning place in Washington. Haley wants to buy some more slaves. He buys Albert without buying his old mother. Haley catches a boat La Belle Riviera on the river Ohio. And overhead in the cabin sit fathers and mothers, husbands and wives and in the deck below sit all the slaves. Shortly Haley catches hold of Lucy and her child whom he had earlier bought of. Even he sells Lucy's son at

Louisville when she is asleep. Once Lucy knows this she commits suicide by drowning in the river. Tom watches all this. Stowe comments on American slavery: "Who does not know how our great men are outdoing themselves, in declaiming against the foreign slave trade? There is a perfect host of Clarkson's and Wilberforce's risen up among us on that subject, most edifying to hear and behold. Trading Negroes from America, dear reader, is so horrid. It is not to be thought of! But trading them from Kentucky,—that's quite another thing!" (p. 146).

Eliza is left at Simeon Holiday's house. Simeon's wife Rachel is the best kind of woman. The Holidays shelter poor Eliza. Even they find Eliza's husband. This makes her more than happy. Stowe writes, "She dreamed of a beautiful country,—a land, it seemed to her, of rest,—green shores, pleasant islands, and beautifully glittering water; and there, in a house which kind voices told her was a home, she saw her boy playing, a free and happy child. She heard her husband's footsteps; she felt him coming nearer; his arms were around her, his tears falling on her face, and she awoke!" (p. 153). Equal was George's joy when he joined his family at the Holidays' house: "This, indeed, was a home—home,—a word that in God, and trust yet known a meaning for; and a belief in God, as, with a golden cloud of protection and confidence, dark, misanthropic, pining, atheistic doubts, and fierce despair, melted away before the light of a living Gospel, breathed in living faces, preached by a thousand unconscious acts of love and good-will, which, like the cup of cold water given in the name of a disciple, shall never lose their reward" (p. 155).

Thereafter, the Holidays make an arrangement and accordingly some people by the name Phineas Fletcher would carry them onward to some place wherefrom they could go to Canada.

Now Haley with his slaves and that of Tom travels in a boat on the River Mississippi. Stowe describes the merchandise of the boat, its two decks and cotton bales. The white people include the family of St Clare and his daughter Evangeline, Eva for short and his cousin Miss Ophelia. Tom reads illegibly his Bible. The girl called Eva is very cute and looks an airy fairy. She walks the whole of the boat. As usual, the girl comes to Tom looking at him. He asks her who she is. She says she is Eva. He entices her with his special kind of toys-like articles. She likes them. She appears to him some kind of angel sent out from his New Testament. Their conversation is beautifully drawn. Shortly the boat stops at a landing to take some wood and Tom helps the boatman have it. Soon Eva falls down into the water and Tom who is there rescues her easily. Her father St Clare appreciates him for this. In fact, Eva asks her father to purchase him as though a playing object. St Clare buys Tom for 1300 dollars.

Stowe writes about St Clare. He is a simple and rich man of Louisiana. The family had its origin in Canada. He had a brother, both doing plantation. Later, his brother settled to his plantation in Vermont. St Clare remained in Louisiana. Their mother was a Huguenot French lady whose family had immigrated to America during the days of settlement. He once saw a woman and wanted to marry her. But her gardians did not help him as they wanted her marry their son. Then, St Clare married a rich but useless lady Marie. When their journey began she was in their house in New Orleans. So St Clare is going to New Orleans now. As Eva wants a good climate, he takes her there. As she, his only daughter, now health-upset, wants Tom, he buys Tom too. His cousin Miss Ophelia is going with him for taking care of his family. Once New Orleans comes St Clare alights. Once back home St Clare is happy to meet his wife and show her his new servant as a better blackie than all at home. Yet she does not like him. Tom is introduced to Adolph, another servant who used to take liberty in the house. Tom settles with his new master and is pleasant to one and all. Eva stays much of her time in his company.

The novel *Uncle Tom's Cabin* is full of discussions and debates about slavery. Yet the matter is clearly divided into two groups amongst the whites. Some of them like Shelby though take part in it denounce slavery. His wife is keen about it. Mr Bird, the Senator, does not like slavery though he cooperates. His wife is as good as Mrs Shelby that way. Then the case of Holidays is considerable. The Holidays do not like slavery.

Likewise, Mr Clare does not like slavery. His cousin Ophelia does not like it for sure. Whereas Mary Clare likes slavery and her ideas about it are harrowing: She says, "Well, at any rate, I'm thankful I'm born where slavery exists; and I believe it's right,—indeed, I feel it must be; and, at any rate, I'm sure I couldn't get along without it" (p. 203).

Eliza and George are united by the efforts of the Holidays. Now they are specially happy though their joy appears to be of short life. Simeon Holiday arranges a cart for their forward journey. Phineas Fletcher who is ready to carry them forward also brings the news of a gang in search of them. The parting journey is marked by joy and sympathy. They look worthy of a painting as the author says. Once they travel as farther as possible they notice Tom Lokher's party. So in a twinkling all of them run off to some hideout. Tom Lokher follows them in a dangerous rout. On knowing this George addresses him thus: "Gentlemen, who are you, down there, and what do you want?"

"We want a party of runaway niggers", said Tom Lokher. "One George Harries, and Eliza Harries, and their son, and Jim Selden, and an old woman. We've got the officers here, and a warrant to take'em; and we're going to have 'em, too. D'ye hear? An't you George Harris, that belongs to Mr Harris, of Shelby Countty, Kentucky?" (p. 215).

Then, Tom Lokher fires at George which he escapes narrowly. This makes George fire back and the same hits Tom and he falls down. Naturally Marks and others following Tom retreat back. So George and his company continue their forward journey. Eliza makes them pity Tom Lokher and they take him to the next station where he is deposited for medicine. Next Harriet Beecher Stowe narrates St Clare's life, attitudes and ideas, focusing on American slavery. We hear that some Americans do not want slavery go off. They make Black people suffer. The instances of Dinah, Prue and others are offered.

One day the poor old Tom with the help of Eva writes a letter to his wife Chloe. The girl exclaims "Oh!, it is a shame you ever had to go away from them!" (p. 257). These days St Clare buys a black girl called Topsy maybe as a company for Eva or just to help the girl to be brought up under the care of Miss Ophelia. Ophelia likes to bring up the girl only after a lot of fuss. One day the old lady asks Topsy for details about her life. The dialogue is amazing showing the flight of the Negroes:

> Sitting down before her, she began to question her.
>
> "How old are you, Topsy?"
>
> "Dunno, Missis," said the image, with a grin that showed all her teeth.
>
> "Don't know how old you are? Didn't anybody ever tell you? Who was your mother?"
>
> "Never had one!" said the child, with another grin.
>
> "Never had any mother? What do you mean? Where were you born?"
>
> "Never was born!" persisted Topsy with another grin. (p. 263)

So we find the little Negro girl in such a flight that she is sold from one person to another. In the deal, she is unaware of her parents, age and upbringing. She has also, due to the problem of living, learnt lying and stealing. Ophelia has to struggle hard to teach her honesty and goodness in life. Topsy learns something in the deal. She is happy to speak to Tom and Eva. These days Tom receives a letter from his wife written by master George. It is said that all are well at home. Emily Shelby, Chloe and George are doing some efforts to buy him back. Accordingly, Chloe is hired in a confectionary factory for earning some money towards their buying him. Tom is happy to know all this. This time Eva meets him and both the good souls talk of hope and heaven. Tom sings of some Bible songs:

> Oh, had I the wings of the morning,
> I'd fly away to Canaan's shore;
> Bright angels should convey me home,
> To the New Jerusalem.

"Where do you suppose new Jerusalem is, Uncle Tom?" said Eva.

"Oh, up in the clouds, Miss Eva. Look in those clouds!—they look like great gates of pearl; and you can see beyond them,—far, far off,—it's all gold. Tom sings about 'spirits bright'."

"I see a band of spirits bright,
That taste the glories here;
They all are robed in spotless white,
And conquering psalm they bear."

"Uncle Tom, I've seen them", said Eva. Tom had no doubt of it at all; it did not surprise him in the least. If Eva had told him she had been to heaven he would have thought it entirely probable.

"They come to me sometimes in my sleep, those spirits"; and Eva's eyes grew dreamy and she hummed, in a low voice,—

"They all are robed in spotless white,
And conquering psalm they bear."

"Uncle Tom", said Eva, "I'm going there."

"Where, Miss Eva?"

The child rose and pointed her little hand to the sky; the glow of evening lit her golden hair and flushed cheek with a kind of unearthly radiance and her spirits bright, "Tom, I'm going before long" (pp. 183-84).

This episode marks something important in the life of Eva as a heaven sent girl. She thinks of good and salvation, maybe because of her going there shortly due to her frail health as bad as her mother's. This time, St Clare's brother Albert and his son Henrique come and stay there for a day at the lake where St Clare has shifted his house for guarding against the heat of the summer. Henrique's slave boy Dodo is harassed and Eva takes the chance to reform Henrique. Once Albert goes off, Eva falls ill. Doctors say she is declining in her health. Another day, she puts it to her papa that she is going to heaven. She says, "The time is coming that I am going to leave you. I am going, and never to come back!" (p. 300). Oh she tells him he should leave the slaves for freedom! She tells him: "And promise me, dear father, that Tom shall have his freedom as soon as—", she stopped and said, in a hesitating tone,—"I am gone!" (p. 301).

We find that gradually Eva develops pain in her heart. This convinces her that she is going to die. So she provides all of them a curl of her hair and she tells them: "I want to speak to you about your souls.... Many of you, I am afraid, are very careless. You are thinking only about this world. I want you to remember that there is a beautiful world where Jesus is" (p. 313). She advises Topsy to well behave. She tells St Clare and Tom that she will see them in heaven. The father tells her, "Farewell, beloved child!" It appears to the grief-stricken man as if the end of the world. He bears the grief heavily and imagines she is calling him to the sky. St Clare thinks of freeing Tom but he thinks of his emotional happiness requiring him for that. Now the Clares return to New Orleans. One day he gifts the child Topsy to Miss Ophelia. One day even he is stabbed of by a ruffian when he was helping them to cease their quarrel. St Clare dies with the word 'Mother' in his mouth.

After the death of Mr Clare, Marie decides the family matters. The first of which is she chastises unruly people like Rosa. Miss Ophelia does not like the measure. Yet, she asks Marie to free Tom as Eva as well as her father wanted it. Marie is stubborn and she refuses. She instead sends all her slaves to Mr Skeggs for auctioning. There, one Mr Simon Legree purchases Tom and others. Legree also purchase a lady Emmaline. He takes them to his cotton plantation in the South. He asks them to pluck cotton balls. Mr Legree is cruel and hard-hearted. He likes Tom though. Yet he wants Tom to become an overseer for his slave servants. But Tom fails in being cruel and hard-hearted as his two servants Quimbo and Sembo or his hounds. Tom's helping Cassy provokes Legree and he lashes him for being 'good' and a 'truly Christian'. This is totally inhuman. He beats Tom badly and the latter often falls ill.

Sometime later, Cassy and Emmeline make an escape. Their escape story is detective in nature. Once they go off partially, Legree beats Tom almost to death. George Shelby arrives to Tom's surprise but Tom is going to heaven now. He breathes his last. Shelby speaks to Legree about life's truth and buries Tom. Soon Cassy makes her escape finally. She joins Shelby. Another woman Madame de Thoux goes with him. When she makes a causal enquiry of her brother George, Shelby speaks of Eliza too. That means Thoux traces George Harries and the same enquiry helps Cassy find out her daughter Eliza, now George's wife. Shelby tells them they are in Canada. So they go to Amherstburg and find out George. Later, Thoux takes George's family with Cassy and Emmeline to France. George will have some university education there. Finally he decides to settle in Africa for the sake of helping the black people.

On the other hand, George Shelby reaches Kentucky and delivers the sad message. Chloe feels very sad. One week, fortunately Shelby frees all his people with the words in reverence of Tom of Uncle Tom's Cabin: "Think of freedom every time you see UNCLE TOM'S CABIN; and let it be a memorial to put you all in mind to follow in his steps, and be as honest and faithful and Christian as he was" (p. 474).

The novel *Uncle Tom's Cabin* is about Tom's suffering as a slave. Stowe asks one important question over the narration: "What is it to be a moral human being?" The novel is quite relevant today as it helped a nation to move to its Civil War. Abraham Lincoln's legendary statement that "So this is the little lady who made this big war", evinces the importance of the novel. The novel, to be brief, is a powerful work that is an essential part of the collective experience of the American people.

NOTES

1. Harriet Beecher Stowe, qt. by Darryl Pinckney, Introduction, *Uncle Tom's Cabin,* A Signet Classic, New York, 1998, p. ix.
2. Harriet Beecher Stowe, *Uncle Tom's Cabin.*
3. Darryl Pinckney, Introduction, *Uncle Tom's Cabin,* p. xvi.
4. All the refrences to the novel are from the edition Harriet Beech Stowe, *Uncle Tom's Cabin,* with an Introduction by Darryl Pinckney, A Signet Classic, New York, 1998.

6

Frederick Douglass's *Narrative of the Life of an American Slave*

Frederick Douglass was born a slave in Maryland. He taught himself to read and write, escaped to Massachusetts by disguising himself as a sailor and became one of the most effective orators of his day, an influential newspaper editor, a confidant of the radical abolitionist John Brown, a militant reformer and a respected diplomat. The first two accounts of his experiences belong to the tradition of fugitive-slave narratives popular in the North before the Civil War; the final volume, published when he was in his mid-sixties, reveals one of the most remarkable and successful lives of the 19th century.

Narrative of the Life of Frederick Douglass, an American Slave[1] (1845) told in 125 pages, the story of his life, from early childhood until he escaped from bondage (and changed his last name from Bailey to Douglass) in 1838. The vivid detail, the dignity of tone and the sincerity of the writing left no doubt that Douglass had in fact suffered the horrors. In 1855 he published a revised version of the *Narrative* under the title *My Bondage and My Freedom*. This work balanced a more detailed account of his life. It told of his intimacy with the abolitionist movement, which demanded immediate freeing of all slaves on moral grounds, of his successful speaking tour of the British Isles, the purchase of his freedom for $700 by a group of his admirers and his move to Rochester, New York, where he brought out in 1847 the first issue of the increasingly outspoken weekly newspaper he published for 13 years (first as *The North Star*, later as *Frederick Douglass's Monthly*). The third of Douglass's autobiographies, *The Life and Times of Frederick Douglass* (1881), subsumes the first two and adds to them the events of his career just before, during and after the Civil War and traces the rising arc of his fame and influence and the ultimately honored recognition of his countrymen, black and white alike.

Wrongly accused of complicity in John Brown's raid on the arsenal at Harpers Ferry in 1859, Douglass was obliged to flee to Canada and thence to England. Once the Civil War began, he took an active role in the campaign to make black men eligible for Union service; he became a successful recruiter of black soldiers, whose ranks soon included two of his own sons. Having helped to enlist these men, Douglass was only acting in character when he took his protests over their unequal pay and treatment directly to President Lincoln. Douglass continued to object to every sign of discrimination—economic, sexual, legal and social. Even after he had been appointed United States Marshal and then Recorder of Deeds for the District of Columbia, he continued to speak out on such matters as the exploitation of black sharecroppers in the South, to demand anti-lynching legislation, to protest the exclusion of black people from public accommodations. He was active in suffrage movements for women. It would be hard to exaggerate the importance for later black leaders such as Booker T. Washington and W.E.B. DuBois of Douglass's exemplary career as a champion of human rights. His life, in fact, has become the heroic paradigm for all oppressed people.

The narrative begins with Douglass's birth in Tuckahoe in Talbot County, Maryland. As a slave he did not know his age as horses do not know theirs. Yet he found out his age as 17 in 1835.

Harriet Bailey was his mother and his father, a white man. Probably his master was his father as people whispered it. He got separated from his mother when he was a child. His mother worked as a farm-hand at another master 12 miles away. She used to see him night time. He was not informed of her death. She died as a stranger. Douglass thinks most mulatto slave children were fathered by their white masters.

Frederick Douglass served many masters—original and hiring. The first one Captain Anthony had 30 slaves in his two farms and the boy Douglass worked under his overseer Plummer, a monster. He remembers that the white master would whip the blacks to wounds and even to death. They would try to justify the use of whip. Worse still the slaves never knew what a full meals was!

Frederick Douglass was in another master, Hugh's house for seven years. Here he learnt reading and writing. The Hughes treated him as though a brute. First his mistress was kind. But the master asked her not to teach the slaves. So as Douglass says, "Slavery proved as injurious to her as it was to him" (p. 838). She decided to keep him in dark as education and slaves were incompatible! He says how he learnt reading: "The plan which I adopted, and the one by which I was most successful, was that of making friends of all the little white boys whom I met in the street. As many of these as I could, I converted into teachers. With their kindly aid, obtained at different times and in different places, I finally succeeded in learning to read" (p. 839).

Douglass, when 12, read a book called *The Columbus an Orator* which had a dialogue between a master and his run away slave. Sheridian denouncement of slavery also encouraged him to run away one day. Douglass thought the whites as captors and monsters. More he read more he hated them. He read about abolition. One day he went to the harbor and helped two Irish workers on his own. Then they sympathized with him and asked him to run away to the north. Douglass says he learnt writing in a shipyard and he explains all the amusing things about it.

Then he left to live with another master Thomas Auld at St Michael's in 1832. The Aulds were cruel and mean. They gave neither good food nor enough of the other. So the boy resorted to begging and stealing as necessary. "Thos did nothing of himself. He was a slaveholder without the ability to hold slaves" (p. 843). Once he got converted he found religious sanction for cruelty. He used to beat Henny, a woman, to blood and would quote the Bible: "He that knoweth his master's will, and doeth it not, shall be beaten with many stripes" (p. 844).

Douglass had his own difference with Thos and the latter entrusted him to the care of Edward Covey, another 'nigger-breaker' in 1833. Mr. Covey gave him enough food but not enough time to eat it. He whipped Douglass heavily. He made him a farm-hand and whipped Douglass for his awkwardness. He was called the 'snake' for his cunningness. Douglass observes, "If at any one time of my life more than another, I was made to drink the bitterest dregs of slavery that time was during the first six months of my stay with Covey. We were worked in all weathers. It was never too hot or too cold; it would never rain, blow, hail, or snow, too hard for us to work in the field. Work, work, work was scarcely more the order of the day than of the night. The longest days were too short for him, and the shorter nights too long for him. I was somewhat unmanageable when I first went there, but a few months of this discipline tamed me. Mr Covey succeeded in breaking me. I was broken in body, soul, and spirit. My natural elasticity was crushed, my intellect languished, the disposition to read departed, and the cheerful spark that lingered about my eye died; the dark night of slavery closed in upon me, and behold a man transformed into a brute!" (p. 847).

One day Covey beat him too much. So Douglass went to the old master for help. As per the conditions, Douglass was to serve Covey for a full year. So he went back and got threatened. Douglass ran away soon. A friend Sandy advised him to have a root and none would beat him. This comes true for a few days. But next Monday Covey tried to tie Douglass and Douglass resisted it. He beat his master. Douglass writes, "This battle with Covey was the turning point in my career as a slave. It rekindled the few expiring embers of freedom, and revived within me a sense of my own manhood. It recalled the departed self-confidence, and inspired me again with a determination to be free" (p. 852). Edward Covey, as a first class slaveholder, did not punish Douglass as his fame was at stake. Slaveholders made slaves to eat molasses, drink rum and made them lose their conscience.

In 1824 Douglass joined another master William Freeland nearby. Douglass observes this master was good. Here Douglass awoke his other slaves to literacy. He called his school as Sabbath school. Many neighborhood slaves joined him. They learnt the 'will of the God'. This work was 'the sweetest engagement' for him. The slaves loved each other and were ready to die.

Douglass was hired again by Freeland in 1835. But he refused service there as he decided of freedom or death. He decided to run away and his friends Henry and John Harries, Henry Bailey and Charles Roberts joined him. He had master William Hamilton's false letter for protection.

But the group was arrested and taken to Michael's for inspection. They were put in Easten jail. After a week, he was taken by his master and sent to his brother Hugh in Baltimore. He was hired in a shipbuilding firm where he worked like an animal. He had a fighting with the white people and got wounded. Hugh then sent him to Mr. Walter Price's shipyard where Douglass calked and earned much money for his master.

NOTE

1. All the textual reference are from Frederick Douglass's *Narrative of the Life of an American Slave*, pt. in *Norton Anthology of American Literature*.

7

Democratic Life in Walt Whitman's Poetry

The 19th century United States of America produced several great writers. Many of them were poets, prose writers and playwrights. Walt Whitman was one of the greatest poets of the times.

American literature found its renaissance in the mid 19th century. If Ralph Waldo Emerson was its harbinger, Henry David Thoreau, Walt Whitman, Nathaniel Hawthorne, Emily Dickinson and many others were its pioneers.

The poetry of Emerson created a stream of inspiration in American literature. Emerson wrote philosophical poetry. Walt Whitman was there to improvise American poetry with his so-called democratic kind of poesy.

Walt Whitman was born in Long Island in 1819. His father was a carpenter-builder by trade. The Whitman family moved to Brooklyn suburb later. He had his basic education there. Soon he began reporting to newspapers such as *Daily Eagle*. It is said he taught people democratic politics, morals, civic virtues and the tendencies of the times.

The youth Walt Whitman was a dreamer and mystic. He was patriotic to the core. He worried about his nation. He was not a family man. He was a Bohemian. Thus, his thoughts are poured in his great work *Leaves of Grass*. Once he said to his friend the Canadian Dr. Ricgard Maurice Bucke: "Out of my life in Brooklyn and New York from 1838 to 1853 absorbing a million people, for fifteen years, with an intimacy, eagerness, an abandon, probably never equaled."[1] Whitman read great writers like Carlyle and Scott and many others daily, in his work of editing and collected an intellectual arsenal for democracy. When American Democratic Party liked to approve slavery he turned from politics to writing poetry. Emerson hailed him as the author of 'the American poem'.

Walt Whitman became rather self-expressive and transcendental. His spiritual intuition was quite strong after he refused political journalism. His masterpiece *Leaves of Grass* is something of a record in world poetry. Walt Whitman defined his work thus:

> An attempt...of a naïve, masculine, affectionate, contemplative, sensual, imperious person to cast into literature not only his own grit and arrogance, but his own flesh and form, undraped, regardless of models, regardless of modesty or law; and ignorant, as at first it appears, of...all outside of the fiercely loved land of his birth.... The effects of the original eye or arm, or the actual atmosphere, of tree, or bird.
>
> I saw, from the time my enterprise and questionings positively shaped themselves (how best can I express my own distinctive era and surroundings, America, Democracy?) that the trunk and center whence the answer was to radiate, and to which all soul, a personality—which personality, after many considerations and ponderings, I deliberately settled should be myself—indeed could not be any other.
>
> *Leaves of Grass*...has mainly been...an attempt...to put *a Person*, a human being (myself, in the latter half of the Nineteenth Century, in America) freely, fully and truly on record. I could not find any similar personal record in current literature that satisfied me.[2]

The first edition of *Leaves of Grass* was published by Walt Whitman himself. The same collection very well pictured is a collector's item today. The book had 12 poems such as "Song of Myself". "Song of Myself", the first poem, so characteristic of Whitman is his best. It is a key to understand the poet. He shows he wanted to be a poet of the new world. It is a poem of 52 loosely grouped verse paragraphs, every para being a turn in the thoughts of the poet. The poem begins with an assertion intended to challenge contemporary literature, particularly poetry. The poet speaks thus,

> I celebrate myself, and sing myself,...
> For every atom belonging to me as good belongs to you...
> I loafe and invite my soul...
> I harbour for good or bad, I permit to speak at every hazard,
> Nature without check, with original energy.

Walt Whitman discovers that there is a world of sense perception in every man and woman. He thinks all people are brothers and sisters. Mankind is a fraternity. It is observed:

> Therefore the self-dramatized Walt Whitman speaks all this, sees himself in all people and all life, speaks for woman as well as man, for evil as well as good, and walking with the tender and growing night feels unspeakable passionate love for such beauty. He accepts time absolutely; in the long run, he says, it is without flaw. He accepts science which explains reality. He trusts the en-masse:
>
> I speak the pass-word primeval, I give the sign of democracy.
> By God! I will accept nothing which all cannot have their
> Counterpart of on the same terms.

Robert Spiller writes, "Now Walt Whitman goes with his vision. Over America, its work and festivals, he wanders, pleased with all his meets, then lifts his imagination to the past. He walks with Christ on the hills of Judaea; he is a free companion, a hero, a slave hounded by pursuers; he was at the Alamo; he fought with Paul Jones. He will save the depressed and the dying by the power of his love, outbidding those old hucksters, the heathen gods:

> I know perfectly well my own egotism,
> Know my omnivorous lines and must not write any less,
> And would fetch you whoever you are flush with myself."[3]

Walt Whitman is said to be an expansionist poet. His writings are prophetic. He asks people to learn things like him, learn to live local and love the global. He asks people to think highly and live plainly. He asks them to love all so that all will love them. He asks them to be good to others as to themselves.

He asks them to be human, hard-working, magnanimous. He asks them to value their bodies as they value their souls. He says body is as important as the soul.

How Walt Whitman has such revolutionary thoughts? One must know. One must know that he came from a radical humanistic family. His father Walter Whitman was a strong individualist. Secondly his mother was from Quakerism which guided man to live by the light of his soul. Quakerism influenced Walt Whitman greatly. Thirdly Walt Whitman learnt from Emerson's transcendentalism. It is observed that: "If, as Whitman learned both from the Quakers and from Emerson, a man could be God's mouthpiece, then God Whitman felt, must be manifest through man's body and all its impulses as well as through his soul. Soul and body were indissolubly interdependent, and blood and spirit were equally important in a true democracy. The common man, lusty, full-blooded, living, especially in America, upon hearty and varied experience, was as important as the saint, the intellectual, or the aristocrat, and in history likely to become more important. The vigorous sexual instinct which keeps the race alive was not merely a means for breeding new candidates for the Heavenly kingdom, nor was it, as the Concordians thought, an animal remainder to be sublimated into a love transcending the flesh. No, if the soul was God, so was the body, and if democracy, and man himself, was to reach an ideal society, then the senses must have their full self-development as part of the expression of the soul. Here was an extension of transcendentalism, adapting it to the need and the facts of an expanding democracy in a new land."[4]

Walt Whitman as tall as six feet, was lusty, vigorous and healthy. It is what he expected in others. These are the passions and things that occur in *Leaves of Grass*. Walt Whitman was physically sympathetic, mentally interpretative, for both sexes, richer perhaps than either taken alone. Yet Whitman's sexual oversensitiveness was grossly misinterpreted in his times. It shocked the religious and puritan. Still he was original though shocking, bold though egoistic and powerful though sometimes in wrong directions. Some of the ideas are seen in his "I Sing the Body Electic" and "Who Learns My Lesson Complete".

A second edition of the *Leaves of Grass* appeared in 1856 with new poems such as "Salut au Monde!", "Song of the Broad Axe", "Crossing Brooklyn Ferry" and "Song of the Open Road". In 1860 Whitman issued the next volume. The sixth edition appeared in 1876 with fine poems such as "Passage to India". The ninth and the last edition appeared in 1892.

The first edition of the *Leaves of Grass* was mainly the nucleus of great poetry which he enlarged later. He sent many copies to writers, intellectuals and reviewers. They took great interest in it and spoke of it well. Yet *Leaves of Grass* did not sell well. Many people did not understand it until the end of Whitman's life. It is observed that: "All this was true of the first *Leaves of Grass*, and unfortunately the shock and clamor with which the relatively few greeted its 'arrogant' verses redoubled when in the 1860 edition Whitman included his 'Calamus' and his 'Children of Adam', poems which, so the outraged critics thought, were only incentives to sexuality and perhaps to perversion. They neglected (with a few exceptions) new poems of moving beauty and emotional depth, such as 'Crossing Brooklyn Ferry'. The critics of later editions did not recognize the deepening of Whitman's religious feeling and his far saner intuitions of human nature in such superb poems of the later fifties and the sixties as 'Out of the Cradle Endlessly Rocking', 'When Lilacs Last in the Dooryard Bloom'd', and 'Passage to India'. Nor did they note, again with a few exceptions, a growth in artistry, until what had been an experiment in 'Song of Myself' became in these later poems the technical excellence of a great and original creator of prosody."[5]

Sometimes Whitman was not happy with his nation, for the people in power were corrupt or manipulating. He did not like slavery. The Democratic Party approved slavery which deepened Whitman's anguish. So he writes,

> Let the people sprawl with yearning, aimless hands!...
> (Stifled, O days! O lands! In every public and private corruption!)

Robert Spiller thinks no one, for example, can fail to notice Whitman's nobility as seen in the poem "Out of the Cradle

Endlessly Rocking". The poem is a reminiscence of childhood. It is a record of loss and love far too passionate and too mature for a child's mind. The poet speaks of two birds that have come from Alabama and now rest at a nest in the shore of Paumanok. He speaks of the he-bird which has lost its mate—the she-bird. The he-bird laments over the loss of its spouse. Its anguish is simply unbearable:

> Hither my love!
> Here I am! Here!
> With this just-sustained note I announce myself to you,
> This gentle call is for you my love, for you.

The poet thinks death is not an end of life. It is the beginning of an afterlife. It is an answer to the insatiable. It is observed: "Death began to seem as important as life, religion more important than self-expression, for only death with its extensions of spiritual continuities growing closer to the mystery of God, solved the irreconcilable contradictions of earthly life. His poetry deepened because his imagination, always aware of spiritual values, now was chastened into reaching far beyond and beneath his sensory experiences."[6]

Whitman's elegy on the death of Abraham Lincoln is greatly moving. All readers have admired the pathos of "When Lilacs Last in the Dooryard Bloom'd". The poem is about the poet's mourning of the death of American President Abraham Lincoln. Whitman makes use of symbols like lilacs, western star and thrush. The bird's singing is a commentary on the poet's mourning of the dear departed leader. Whitman calls the leader as 'a powerful western fallen star!' He writes,

> O what shall I hang on the chamber walls?
> And what shall the pictures be that I hang on the walls,
> To adorn the burial-house of him I love?
> ...
> Lilac and star and bird twined with the chant of my soul,
> There in the fragrant pines and the cedars dusk and dim.

The poet has both the knowledge of death and thoughts of death. He laments that death is not the end of life, it is a gateway for the other world. It opens the world of love.

Walt Whitman's poem "Passage to India" is still nobler. The poem is an answer for the youths who ask the question "Whither, O Mocking Life?" the marriage of the seas in the Suez Canal, the crossing of the continent by steel, do not satisfy, they are but shadows of a greater dream. Whitman says there must be a passage to more than India. So one must sail for deep waters of life. The poet writes,

Passage to India!
Cooling airs from Caucasus far, soothing cradle of man,
The river Euphrates flowing, the past lit up again.

Lo soul, the retrospect brought forward,
The old, most populous, wealthiest of earth's lands,
The streams of the Indus and the Ganges and their many affluents,
The tale of Alexander on his warlike marches suddenly dying,
On one side China and on the other side Persia and Arabia,
To the south the great seas and the Bay of Bengal,
The flowing literatures, tremendous epics, religions, castes,
Old occult Brahma interminably far back, the tender and junior Buddha,
Central and southern empires and all their belongings, possessors,
The wars of Tamerlane, the reign of Aurangzebe,
The traders, rulers, explorers, Moslems, Venetians, Byzantium,
The Arabs, Portuguese,
The first travelers famous yet, Marco Polo, batouta the Moor,
Doubts to be solved, the map incognita, blanks to be filled,
The foot of man unstayed, the hands never at rest,
Thyself O soul that will not brook a challenge

Passage to more than India!
O secret of the earth and sky!

O my brave soul!
O farther farther sail!
O daring joy, but safe! Are they not all the seas of God?
O farther, farther, farther sail!

There are controversies about Walt Whitman's poetic style. As we know there are as many styles as there are as many great poets. Walt Whitman is one of the greatest poets. He was quite different from others of his time. Just like Emily Dickinson, Whitman had his own way of writing poems. His language was prosaic rather. He did not care for traditional styles. Shakespearean language and Italian and French operas influenced him. His style was best suited to write about a new nation, human passions and democracy. Walt Whitman used symbols too as we see in poems like "When the Lilacs Dooryard Bloom'd". And his symbolism is confident, controlled, expressive and beautiful.

Walt Whitman has written many other works. His *Democratic Vistas* (1871) may be read for its emphasis on the use of democracy. He thinks democracy can help every man to materialize his aims and objectivities. It can be a humanism, a welfare state at the same time. Whitman was a chanter of democracy. He was a bard and seer. He was simply revolutionary. Such a great man died in 1892 after a bout of paralysis. Emerson's tribute to him is still relevant today. Emerson said: "Americans who had been seeking abroad for some powerful expression of their phase of earth history could come home—unto us a man has been born."[7]

NOTES

1. Robert Spiller, "Walt Whitman", *Literary History of the United States*, ed. by Robert Spiller, p. 474.
2. Walt Whitman, qt. by Robert Spiller, "Walt Whitman", *Literary History of the United States*, ed. by Robert Spiller, p. 474.
3. Robert Spiller, "Walt Whitman", *Literary History of the United States*, ed. by Robert Spiller, p. 79.
4. *Ibid.*, 482.
5. *Ibid.*, 487.
6. *Ibid.*, 490.
7. *Ibid.*, 498.

Herman Melville's *Moby Dick*

8

Herman Melville is an American novelist. He was born in New York. After primary education, he sailed to Liverpool. He did a whaling trip and lived with the Typee cannibals in the Marquises. This is seen in *Typee* (1846). *Omoo* (1847), *Mardi* (1849), *Redburn* (1849) and *White-Jacket* (1850) are about sea life. He lived with Nathaniel Hawthorne and dedicated his novel *Moby Dick* (1851) to him, which is, by some considered as the best American fiction. His last two novels are *Pierre* (1852) and *The Confidence-Man* (1857) and *Billy Budd* (1924) is his unfinished story. He wrote poetry and short stories too.

Herman Melville's *Moby Dick* is a complex plot of adventure, fact, superstition, history and philosophy narrated by meditative wanderer Ishmael. Captain Ahab's boat Pequod and his act of trying to destroy a white whale called 'Moby Dick' is a prominent concern here. Ishmael's story of joining the ship is equally important. So rich are the novel's symbols and themes. "In essence Melville tried to explore humanity's place in the physical and metaphysical world in all its ambiguity and complexity. To do this he juxtaposed such ideas as Christian and pagan beliefs, civilization and savagery, science and superstition, gods and devils, free will and fate, the physical and the spiritual, and light and darkness."[1]

The title of chapter 1, "Loomings" sets a portentous mood to the actions. The narrator introduces himself with the famous line, "Call me Ishmael", the name of the outcast son of the biblical Abraham. He then begins the story of 'some years ago' when, destitute in Manhattan, he decides to go to sea, a habitual antidote to his discontent. He—and all men, he maintains—are mystically attracted to the ocean because in it they see 'the image of the ungraspable phantom of life'. However, this time he goes to sea 'not as a merchant sailor but as a whaler', he initially believed he was motivated by his 'own unbiased freewill and discriminating judgment', when in fact the Fates, he claims, were deluding him.

Ishmael arrives in New Bradford to find he has missed a boat to Nantucket. He rejects two inns as expensive before deciding upon the third, The Spouter-Inn, whose landlord is named Peter Coffin. The number of three in *Moby Dick* frequently has ominous significance.

Some of the novel's few comic moments take place during Ishmael's first night and morning at The Spouter-Inn and involve his acquaintance with the cannibal Queequeg. Ishmael is horrified at the sight of the pagan. Ishmael explores New Bradford, attends a whale men's Chapel Sunday service and forms a 'bosom' companionship with Queequeg. The chapel holds a congregation of 'sailors and sailors' wives and widows', who focus on memorial tablets of men who died at sea—some killed by whales. Realizing his potential fate, Ishmael raises several unanswerable questions about death. He then looks at what for him is the bright part of his being—his soul. The old chaplain, a former harpooner named father Mapple, mounts his pulpit, which resembles a ship's bow and addresses the congregations. His sermon includes two lessons. He tells the story of the prophet Jonah, who, after being swallowed by a whale, 'leaves all his deliverance to god' and achieves 'true and faithful repentance; not clamorous for pardon, but grateful for punishment'. He then says that because, he therefore feels a greater responsibility not just to heed the lessons, but to preach 'the truth to the face of falsehood'.

Back at The Spouter-Inn, Ishmael and Queequeg become close friends. With his simple, honest heart and brave spirit Queequeg, a significantly not Father Maple, seems to turn Ishmael's soul toward goodness. Ishmael and Queequeg journey to Nantucket to sign up with a whaler and board Ahab's ship. Aboard the *Moss*, which takes them from New Bradford in Nantucket, to the two lodge at the Try Pots, over whose doorway hangs a topmast resembling a gallows. After Ishmael surveys three ships, he selects the third—the Pequod—a noble yet melancholy craft. Ishmael applies to two old former whaleship captains and investors in the Pequod, the Nantucket Quakers Bildad and Peleg, whose job it is to prepare to pay Ishmael, they decide on a lower 'lay' than Ishmael had proposed, but he accepts their offer and promises to bring his harpooner friend Queequeg to meet them the next day. Prejudiced against the pagan, Peleg and Bildad first balk at hiring Queequeg. But after Ishmael declares that Queequeg is a member of the 'whole worshipping world's church' and after Queequeg impressively throws his harpoon, he is signed for a lay larger than Ishmael's. In the first of the novel's many prophecies and warnings, Peleg warns Ishmael about the forbidding ocean; describes the Pequod's captain, Ahab as mysteriously 'sick' since his leg was chewed by a whale and tells him of the prophetical name given to Ahab by his widowed, crazy mother, who saw in him a vile king, 'grand, ungodly, godlike'. Ishmael and Queequeg next meet a shabbily dressed puzzling old sailor named Elijah, who, after learning that they have signed on with the Pequod, asks whether there was anything in the agreement about their souls. He then hints at Ahab's tormented history and the circumstances surrounding the loss of his leg. At dawn on the day they are to sail, they again meet Elijah, who asks if they saw some men heading toward the ship. Ishmael explains that 'it was too dim to be sure'. Elijah replies 'see if you can find 'em now', hinting at the deaths of sailors before them. The Pequod sails on Christmas Day.

In chapters 24 to 36 the rest of the major characters are introduced and Ahab's purpose to pursue Moby Dick—at any cost—is clearly established. Chief mate Starbuck is a careful Nantucket Quaker, a man of deep national reverence who kills whales only for the industrial products they provide. Stubb, the second mate, is a jolly Cape Cod native whose fearless philosophy is that one should worry about danger and death when they come. Third mate Flast of Martha's Vineyard is dull and unconsciously fearless. Ahab, who finally appears on deck after a mysterious reclusiveness, is most marked on the right side of his otherwise scorched face. Starbuck's head harpooner is

Queequeg; Stubb's is Tashtego, a Native American from Gay Head, Martha's Vineyard; Flask's is the imperial Daggoo, a black African. Dough-Boy, the steward is instrumental in informing the crew of Ahab's Macbeth-like nightmare-ridden sleeping habits. The Manxman is an old sepulchral man respected as having 'preternatural powers of discernment'. Tambourine-playing Pip, a young black shipkeeper, is hinted as destined to be among the angels.

Ahab spends his time gazing at the sea, steadying his whalebone leg in specially made notches on deck. In these chapters, Ishmael's intermittent whaling discourses appear. In "The Quarter-Deck-Ahab reveals his design to exact vengeance on the instructable supernatural forces that have insulted him, symbolized for him by the physical, natural being Moby Dick. He then conducts a dark ritual to further guarantee the crew's loyalty. All swear "Death to Moby Dick. God hunt us all, if we do not hunt Moby Dick to his death!" Chapters 37 to 42 present soliloquies by Ahab, Starbuck and Stubb; information on Moby Duck; and explanations for the signification of his whiteness. Ahab sees his own soul as 'damned in the midst of paradise'. Too dark now to recognize beauty; Starbuck feels he must succumb to the plan of Ahab whom he now hates and pities. Ishmael develops his vision of the whale. Moby Dick is considered the most perilous whale of the seas.

Before the first whale chase, Starbuck orders Ishmael in his boat because he senses a shared fear of whales. A storm approaches as they lower the boats. Queequeg harpoons a whale, but Starbuck's boat is swamped and the whale escapes. Separated from the Pequod by the storm, they spend the night alone on the sea and are nearly killed when at dawn the ship sails at the mist and smashes into their boat. One serene night some time later Fedallah sees the silvery celestial jet of a whale, which for nights is repeatedly seen and is believed to belong to Moby Dick. The crew enquires many ships about its location. After a chase in which Stubb harpoons a whale the whale experiences a gruesomely described death. When the Pequod meets the ship Jeraboam, its captain Mayhew, refuses any physical contact between the crews. Although there seem to be no symptoms, one of the Jeraboam's crew, a fanatical shaker and self-declared prophet who calls himself Gabriel, has convinced his shipmates that he cast an epidemic from a vial. While Meyhew, from a drop boat tells the foreboding story of how his chief mate was killed by Moby Dick. Gabriel repeatedly shouts warnings against hunting the whale. In the next three chapters, Ishmael's discourse on whaling becomes increasingly prominent. In chapters 73 to 105 Pequod meets three more ships. The Pequod meets the English ship Samuel Enderby, whose captain Boomer has an ivory limb in place of an arm lost to Moby Dick. Boomer has recently seen the white whale but will not pursue Moby Dick again, saying, "Aint one limb enough?" As Ahab is leaving the Enderby, he splinters his leg and later has the carpenter make another. In chapters 106 to 135 the Pequod meets three final ships that had encountered Moby Dick. Oil is discovered in the Pequod's hold, but Ahab does not want to interrupt his pursuit of Moby Dick, to locate and repair the leak.

The day after the Pequod meets the homeward-bound ship Bachelor—which has encountered nothing but good luck—four whales are slain, one by Ahab. While Ahab's whale boat is waiting to be picked up by the Pequod, his dark shadow, the Parsee repeats three prophecies he has earlier made, that 'neither hearse nor coffin' can be Ahab's; that Ahab will not die until he sees two hearses on the sea—the first 'not made by mortal hands'.

On a further note of loss, the Pequod meets the ship Rachel. Though its captain has encountered Moby Dick, he is searching not for the whale, but for a son lost at sea during the chase. Refusing to help in the search, Ahab says, "May I forgive myself". The Pequod meets a last, miserable ship, the Delight, whose hollow-cheeked Nantucket captain reveals that the day before, Moby Dick killed five of his men, all but one of whom was buried by the sea.

The last chapter comprises three chases of Moby Dick. On the first day, the whale bites Ahab's boat in half. On the second day, the boats are lowered and Moby Dick, after becoming entangled in harpoons, takes the boats of Stubb and Flask underwater, flips Ahab's boat and crew into the air and flees.

Although there are no fatalities, men are wounded, boats are damaged, Ahab's special harpoon is lost and his leg is again splintered. After the crew is assembled on the Pequod's deck everyone realizes that the Parsee is missing and is perhaps dead—one of his prophecies fulfilled. Thinking of Moby Dick, Ahab declares that things that are drowning rise twice but the third time sink forever. But when the carpenter makes him a third leg, Ahab fails to realize the portentous symbolism.

On the third day, Ahab declares himself, 'nobler' than the 'noble and heroic', unconquerable wind, against which the Pequod has been sailing. Ahab orders the crews of the damaged boats to return to Pequod, leaving only his boat to find the whale. Moby Dick snaps the line and proceeds to attack the Pequod, biting its prow. As the ship begins to sink, the crew says their last prayers. Ahab recognizes the Pequod as another of Fedallah's prophecies—the man-made hearse of American wood that cannot be his. His final cry is "Oh lonely death on lonely life!" resounds. He darts the whale for the last time and the line catches him around the neck and he is dragged underwater. Everything is shrouded by the ancient sea. Ishmael who could not take part in the finale act of tragedy, witnesses how Ahab and his crew lost to the whale Moby Dick. Melville provides an epilogue where the tragic flair blooms.

Melville's *Moby Dick* is a famous American tragic novel. It is a great sea story about whaling expedition. This is about man's great strength and also of his failure before the mighty nature. D.H. Lawrence observes, "Melville's biggest book is *Moby Dick*, or *The White Whale*. It is the story of the last hunt. The last hunt, the last conquest—what is it?"[2]

NOTES

1. Viva Notes on Herman Melville's *Moby Dick*, with an introduction by Herold Bloom, Viva Ltd., New Delhi, 2007, p. 12.
2. D.H. Lawrence, "Hunting Moby Dick", p. 29.

9 Emily Dickinson as a Mystic Poet

Poets are born and poets die but poets who remain as long as the sun are only a few. Poets who deal with the themes that are universal such as love, death and immortality are always enduring. Their influence upon the younger generation is there. Such poets are the interpreters of human life appreciating the beauty of divine gifts to man.

Emily Dickinson is certainly a great poet whose life is a tale of poetic beauty and truth—a tale always useful for the posterity. Emily Dickinson is a poet at that who lived a life of simplicity, chastity and divinity. Today she is regarded as one of the greatest American poets. Her forthright examination of philosophical and religious skepticism, her unorthodox attitude towards her gender and her distinctive style have earned her a widespread acclaim. So Emily Dickinson's poetry has become most curious, mystical and distinct from the mainstream of English poetry.

Philosophically speaking the most characteristic feature of Emily Dickinson's poetry is its mystical tendency. Her life too is like her poetry. The very fact that contrasts her philosophically is her experiencing of life that is transcendental. Like St Theresa of Avila and St John of the Cross of the West, like Akkamahadevi and Mirabai of the East, or more like Emerson and Thoreau, her own contemporaries, Emily Dickinson is a poet of her own conviction. She approached life in her own way. Donald Thackeray observes:

> The most desultory of the poems of Emily Dickinson reveals their remarkable divergence from the customary approach to the problems of human experience. Ordinarily

> one thinks of life in terms of the facts of environment, the interrelationship of persons within a social situation, and the possibilities of various courses of action. All this can be found in Emily Dickinson's poems, but there is something more. The 'something more' most often takes the form of a pervasive atmosphere—not precisely definable, yet felt as a real, and indispensable aspect of her poetry. The essence of this aspect appears to be attitude which permeates her poems and which I should call a mystical attitude.[1]

Be it as it may, critics are of the divided opinion about Emily Dickinson's mysticism. Genevieve Taggard, R.P. Blackmur, Yvor Winters think Emily Dickinson is not a mystic. The reasons they enlist for this are: (a) Emily Dickinson had paradoxes of duality and (b) Emily Dickinson did not completely experience the transcendental unity with divinity. Genevieve Taggard observes: "If the voice of heavenly vision had spoken alone in Emily Dickinson, she would have been a mystic poet. She is not a mystic poet.... The real mystic experiences ecstasy, and his invariable report is that life is single and divine: he abhors a double."[2] These critics tend to regard mysticism only as a secret and exclusive cult wrapped in mystery without knowing that in everyone of us there lies an element of it. R.P. Blackmur thinks Emily Dickinson's mystical tendency stems from many factors: "It is not mystical itself. It is an attitude composed partly of the English hymnal, partly of human sensibility bred with experience of composition at work, which is the most important of all the distinguishable elements."[3] However, when one searches for a deeper reality about mysticism, the true tenets of it are available. Evelyn Underhill who is a great authority on mysticism writes that mysticism is "The expression of the innate tendency of the human spirit toward complete harmony with the transcendental formula under which that order is understood."[4] As per this interpretation, Emily Dickinson is surely a mystic poet, for the reason, much of her poetry is incomprehensible to readers. Emily Dickinson's felt-experience transcends our observation. Paul Tillich says, "An expression in language of this personal quality we call poetry; expressed in action, as a mode of life concerned with the dialectic between experience and culture and with respect to man's ultimate values it is mysticism."[5] Besides, Emily Dickinson's way of life—her withdrawal from society, her rebellion against the orthodox religion and abandonment of Calvinism—prove this. Her acquaintance Mobel Loomis Todd writes: "I must tell you about the character of Amherst. It is a lady whom the people call the *Myth*. She is a sister of Mr. Dickinson and seems to be the climax of all the family oddity. She has not been outside of her own house in fifteen years, except once to see a new church, when she crept out at night and viewed it by moonlight.... She dresses wholly in white and her mind is said to be perfectly wonderful. She writes finely, but no one ever sees her. Her sister...invited me to come and sing to her mother sometime.... People tell me that the *myth* will hear every note—she will be near, but unseen."[6]

Mobel Todd thinks Emily Dickinson's life and poetry are distinct from the ordinary. Donald E. Thackeray states, "Emily Dickinson was able to contemplate and experience aspects of human existence which ordinarily escape notice. Furthermore, her concern with religious thought, with death and immortality gave her stimulus to attempt to comprehend a greater, more complete knowledge than is possible for the rational intelligence. Thus she had both the capability and incentive to attempt a mystical development."[7] No doubt, Emily Dickinson is a mystic poet and there are hundreds of books and thousands of articles—all unearthing her implicit mystical tendency.

Most mystics are non-conformists. Or non-conformists are mystics. Emily Dickinson is just one of them. She did not believe the Trinitarian theology; she abandoned Calvinism; and she did not become a church member. Even she had no belief in the ways of the world. Emily Dickinson was a rebel. She was what Jean de Menesce says: "For their part, the mystics are often uneasy with ecclesiastical authority, and anxious to avoid heresy. Their writings, consequently, are less a result of artistic aspiration or pathological confession or mere individualism, than the desire to bring forward, in order to examine and be examined and thereby clarified the extraordinary thing they have encountered."[8]

It is observed that as long as man is in mortal body he is prone to suspect any divine objects. Atheists belong to this category of doubting Thomases. Accordingly, even the most devout, doubt of God's existence and benevolence. This is what we see in Emily Dickinson's early poetry. The following extracts show this:

Those—dying then,
Knew where they went—
They went to God's Right Hand—
And God cannot be found

This recalls A.C. Swinburne's atheistic poetry quoted below:

By the name that in hell-fire was written, and burned at
The point of thy sword,
Thou art smitten, thou God, thou art smitten: thy death
Is upon thee, O Lord.
And the love-song of earth as thou diest resounds through
The wind of her wings—
Glory to Man in the highest! For Man is the master of
Things.

Like the atheist existentialist thinker Nietzsche or the atheist poet Thomas Hardy, Emily Dickinson is a woman of enquiring spirit unable to accept anything without a clear personal examination.

First Emily Dickinson did not believe in Heaven as of God. Here her enquiry of heaven or its bliss is genuine:

We pray—to Heaven—
We prate—of Heaven—
Relate—when Neighbours die—
At what clock to Heaven—they fled—
Who saw them—wherefore fly?
Is Heaven a Place—a Sky—a Tree?
Location's narrow way is for Ourselves—
Unto the Dead
There's no geography—
But state—Endowed—Focus—
Where—Omnipresence—Fly? (Poem 489)

Emily Dickinson criticizes heaven:

I went to Heaven—
'Twas a small town—

Lit—with a Ruby—
Lathed—with Down— (Poem 374)

Emily Dickinson is unhappy about heaven when she thinks, "In Heaven—they neither woo nor are given in wooing—what an imperfect place?"[9] Still in another poem:

What is—'Paradise'—
Who live there—
Are they 'farmers'—
Do they 'Hoe'—
Do they know that this is 'Amherst'—
And that I—am coming—too— (Poem 215)

In the following poem Emily Dickinson shows how she is unhappy both with the world and with the idea of heaven:

I never felt at Home—Below—
And in the handsome Skies
I shall not feel at Home—I know—
I don't like Paradise— (Poem 413)

After God and Heaven, Emily Dickinson thinks of Jesus Christ but in terms of human relationships:

The savior must have been
A docile gentleman—
To come so far so cold a Day
For little Fellowman— (Poem 1487)

Emily Dickinson's regard for the Bible was as low and earthly as her evaluation of the Son of God. In her view, the Holy Book is not at all a holy book, but:

An Antique Volume
Written by faded Men
At the Suggestion of Holy Specters (Poem 1545)

Emily Dickinson who did not go to church, nor listen to holy sermons, expresses thus:

Some keep the Sabbath going to Church—
I keep it, staying at Home—
With a Bobolink for a Chorister—
And an Orchard, for a Dome—

Some keep the Sabbath in Surplice—
I just wear my Wings—
And instead of tolling the Bell, for Church,
Our little sexton—Sings.

Emily Dickinson was a gross non-conformist. She would not go by the appearance of things.

I took my power in my hand—
And went against the World— (Poem 540)

It is natural that she did not believe the corrupt orthodox and ignorant world. Her very originality of thought, her adherence to her own life ethics and her inner religion made her hate bad elements. An angry Emily Dickinson speaks in 1859:

How martial is this place!
Had I mighty gun
I think I'd shoot the human race
And then to glory run! (Poem 118)

Denis Donoghue observes, "This is her way. Emily Dickinson tested everything whether it was given by experience or by imagination. Every house had to be searched for ghosts. Many of her poems apply to the great religious doctrines the same interrogative pressure of her own religious faith, virtually anything may be said, with some show of evidence. She may be represented as an agnostic, a heretic, a skeptic, a Christian. She grew up in a Christian family, but she was not devout. She did not possess a talent for conviction."[10]

However, once this doubt in God and Heaven, hatredness for the ills of the world and other things was over, the provincial young lady started to return to the faith yet in an otherworldly sense. Faith in her returned and she thought of God in a friendly way:

My faith is larger than the hills,
So when the hills decay,
My faith must take the purple wheel
To show the sun the way

...

How dare I therefore stint a faith
On which so vast depends,
Lest Firmament should fail for me—
The rivet in the bands (Poem 305)

Subsequently faith for Emily Dickinson becomes a bridge and she writes:

Faith—is Pierless Bridge
Supporting what we see
Unto the scene that we do not—
Too slender for the eye.

A turned believer Emily Dickinson loves God. Like Radha, Krishna's lover, she turns God's beloved. She thinks soon after her death, she will be one with God through her marriage with Him. Albert Gelpi thinks, "This kind of speculation about the nature of death and the after-life gave Emily Dickinson a new faith in the believable, comprehensible resurrection."[11] The forthcoming death and a happy life afterwards for Emily Dickinson are seen below:

I'll tell Thee All-how Bald it grew—
How Midnight felt, at first—to me—
How all the Clocks stopped in the World—
Then how the Grief got sleepy—some—
As if my Soul were deaf and dumb—
Just making signs—across—to Theee—
That this way—thou coulds't notice me— (Poem 577)

As the Empress of Calvary, Emily Dickinson thinks soon after her death she will have a crown reserved for her in heaven. Therefore, she is not afraid of death's icy hand:

Afraid! Of whom am I afraid?
Not death—for who is He?
The Porter of my Father's Lodge
As much abasheth me! (Poem 608)

Mysticism is a personal religion. Hence, mystics know God in their personal ways, which the worldly-wise, cannot understand. Supporting this, the mystic William of St Thierry observes: "Mystics claim to know the secret things of God disclosed in a particular way to their innermost selve and then undertake to express their knowledge for the benefit of humanity at large."[12] So Emily Dickinson understands God and establishes her own rapport with Him. For Emily Dickinson life is a form of death and once she dies, she thinks, she will get resurrection to find what she could not find in her mortal life. This is the dawn of her celestial wedding:

A wife—at daybreak I shall be—
Sunrise Hast thou a Flag for me?
At Midnight, I am but a Maid,
How short it takes to make it Bride—
Then—Midnight, I pass thee
Unto the East, and Victory—
Midnight—Good Night! I hear them call,
The Angels bustle in the Hall—
Softly my Future climbs the Stair,
So soon to be a child no more—
Eternity, I'm coming—Sir,
Saviour—I've seen the face—before! (Poem 461)

As the intensity in her position as the Queen of Calvary is strengthened, Emily Dickinson thinks God more as her man of destiny resembling the Indian mystic-poets Akkamahadevi and Miradevi. The worldly suffering Emily Dickinson thinks will bring her divine bliss—a white election, a marriage, a union—combining an earthly crown of thorns with a heavenly crown of bliss. She writes:

Title divine—is mine!
The Wife—without the Sign!
Acute Degree—confined on me—
Empress of Calvary!
Royal—all but the Crown!
Betrothed—without the swoon
God send us Women—
When you—held—Garnet to Garnet—
Gold—to Gold
Born—Bridalled—Shrouded—
In a day—
"My Husband"—woman say—
In this—the way? (Poem 1072)

Emily Dickinson's sense of heavenly wedding is seen at best in the following poem:

Given in Marriage unto Thee
Oh Thou Celestial Host—
Bride of the father and the Son
Bride of the Holy Ghost.

Other betrothal shall dissolve—
Wedlock of will, decay—
Only the Keeper of this Ring
Conquer Mortality—

This heavenly consumption of human passion is something unparalled in the western mysticism. An Indian woman mystic like Akkamahadevi evinces her wedding with God thus:

O Sir, I love the beautiful One,
The formless One, who is beyond
Or death or dissolution
Chennamallikarjun is my groom:
All other husbands in the world
Are naught to me![13]

Emily Dickinson bears a comparison with Akkamahadevi who said she married God Chennamallikarjun and with Mirabai who said she married Krishna. Even Emily Dickinson reminds Emerson's aunt Mary Moody who to go to heaven safe and soon, slept in a bed fashioned in the form of a coffin. Though the world did not like her, Emily Dickinson was not afraid of it. In spite of her occasional disbelief in God, Emily Dickinson walked ahead without bending her head. Her white robe became her battle standard against an uncomprehending world that called her an infidel and a pagan, while she was conscious that her mystic union with God was satisfactory. This mystical phase of Emily Dickinson's life bears a comparison to Robert Browning's doomed child bride, Pompilia who dreams of celestial reunion with her priest-lover Caponsacchi in the poet's *The Ring and the Book* (1868). Emily Dickinson who was deprived of a happy earthly life dreamed of a heavenly life. This is shown in her poem, "I cannot live with you", which secularizes Christ-centred fervor. She writes,

I cannot live contained here
Without some glimpses of thy face;
And heaven, without thy presence there,
Will be a dark and tiresome place.

Emily Dickinson was religious in an entirely different sense of the word. Never she followed any dogmatic customs or observed religious austerities. Like St Theresa, she followed her own creed often rebelling against the ways of the world. Like Thoreau, she says to live on the earth is a joy. She wrote to Higginson that "to be human is to be more than divine, for when Christ was divine he was uncontented till He became human". Emily Dickinson writes, "I have perfect confidence in God and His promises and yet I know not why, I feel that the world holds a predominant place in my affection."[14] She writes,

If I can stop one Heart from breaking
I shall not live in vain
If I can ease one Life the Aching
Or cool one Pain
Or help one fainting Robin
Unto his Nest again
I shall not live in Vain (Poem 919)

St Theresa affirms the same: "If you see a sick woman to whom you can give some help never be affected by the fear that your devotion will suffer, but take pity on her.... That is a true union with His will."[15]

Emily Dickinson believes the Biblical precept—the kingdom of god is within us:

Who has not found the heaven below
Will fail of it above
God's residence is next to me
His furniture is love.

So there exists a close link between mysticism and humanism. Mystics of all sorts and of all ages have advocated others to do social services as much as they have done it. Many mystics had been social reformers. Christ himself was a mystic. So were St Joan of Arc, St Theresa, St John of the Cross, Rolle, G.M. Hopkins and many more. In fact, many of us are mystics since we have within us the seeds of mystical experience, which we detect by reflection on the fiduciary character of ordinary knowledge.

Great suffering made Emily Dickinson think of God as much, as death compelled her to have friends. Emily Dickinson even made use of writing to fend off whatever private devil that lurked in the shadows of her earthly fear. Life for Emily Dickinson brought more sorrow and happiness. This made her live in solitude, which helped her for enhancing her life with subtlety of feeling, compassion and understanding. This solitude and suffering made Emily Dickinson sing like the 14th century English mystic Rolle who says, "Then and there my thinking itself turned into poem.... The effect of this inner sweetness was that I began to sing what previously I had spoken: only I sang inwardly and that for my Creator."[16] Emily Dickinson's urge to sing is perennial. She sings thus:

Bind me—I still can sing—
Banish—my mandolin
Strikes true within—

Slay—and my Soul shall rise
Chanting to Paradise—
Still thine.

Just like mystics Rolle, Blake, Wordsworth, Emerson and others, Emily Dickinson sings on her inner religion. For woman like Emily Dickinson who lived in solitude and suffering, deliverance was worth the terrible price of living in a world ruled by such bad circumstances posed continually.

Mystical overtones are seen in Emily Dickinson's nature poetry. Her poems on the lines of hills, fresh and fragrant air, rain-bearing clouds, flora and fauna, drive home the fact that nature is a divine embodiment. The nature's aspects are seen in a pantheistic vein:

Spring is the period
Express from god
Among the other seasons
Himself abide.
But during March and April

None stir abroad
Without a cordial interview
With god.

An understanding of mystical tendency in Emily Dickinson's nature poetry is in line with Evelyn Underhill's statement: "Where we received hints, he (the mystic) would have communion with certainties. The freshness of the eternal springs would speak to him in the primrose and the budding tree.... Spirit find spirit in the Unknowable Abyss."[17]

Love is a means for the realization of things worldly or otherworldly. It is through love that man and woman unite with each other. Again it is through love, of course, on a higher plane, that man tries to unite with God. Love plays an important role in man-God relationship. Love is eternity there. Psychologists like Henry Bergson admit it: "God is love and the object of love.... But what he does not state clearly is that divine love is not a thing of god: it is God Himself."[18]

Be it as it may Emily Dickinson, born and brought up in Victorian tradition accepts Neo-Platonic love as the most ideal for the realization of human aspirations. For Emily Dickinson love is a cosmic force responsible for creation, preservation and destruction. She writes,

Love—is anterior to me
Posterior—to Death—
Initial of Creation, and
The Exponent of earth—

The world is a divine dream or a book written by God in the wake of His love for the earthlings. In Emily Dickinson's view this living world is a shadow of divine love. She writes,

Unable are the Loved to die
For Love is Immortality,
Nay, it is Deity— (Poem 809)

Since man is a relic of God, in him rests a divine spark. This is best exemplified for Emily Dickinson in the curious phenomenon of the emergence of butterfly from cocoon. Emily Dickinson is inclined to think that the secret of the 'cocoon perched in ecstasy/Defies imprisonment'. This love is the primal cause of metamorphosis and growth. This ecstatic impulse in natural evolution is a manifestation of love. Emily Dickinson's idea of love reminds Emersonian saying, "Give all to Love".[19]

It seems Emily Dickinson is sure of immortality. She writes,

Do people moulder equally,
They bury, in the Grave?
I do believe a Species
As positively live
I need not further argue—
That statement of the Lord
Is not a controvertible—
He told me, death was dead— (Poem 432)

Emily Dickinson's concept of immortality is that of the primitive belief in the imperishability of the soul even after death. The Dionysian and Pythogorecian view of immortality which came to the Christian world can be seen there. This is vividly seen in her famous poem, "The Soul Selects Her Own Society",

The Soul selects her own society—
Then—shuts the Door—
To her divine Majority—
Present no more—
Unmoved—she notes the Chariots—pausing—
At her low Gate— (Poem 303)

Emily Dickinson stresses upon intuition in mystical life. She says,

By intuition mightiest things
Assert themselves, and not by terms—

Thus, we see a greater portion of Emily Dickinson's poetry mystical related to death, divinity, salvation and immortality. Much of her poetry is about the other world. Emily Dickinson, through her mystical eye, has written a species of poetry that is rarely written by others. Her poetry has become a challenge to critics for interpreting it properly.

NOTES

1. Donald Thackeray, *Emily Dickinson's Approach in Poetry*, Cambridge: Univ. of Nebraska Press, 1954, p. 29.
2. Genevieve Taggard, *The Life and Mind of Emily Dickinson*, New York: Alfred Knapf, 1930, p. 29.
3. R.P. Blackmur, *The Expense of Greatness*, New York: Arrow Editions, 1940, p. 113.
4. Evelyn Underhill, *Mysticism*, London: Methuen, 1926, p. x.
5. Paul Tillich, qt. by Patrick Grant, *Literature of Mysticism in Western Tradition*, London: Macmillan, 1983, p. 8.
6. Mabel Todd, qt. by John Cody, *After Great Pain: The Inner Life of Emily Dickinson*, Cambridge: The Harvard Univ. Press, 1971, p. 12.
7. Donald Thackery, *Emily Dickinson's Approach in Poetry*, p. 30.
8. Menesce Jean, qt. by Patrick Grant, *Literature of Mysticism in Western Tradition*, p. 10.
9. Emily Dickinson, qt. by P.T. Anantharaman, *The Sunset in a Cup: Emily Dickinson and Mythopoeic Imagination*, New Delhi: Cosmo Publication, 1985, p. 127.
10. Denis Donoghue, *Emily Dickinson,* Minneapolis: Univ. of Minnosota Press, 1969, p. 4.
11. Albert Gelpi, *Emily Dickinson and Her Culture*, Cambridge: CUP, 1984, p. 136.
12. William St Thierry, qt. by Patrick Grant, *Literature of Mysticism in Western Tradition*, p. 1.
13. Akkamahadevi, qt. in *Sunyasampadane.*
14. Emily Dickinson, qt. by P.T. Anantharaman, *The Sunset in a Cup: Emily Dickinson and Mythopoeic Imagination*, p. 132.
15. St Theresa, qt. by Patrick Grant, *Literature of Mysticism in Western Tradition*, p. 2.
16. Rolle, qt. by Patrick Grant, *Literature of Mysticism in Western Tradition*, p. 93.
17. Evelyn Underhill, *The Mystic Way*, London: J.M. Dent and Sons Ltd., 1913, p. 31.
18. Henry Bergson, *Emily Dickinson's Poetry*, New Delhi: Bahri Publication, 1983, p. 125.
19. *Ibid.*, p. 123.

Mark Twain's *Huckleberry Finn* 'as a Satire on Slavery' 10

Samuel Langhorne Clemens, well-known with his pseudonym, 'Mark Twain', is the greatest American humorist writer. He is one of the greatest writers of the world. He is known for the novels of his boyhood on the river Mississippi—*Tom Sawyer* and *The Adventures of Huckleberry Finn*. He was an annalist of American heritage. He witnessed the epic of America, the westward full.

Samuel Langhorne Clemens was born in Florida in 1835. His parents John Marshall Clemens and mother Jane Lampton Clemens were Virginians. His father moved the family to Hannibal and Clemens spent his boyhood there. Mark Twain had little education and he spent his early years in a printing press. He began writing burlesques. His one hobby was boating on Mississippi and he knew the river like a book. There was the disturbance of Civil War.

Soon Mark Twain worked as a journalist. In 1863 he adopted the pseudonym 'Mark Twain', a river phrase meaning 'two fathoms deep'. Mark Twain went to San Francisco as a reporter and faced problems because of his frank reporting. His career as a humorist began. Even he lectured. In 1867 he went to a tour of the Quaker City and later he made a trip to Europe. The result was his travelogue *The Innocents Abroad* (1869). When William Dean Howells wrote its review Mark Twain was happy to say, "When I read that review of yours, I felt like the woman who was so glad her baby had come white." Mark Twain was like a wild man from the west.

Soon after he returned from Europe Mark Twain married (in 1870) Olivia Langdon of Elmira of New York. Yet she did not suit to his taste. Even she was an invalid. They lived together for 34 years and had three daughters—Susa, Clara and Jean and possibly a son. Mark Twain, like his father, was not systematic. In fact, he was rather 'innocent'. He is described as "the generous, erratic, moody, and vulnerable human being".[1] He needed a critic always. His wife was one of them. His friend William Dean Howells was another. The couple lived in Buffalo where he edited *Buffalo Express*. Yet Mark Twain's investment in printing was never a success. His next book *Roughing It* (1872), another travelogue was good enough. Next he moved to Hartford and stayed as a neighbor of Harriet Beecher Stowe. He published *The Gilded Age* in 1873, a satire written with Charles Warner. His *Old Times in the Mississippi* (1875) was a book of sketches, while *Tom Sawyer* (1876) was about his times in Mississippi. And finally there was his masterpiece *The Adventures of Huckleberry Finn* (1884) for the writing of which he took seven years and even he wanted to burn it.

Meanwhile, Mark Twain involved in some projects. He, in collaboration with Bret Harte wrote a play; toured Europe and published *Tramps Abroad* (1880) and *The Prince and the Pauper* (1882), a children's book. His next in-land travel book was the famous *Life on the Mississippi* (1883). Mark Twain put a lot of money in publishing business and lost much. Only the oil tycoon Henry Rogers' help consoled him. Twain wrote the work *Personal Recollections of Joan of Arc* (1896) which was the best work for him. Mark Twain was not happy with his project and he undertook a world tour and lecturing and when he was just off, he heard the illness of his daughter Susa. His *Following the Equator* (1897) is an account of his tour to Australia and India. In 1904 his wife Olivia died; and his last phase of life began. Now he settled in Stormfield and he wrote his *Autobiography* (1924). When his daughter Clara married and his daughter Jean died in 1909 Mark Twain became alone. He died the following year. Earnest Hemingway said, "*The Huckleberry Finn* is both the first and the best book in American literature". Twenty years later William Faulkner said much the same thing. Mark Twain discovered both the American language and American consciousness. He was the 'writer's writer'. The unique characteristics of his style are that his style was clear. Language mastery was his trademark. He had a command over American vernacular. It is said, "Mark Twain's style was easy, incisive to nuances of dialect, rich in the resources of comedy, satire, irony and corrosive anger."[2] Finally there was Mark Twain's humor. Twain's humor was an art. He excelled all others in his sketches of people. He imitated current funny men like Ward, Orpheus C. Kerr, and Josh Billings. He was often called 'phunny phelow'. It is said, "In his heart Mark Twain must have realized that essentially he was a man of feeling, too sensitive to serve merely as a comedian, too undisciplined to be the philosopher he sometimes fancied himself. His forte was to recapture the sheer joy of living, when to be young was very heaven. A great river flowing through the wilderness set the stage for a boy's own dream of self-sufficiency, of being a new Robinson Crusoe on Jackson's Island. In the background moved the pageantry of life, colored by humor, make believe, and pure melodrama; but the complexity of the machine age and the city lay far, far away."[3]

Mark Twain's novel *The Huckleberry Finn* is really great. Like Harriet Beecher Stowe's *Uncle Tom's Cabin*, it depicts a white boy Finn's effort to rescue a black man Jim. Mark Twain was essentially a humanist. He too knew how the Civil War was fought for the sake of abolition of slavery. He had deep sympathy for the nigro. So Mark Twain became a warm friend of the nigro and his rights. Mrs. Clemens once suggested "Consider everybody colored till he is proved a white." Twain had read many such novels on slavery. The works of Thomas Aldrich's *Story of a Bad Boy*, Howell's *A Boy's Town*, Stephen Crane's recollection on Whilomville and William White's of Bayville. The Twain novel is a picaresque novel. It is a fine book. To a stranger in 1887 he described this book as "'simply a hymn', put into prose form to give it a worldly air". More than that, "*Huckleberry Finn* is clearly the finest book, showing a more mature point of view and exploring richer strata of human experience. A joy forever, it is unquestionably one of the masterpieces of American and of world literature. Here Twain returned to his first idea of having the chief actor tell the story, with better results. Huck's speech is saltier than Tom's, his mind freer from the claptrap of romance and sophistication. Huck is poised midway between the town-bred Tom and that scion of woodlore and primitive superstition Nigger Jim, toward whom Huck with his margin of superior worldliness stands in somewhat the same relation that Tom stands toward Huck. When Tom and Huck are together, our sympathy turns invariably toward the latter."[4]

The Adventures of Huckleberry Finn is a long novel with numerous chapters with their titles. Chapter I is "I Discover Moses and the Bulrushes" is about Mark Twain's youthful-hero Huckleberry Finn's (Huck Finn for short) early life as an orphan in the house of a benign widow Mrs. Douglas. The author hints that those who want to read about him must also read the life of his friend Tom Sawyer as depicted in the novel of that name. In fact, these two novels and the third *The Life on Mississippi* are a trilogy—all dealing with Tom, Huck and Jim. In fact, Tom appears in the present novel. There is a reference to his aunt Polly. Be it as it may, the widow Douglas is a dismal and decent lady. She has a sister Miss Watson—both very pious people. They are Christians. They believe in essential humanity. So they shelter black people as much as they help the poor whites like Huck Finn. Mrs. Watson tells the boy Finn "Set up straight". She spoke to him of providence. The women sent the boy to a school. The latter, however, tried to resist their move though he learns the beauty of education a little later. In the second chapter "Our Gang's Dark Oath" portrays Huck being with his friends Tom, Ben Rogers, Joe Harper, Tommy Barnes and others. Tired of the women's wisdom and piety Huck goes out to them and all of them go to a cave and plan to start a robbers' gang. They like to loot people. This is an adventure for them. They even get some gold there and they sell it to Judge Thatcher for money. Yet Huck deposits his money on interest. Their very idea of robbery is based upon Cervantes' *Don Quixote* as Tom says in the chapter "We Ambuscade the A-rabs". Yet they do not rob any. This is all boyish plans. The chapter "The Hair Ball Oracle" first speaks of Huck's fortunes. Later he gets a horse shoe nail worth 150 dollars which he deposits with the same man and the latter provides him with a dollar interest a day. Their conversation is vivid:

> "No, sir", I say, "I don't want to spend it. I don't want it at all—nor the six thousand, nuther. I want you to take it; I want to give it to you—the six thousand and all."
>
> He looked surprised. He couldn't seem to make it out. He says:
>
> "Why, what can you mean, my boy?"
>
> I say, "Don't you ask me no questions about it, please. You'll take it—won't you?"
>
> He says:
>
> "Well, I'm puzzled. Is something the matter?"
>
> "Please take it", I say, "and don't ask me nothing—then I won't have to tell no lies."
>
> He studied a while, and then he says,
>
> "Oho-o! I think I see. You want to sell all your property to me—not give it. That's the correct idea."
>
> Then he wrote something on appear and read it over, and says:
>
> "There: you see it says 'for a consideration'. That means I have bought it of you and paid you for it. Here's a dollar for you. Now you sign it."
>
> So I signed it, and left.[5]

Jim is a nigger at Douglas's house. He is almost an aged man. Still he is treated as a young one. He is illiterate, superstitious and dull-headed. He says he can speak to ghosts at night.

Shortly thereafter Huck goes to his house and finds his pap (father). His father who had been absent for two years, appears now. He wants to take care and control his son. He asks him for all his money that it is with Judge Thatcher. The latter takes the case to a court of law and the new judge decides that pap should not be disturbed much. The father does not like the boy learn much, as he would outwit him. He takes the boy three miles off to Illinois and puts him in a cabin. He locks him three days at times. The boy who does not want to be with his father—a drunkard and wastrel—plans to escape. He saws the door of his cabin and escapes one day in a canoe. He goes to Jackson Island where he meets his friend Jim, who has escaped the next day after Huck's departure. Initially Jim does not believe that Huck is a natural man because he has heard that he is dead. The point is that already there is a rumour that Huck is murdered probably by his father. So Huck, knowing it, wants to remain an isolato for some months. Another thing is that Jim escapes when Huck gets off. This makes people belive that Jim should have been Huck's murderer. So he should have escaped. Actually Jim escaped once he heard his aunt's planning to sell him for a southerner for 800 dollars. Both now live happily. Jim teaches Huck some art of magic. Both plan to go off to New Orleans where Jim can live as a free man. Huck needs to help him greatly. Huck to help Jim wants to know the slave-situation at Illinois. So one day he dresses as a girl and goes off to St Petersburg near Illinois. There he meets a woman—Judith Loftus. She draws his attention at his fears. She is a native of Douglas's town; she says Douglas's boy Huck was taken away by his father and he is killed. Her nigro escaped the next day and the woman wants him back and she has offered 300 dollars for him who gets him; and also 200 dollars for those who get back Huck. And she says she is a slave hunter which frightens Huck. She asks him for his name. He tells Sarah Williams. Later on she asks him her name and he says Mary Williams. What a wonder she declares. He tells her it is Sarah Marry William. She asks him to do some work and finds out that it is he not she. She asks him for the reality and he declares that he is really a he—his name being George Peters—and he wore woman's clothes just to escape a tyrant farmer. He says he is going to meet his uncle at Goshen.

Huck and Jim start their run away journey. They reach St Louis. They find a raft of robbers. They continue their journey and face a boat, belonging to slave-hunters. Huck tells them, on an enquiry—that he is taking his ailing father. Yet they suspect him. Meanwhile Jim is hidden in the waters of the river to avoid them. Now they depart from each other. That is to say they miss each other. Huck goes with two strangers said to be King—a descendent of French Louse XVI and a Duke of Bridgewater. But these two men are frauds capable of any mischief and crime. They all go to a village and find preaching there. The king and duke are skilled cheaters. They can stage a play of Shakespeare and even dance and sing. Thus, they advertise for such shows and do acting and earn some money. In another incident they hear some folks about the death of a certain Peter Wilkes and about his two brothers—William and Harvey in England. They hear that Peter has three daughters Mary Jane, Susan and Johanna. So the king and duke go to the house of the daughters and say that they are their England uncles. Of course, Huck is with them. They arrange the funeral of Peter and steal thousands of dollars from the house. They keep it in a room upstairs. But Huck, knowing their scheming, steals that and keeps it in the body of the Peter's corpse in coffin. Later on the two are unhappy. Once he is safe, Huck escapes. Later Peter's real brothers arrive and when they put them to trial, king and duke summon Huck for service and finally on his advice they dig up the corpse and find out the money. The king and duke are scolded of. Actually Huck exposed the two and the latter are unhappy of Huck for that. Thereafter, they follow Huck and Jim. Some days later even they sell Jim to Sylas Phelps. This makes Huck annoyed. So he thinks why he should take a lot of pains for nigger Jim's sake. So why he should also cheat the old Mrs. Douglas. Then he writes a letter to his friend Tom Sawyer stating that he may convey the massage to Douglas that her servant Jim is with the Phelps, just two miles away from the town. Another event related to Huck's adventures is his witnessing the feud between Shepherdson and Gangerbirds.

This Phelps is a slave hunter. He has a big farm. He has lots of nigger-servants. Once he goes to the Phelps he is warmly welcomed by Mrs. Sally Phelp, the landlady. She mistakes him for Tom, her nephew. On hearing about the lady that Tom is her nephew, he changes his name and he says her that he is not Tom but his brother Sid. She says him Tom is visiting her shortly.

2. *Ibid*., p. 925.
3. *Ibid*., p. 929.
4. *Ibid*., p. 931.
5. All the references to the text are from Mark Twain, *The Adventures of Huckleberry Finn*.
6. Claude Simpson, Introduction, *Huckleberry Finn*, Critical Interpretations, New Jersey, Prentice-Hall, 1968, p. 6.
7. Leo Marx, "Mr. Eliot, Mr. Trilling and Huckleberry Finn", *Huckleberry Finn,* ed. by K.S. Lynn, Harcourt Brace, New York, 1900, p. 204.

11

Psychological Realism in Henry James's *The American*

Henry James is one of the greatest American novelists of the 20th century. He was the greatest living American writer of his time. As a thinker and writer of English novel he is still an authority.

Henry James was born in 1843 to Senior Henry James. His father was a great theologian and teacher. As a strong-willed man he influenced his children, particularly Henry James, the novelist and William James, the psychologist. As they were rich, the James brothers got their education at home. Great writers like Carlyle and Emerson were Senior James's friends.

Henry James spent his boyhood in his native New York City. In 1855 the James family toured Geneva, London and Paris. They returned to Newport R.I. in the USA in 1858. Henry James went to Geneva again and learnt French. In a way much of his education was done abroad.

Henry James, in his young age, came under the influence of a great painter John La Farge. So his fiction is rich in art imagery and even characters. He had some education at Harvard in 1862. Shortly the family moved from New York to Boston and then to Cambridge in Massachusetts. Now he began writing articles to *Atlantic Monthly* whose well-known editor William Dean Howells became his lifelong friend.

Henry James wrote his first novel *Watch and Ward* in 1870. His short story *The Passionate Pilgrim* appeared in 1871. He spent a year at Rome where he began writing his novel *Roderick Hudson* (1875). This is about an expatriate American artist. Next year he went to Paris and befriended Turgenev, Flaubert and Zola. In 1876 he moved to London and stayed there for two decades. He became a good businessman and a socialite.

One of James important early works was *The American* (1877) which was serialized in *Atlantic Monthly* in 1876. The novel is about Christopher Newman who, as an American, goes to Europe in search of culture and aesthetic sensitivity. Honest, candid and generous, he meets an aristocratic Bellegarde family in moral decline. The novel contrasts Newman's idealistic morality and the moral decadence of the Bellegardes.

Henry James's next novel *Daisy Miller* is a feminine version of *The American*. Soon came his *The Portrait of a Lady* in 1881 establishing his reputation. James wrote works like *Washington Square* (1881), *The Princess of Casamassima* (1886) and *The Bostonians* (1886). He tried his hand at playwriting between 1890 and 1895 but in vain.

In 1897 Henry James purchased Lamb House in Rye, Sussex and he lived there the rest of his life. Here he wrote his *The Turn of the Screw* (1898), two of his five volumes of autobiography and later works. Now in 1915 he became a British subject and he passed away in 1916 unhappy of his rootlessness.

The Ambassadors is James' mature work. The novel portrays the mind of an American. The novel is known for James' masterful blending of character, action, setting and symbolism. His *The Golden Bowl* is equally interesting.

The novel The American is set in the mid-19th century Paris. It was first published in 1877. The principal characters are Christopher Newman, an American; Mr. Tristram, a friend and his wife; M. Nioche, a shopkeeper; Mlle, Nioche's daughter; Madame de Bellegarde, a French aristocrat matron; Claire de Bellegarde, her daughter; Marquis de Bellegarde, Madame's eldest son; Valentin, Madame's youngest son; and Mrs. Bread, the Bellegarde's English servant.

Henry James's *The American* is known for its psychological realism. It is an international fiction. It has cosmopolitan look. It is said, "In this novel, James shows the interaction of two cultures, the American and the French. His primary interest is not in the action; his aim is to analyze the various psychological situations created by the events of the plot. The author scrutinizes the inner lives of his characters and writes about them in an urbane and polished style uniquely his own."[1]

The story of the novel is as follows: As Americans had a great fascination they liked to tour or stay in Europe for long. One such Mr. Christopher Newman, a millionaire withdrew from business and sailed for Paris. He wanted to live and enjoy his life and to find a wife for himself there. He wandered in the Louvre and made acquaintance with Mille Niche, a young copyist. She introduced him to her father, an unsuccessful shopkeeper. She was an artist. The American Newman bought a picture from Mille Nioche. He liked to learn French from her father. Later, through the French wife of an American friend named Tristram, he met Claire de Cintre, a young widow, also a daughter of an English mother and a French father. As a young girl she had been married to Monsieur de Cintre, an evil old man. Unfortunately he died soon leaving his young wife disliking second marriage. But she was young and beautiful and Newman liked her as the best woman for him. However, as an American businessman, he was not to the expectation of the French. He was out and out a democrat and they simply aristocratic. For example, when he went to see her brother Marquis de Bellegarde did not allow him.

Yet true to his word the father M. Noche started to teach the American lessons in French. Claire had dominated him and he was at her mercy or she would desert him for another man. M. Nioche assured the outsider that he would shoot her if she left him. Newman pitied the old man and promised him enough money. He wanted some more paintings from her.

Thus, Newman stayed in Paris and made occasional tours in Europe. When he returned to Paris in autumn he learned that the Tristrams were helpful. Even the Bellegardes were ready to receive him. One evening Claire's brother Valentin met Newman and the two became friends. Valentine envied Newman's liberty to do as he pleased; Newman wished himself acceptable to the society in which the Bellegardes moved. Taking this opportunity Newman asked Valentin to persuade his sister to marry him.

The latter, however, liked the idea but he warned that Newman's social standing was contrary to the Bellegardes.

One day Newman met Claire and expressed his wish for her hand. He requested the matron and Claire's elder brother too. Finally the family agreed to his wish as they needed money. Newman visited Louvere to see the paintings. There he introduced Valentin to the young lady painter. These years Mrs. Bread, the old English servant encouraged Newman about his stand. Valentin had quarrels and left for Switzerland. The next day when Newman went to see Claire he heard from the servant that the Bellegardes were unwilling to marry her to a commercial person like Newman. On reaching his house, he had a telegram from Valentin to the effect that he needed his help in Switzerland.

This was a kind of double sorrow for the good outsider. Still he liked to help Valentin and went to Switzerland. Valentin was near death. Valentin guessed Newman's misfortune and alluded to Mrs. Bread who knew the family secret. He advised Newman to know it from her and win Claire's hand. Valentin died the same day. Newman attended the funeral. He met Claire after three days and found that she was willing to enter a convent. Newman prayed her not to do so. Desperate he threatened the Bellegardes about the family secret. Mrs. Bread told Newman that Madame de Bellegarde had killed her invalid husband as he opposed Claire's marriage to M. de Cintre. Bread gave a related document to Newman.

Soon Mrs. Bread left Bellegarde employment and started serving Newman. She also told Newman that Claire joined a convent. Newman went to the convent the next Sunday. After the service he threatened the Bellegardes, who were there, about the document. The next day the marques offered Newman money for the document. Newman refused to sell it. Instead, he wished to have Claire's hand for it which her brother refused.

During the deadlock, Newman traveled the English countryside. Then he went to America. Restless he returned to Paris and learned from the Tristrams that Claire became a nun. Now he thought exposing of the Bellegardes was a useless tactics. He liked to leave Paris forever. Robert Spiller thinks

"Newman is victimized by Europe. It is disillusion for Newman."[2] A similar theme is present in James's another novel *The Portrait of a Lady* (1881) where Isabel Archer faces a bad situation in Europe. Europe is an evil and treachery for her. In fact, James himself acquired the British citizenship and repented for it.

NOTES

1. *The Masterplot*, Vol. 1, p. 94.
2. Robert Spiller, *Literary History of the United States,* Amerind Pub. Co., New Delhi, 1963, p. 1056.

Theodore Dreiser's *The American Tragedy*

12

Theodore Herman Albert Dreiser was born in Terre Haute, Indiana in 1871, the twelfth of thirteen children. His mother was gentle and devoted but illiterate; his German immigrant father was severe and distant. From the former he seems to have absorbed a quality of compassionate wonder; from the latter he seems to have inherited moral earnestness and the capacity to persist in the face of failure and disappointment.

Dreiser's childhood was decidedly unhappy. The large family moved from house to house in Indiana dogged by poverty and insecurity. One of his brothers became a famous songwriter under the name Paul Dreiser, but other brothers and sisters drifted into drunkenness and squalor. Dreiser as a youth was as ungainly, confused, shy and full of vague yearnings as most of his fictional protagonists. Dreiser's novels are direct projections of his life rather.

From the age of fifteen Dreiser was essentially on his own, earning meager support from a variety of menial jobs. A high-school teacher staked him to a year at Indiana University in 1889, but Dreiser's education was to come from experience. This education began in 1892 when he wangled his first newspaper job with the *Chicago Globe.* Over the next decade Dreiser groped his way to authorship, testing what he knew from direct experience. He read Charles Darwin, Ernst Haeckel, Thomas Huxley and Herbert Spencer and learnt that nature and society had no divine sanction.

Sister Carrie (1900), which traces the material rise of Carrie Meeber and the tragic decline of G.W. Hurstwood, was Dreiser's first novel. Because it depicted social transgressions by characters who felt no remorse and largely escaped punishment and because it used "strong" language and used names of living persons, it was virtually suppressed by its publisher, who printed but refused to promote the book. Since its reissue in 1907 it has steadily risen in popularity and scholarly acceptance as one of the key works in the Dreiser canon. Indeed, readers found Dreiser's point of view crude and immoral. In this early period some of his best short fictions were written, among them *Nigger Jeff* and *Old Rogaum and His Theresa.* The best of his short stories like all of Dreiser's fiction have the unusual power to compel our sympathy for and wonder over characters whose inner life we never really enter, but the urgency of whose desire we are made to feel.

In the first years of the century Dreiser suffered a breakdown. With the help of his brother Paul, however, he eventually recovered and by 1904 was on the way to several successful years as an editor, the last of them as editorial director of the Butterick Publishing Company. In 1910 he resigned to write *Jennie Gerhardt* (1911), one of his best novels and the first of a long succession of books that marked his turn to writing as a full-time career.

In *The Financier* (1912), *The Titan* (1914) and *The Stoic* (1947), Dreiser shifted from the pathos of helpless protagonists to the power of those unusual individuals who assume dominant roles in business and society. The protagonist of this "Trilogy of Desire" is Frank Cowperwood. These novels of the businessman as buccaneer introduced, even more explicitly than had *Sister Carrie*, the notion that men of high sexual energy were financially successful, a theme that is carried over into the rather weak autobiographical novel *The Genius* (1915).

The identification of potency with money is at the heart of Dreiser's greatest and most successful novel, *An American Tragedy* (1925). The center of this immense novel's thick texture of biographical circumstance, social fact and industrial detail is a young man who acts as if the only way he can be truly fulfilled is by acquiring wealth through marriage if necessary.

During the last two decades of his life Dreiser turned entirely away from fiction and toward political activism and polemical writing. He visited the Soviet Union in 1927 and published *Dreiser Looks at Russia*. In the 1930s, like many other American intellectuals and writers, Dreiser was increasingly attracted by the philosophical program of the Communist Party. Unable to believe in traditional religious credos, yet unable to give up his strong sense of justice, he continued to seek a way to reconcile his determinism with his compassionate sense of the mystery of life.

It is said, "In his lifetime Dreiser was controversial as a man and as a writer. He was accused, with some justice by conventional standards, of being immoral in his personal behavior, a poor thinker, and a dangerous political radical; his style was said (by critics more than by fellow authors) to be ponderous and his narrative sense weak. As time has passed, however, Dreiser has become recognized as a profound and prescient critic of debased American values and as a powerful novelist."[1]

When Clyde Griffiths was still a child, his religious-minded parents took him and his brothers and sisters around the streets of various cities, where they prayed and sang in public. The family was always very poor, but the fundamentalist faith of the Griffiths was their hope and mainstay throughout the storms and troubles of life. Theirs was a bagger's opera.

Young Clyde was never religious, however, and he always felt ashamed of his parents' way of life. As soon as he was old enough to make decisions for himself, he decided to go his own way. At sixteen he got a job as a bellboy in a Kansas City hotel. There the salary and the tips he received astonished him. For the first time in his life he had money in his pocket and he could dress well and enjoy himself. Then a tragedy overwhelmed the family. Clyde's sister ran away, supposedly to be married. Her elopement was a great blow to the parents, but Clyde himself did not brood over the matter. Life was too pleasant for him; as he enjoyed the luxuries which his job provided. He made friends with the other bellhops and joined them in parties that centered around liquor and women. Clyde soon became familiar with drink and brothels.

One day he discovered that his sister was back in town. The man with whom she had run away had deserted her and she was penniless and pregnant. Knowing his sister needed money, Clyde gave his mother a few dollars for her. He promised to give her more. One night he and his friends went on a party in a car that did not belong to them. Coming back from their outing, they ran over a little girl. In their attempt to escape, they wrecked the car. Clyde ran to Chicago.

In Chicago he got work at the Union League Club, where he eventually met his wealthy uncle, Samuel Griffiths. The uncle, who owned a factory in Lycurgus, New York, took a fancy to Clyde and offered him work in the factory. Clyde went to Lycurgus. There his cousin, Gilbert, resented this cousin from the Middle West. The whole family, with the exception of his uncle, considered Clyde beneath them socially and would not accept him into their circle. Clyde was given a job at the very bottom of the business, but his uncle soon made him a supervisor.

In the meantime Sondra Finchley, who disliked Gilbert, began to invite Clyde to parties she and her friends often gave. Her main purpose was to annoy Gilbert. Clyde's growing popularity forced the Griffiths to receive him socially, much to Gilbert's disgust.

In the course of his work at the factory Clyde met Roberta Alden, with whom he fell in love. Since it was forbidden for a supervisor to mix socially with an employee, they had to meet secretly. Clyde attempted to persuade Roberta to give herself to him, but the girl refused. At last, rather than lose him, she consented and became his mistress.

At the same time, Clyde was becoming fascinated by Sondra. He came to love her and hoped to marry her and thus acquire the wealth and social position for which he yearned. Gradually he began breaking dates with Roberta in order to be with Sondra every moment that she could spare him. Roberta began to be suspicious and eventually found out the truth. By that time she was pregnant. Clyde went to drug stores for medicine that did not work. He attempted to find a doctor of questionable reputation. Roberta went to see one physician who refused to perform an operation. Clyde and Roberta were both becoming desperate and Clyde saw his possible marriage to the girl as a dismal ending to all his hopes for a bright future. He told himself that he did not love Roberta, that it was Sandra whom he wished to marry. Roberta asked him to marry her for the sake of her child, saying she would go away afterward, if he wished, so that he could be free of her. Clyde would not agree to her proposal and grew more irritable and worried.

One day he read in the newspaper an item about the accidental drowning of a couple who had gone boating. Slowly a plan began to form in his mind. He told Roberta he would marry her and persuaded her to accompany him to an isolated lake resort. There, as though accidentally, he lunged toward her. She was hit by his camera and fell into the water. Clyde escaped, confident that her drowning would look like an accident, even though he had planned it all carefully.

But he had been clumsy. Letters that he and Roberta had written were found and when her condition became known he was arrested. His uncle obtained an attorney for him. At his trial, the defense built up an elaborate case in his favor. But in spite of his lawyer's efforts, he was found guilty and sentenced to be electrocuted. His mother came to see him and urged him to save his soul. A clergyman finally succeeded in getting Clyde to write a statement—a declaration that he repented of his sins. It is doubtful whether he did. He died in the electric chair, a young man tempted by his desire for luxury and wealth.

It is observed, "*An American Tragedy* is probably Dreiser's best novel. The title itself is, of course, significant. Dreiser believed that Clyde's downfall was due to the American economic system and he presents a strong indictment against that system. If Clyde had had the privileges of wealth and social position, he would never have been tempted to a moral decision and his consequent ruin. The novel is a powerful document on the theme of social inequality and lack of privilege." The novel is said to be "the worst written 'great novel in the world'".[2]

This is the story of a boy who failed to adjust with American society.

NOTES

1. *Norton Anthology of American Literature*, p. 1611.
2. Robert Spiller, *Literary History of the United States*, Amerind, New Delhi, 1963, p. 198.

Robert Frost's Poetry as a Meditation

13

Robert Frost is one of the pioneers of American poetry. Though he was unhappy of the delay in Americans' recognition of his poetry, he got what he deserved. We know that when Rabindranath Tagore got Noble Prize for Literature, Frost said the world did not recognize him though it recognized Tagore of India. Of course, afterwards, he was an unofficial poet laureate of America. He won the Pulitzer Prize four times and the American senate honored him twice. The then American President John Kennedy invited him to read his famous poem "The Gift Outright" at an inauguration in 1961. He sent him as a cultural envoy to the then USSR. Frost's career presents a number of intriguing tensions even though he was best known as a poet of New England.

Robert Frost was born in San Francisco, California in 1874 as the son of William Prescott Frost, a journalist and Isabelle Moodie Frost, a Scottish immigrant and school teacher. Frost had a sister called Jeanie. After his father's death in 1885 the family returned to Lawrence, Mass, the home of Frost's paternal grandparents. He had his high school education there. He married his schoolmate Elinor White. He studied at Harvard and then moved to Derry in New Hampshire and did chicken farming. Even he worked in other capacities as a mill hand, newspaper reporter and teacher in his mother's school.

Robert Frost at Derry worried as he could not do farming. For a while he taught at the Pinkerton Academy in Derry. He read Emerson, Thoreau and Dickinson seriously. The romantic poets like Keats and Shelley influenced him. In 1912 Robert Frost took his family to England hoping to find a publisher for his two collections of poems, *A Boy's Will* (1913) and *North of Boston* (1914). David Nutt was that publisher there. His first book was admired by Ezra Pound and he helped him to get his second book published. In England Frost was instantly famous. He befriended many Georgian poets like Lascelles Abercrombie and Wilfred Gibson. The critic Edward Thomas appreciated his poetry. Norman Douglas observed that "There is an image of things really heard and seen in Frost's poetry." He said, "It would be quaint indeed if Americans, who are opening their hospitality to Mr. Rabindranath Tagore's spiritual poems of Bengal life, should rest oblivious of their own countrymen."[1]

Then Robert Frost moved back to America and continued to be a teacher-farmer. Of course, he was a farmer-poet always. Now Frost became steadily famous. Then he went on publishing many books of poetry one after another. His books of poems are *New Hampshire, A Writers Tree* and *Further Range*.

However, Robert Frost's family grief was overwhelming later. He lost his wife Elinor White soon; his sister became insane, his sisters Lesley and Irma had unhappy marriages, his daughter Marjorie died soon after a delivery, his son Carol committed suicide feeling that his life was a failure.

Robert Frost was primarily a poet. He was a nature poet, even a mystic. He achieved poetic maturity before the beginning of modern poetry. It is said, "Frost on the surface seems a very traditional poet. He felt that the demands and challenges of strict form were necessary dynamic tension (he famously compared writing free verse to playing tennis without a net). But in his spare and understated way he helped effect a revolution against the overwrought poetic standards of the time; the understatement was itself the very essence of that revolution."[2] So Frost followed more the Georgian poetry of Victorian vein than modern poetry of Ezra Pound, T.S. Eliot and of their imagism. He was a sort of a bridge between the 19th and the 20th centuries. It is said that Frost was an 'outsider', for his poetry is not something like it should be. O, it simply means. His rhetoric is measured and precise as he strives, like Wordsworth a century earlier, to catch the rhythms of the language as it is actually used, to catch, in his phrase, 'the sound of sense'. For him poetry 'begins in delight and ends in wisdom'. Often Frost sums up the 'wisdom' at the end of a poem as in 'The Tuft of Flowers':

> 'Men work together', I told him from the heart,
> 'Whether they work together or apart.'

The unique characteristics of Frost's poetry are that "He adheres to meter as the necessary form of a poem, his use of dramatic monologues and dialogues to convey a psychological narrative; the dark intensity of his lyrics; and his argument that a poem must strive toward clarity and understanding of the world."[3] Critics thought that Robert Frost's poetry is a bit 'old fashioned'. Hyatt H. Waggoner observes, "In the philosophical climate, too, there was little tolerance for many of Frost's attitudes and deepest loyalties."[4] Frost, however, was a religious man to the core. His poems like "Sitting by Bush in Broad Sunlight" and "Not all There" imply religious attitudes. Later ones—"A Masque of Mercy" and "Kitty Hawks"—are explicitly religious. Poems like "Spring Pools", "A Leaf Trader", "Design" and "The Draft Horse" express tragic moods rather than hard-won and tenaciously held convictions. There are poems of endurance, like "Stopping by the Woods on a Snowy Evening" appearing more deeply felt and more perfectly executed. Frost completed his last collection under the title *In the Clearing* in 1962. In the words of Hyatt H. Waggoner, Frost did survive in spite of emerging brands of modernism.

It is said, Robert Frost is one of the best American poets today. It is said, "Frost has been embraced by the American public, and his poetry continues to be a part of an American culture."[5]

Robert Frost was a regional poet and his region was New England. He was not an idealist as that of Vachal Lindsay. He did not worry about poetic unity. His characters are isolated, like their farms and wood lots, or they are caught in a net which tragically or ironically encloses at most the fate of only two or three. His regionalism is that of Emily Dickinson or Sarah Orne Jewett's. It is said, "His regionalism has him a place to stand where he could see what was close by in field or cellar hole, and as well, a clear view above his hills to the 'further range' beyond."[6]

Frost is a metaphysical poet in the sense Emerson and Dickinson were. He wanted to go beyond the seen and heard. In all great metaphysical poetry the tension increases between the simple fact and the mystery which surrounds it, until the total meaning flashes in the final words. As one critic has observed Frost's art consists in 'his careful and deliberate laying of the material for a poetic bonfire'. Frost said poetry for him was essentially dramatic. Frost, like Robert Browning and later E.A. Robinson, excelled in using dramatic monologues. The same is seen in his poems like "Storm Fear" and "The Mountain". His forte is meditation in poetry. The most well-known poem "Birches" is an example. The poem turns on an episode: what it means, in several modes, to be a small boy swinger of birches. But before the poem is finished it has become a meditation on the best way to leave earth for heaven. Frost writes,

> When I see birches bend to left and right
> Across the lines of straighter darker trees,
> I like to think some boy's been swinging them.
> But swinging does not bend them down to stay
> As ice storms do....
>
> .... Earth's the right place for love:
> I don't like to go by climbing a birch tree,
> And climb black branches up a snowy white trunk
> Toward heaven, till the tree could bear no more,
> But dipped its top and set me down again.
> That would be good both going and coming back.
> One could do worse than be a swinger of birches.

About Robert Frost's poetic technique it is observed: "Though Frost seldom strayed to alien country beyond the sight of his New England upland pastures and back meadows, his poetry widened in content and technique from book to book. Each volume disclosed a particular facet of his genius, some new attitude or tone or approach. Few modern poets have shown such a new attitude for growth, on into the old age."[7]

Robert Frost's poetry shows a remarkable growth in form and substance. His new volume *New Hampshire* has a new consciousness. Poems like "I Will Sing You One-O" are in a riddling manner. There is crypticism in his poetry. But poems like "The Need of Being Versed in Country Things" and "Stopping by the Woods on a Snowy Evening" are quite clear and magical. See for example, the world famous snow poem:

Whose woods these are I think I know
His house is in the village, though;
He will not see me stopping here
To watch his woods fill up with snow.

My little horse must think it queer
To stop without a farmhouse near
Between the woods and frozen lake
The darkest evening of the year

He gives his harness bells a shake
To ask if there is some mistake.
The only other sound's the sweep
Of easy wind and downy flake.

The woods are lovely, dark, and deep,
But I have promises to keep,
And miles to go before I sleep,
And miles to go before I sleep.

The next volume *West-Running Brook* (1928) has descriptions of a river which flows in a different direction from others. The narrator wants to choose contraries. The black stream, striking a barrier, flings back one white wave. The stoic theme of resistance and self-realization is found in other poems in this book. The poem, probably of this collection, "The Road that not Taken" is worth reading. The tension between man and nature, hitherto always exciting and often harmoniously resolved, has loosened. Nature has grown more hostile, man more heroic. The sonnet "A Soldier" runs thus:

But this we know, the obstacle that checked
And tripped the body, shot the spirit on
Further than target ever showed or shone.

In *A Further Range* (1936) there are fine poems. "A Lone Striker" speaks of individual freedom; "The Gold Hesperidia" talks of pride; and the poem "Two Tramps in Mud Time" preaches the necessity of uniting avocation and vocation. Frost writes,

Only where love and need are one,
And the work is play for mortal stakes,
Is the deed ever really done?
For Heaven and the future's sake.

Frost finds the world bleaker in his old age. He turns rather spiritual and mystical. He is not much earth-bound now.

However, Robert Frost is essentially a poet of nature. In his early verse one feels the joy in the sensuous pleasure which nature has given most modern poets. But he knows when to avoid the company of nature as it is hostile to him sometimes. So there is a kind of hide and seek attitude. In the earlier poems, nature and man confront each other across the wall, as the buck and the doe in "Two Look at Two" face the wondering man and woman, each pair in its pasture. It is observed, "Man has need of nature, though he should never make the mistake of crossing the wall into her pasture. The woods are lovely, dark and deep against the snowfall, a place to linger and forget duty; but to linger only, and not to stay. Man is most himself when he measures himself against nature's pace and the barriers she places before him.

Well there's—the storm. That says I must go on.
That wants me as a war might if it came
Ask any man.[8]

Robert Frost was a nature poet. As well as he was a thinker, a skeptic, a relativist and a sensibilist. Frost knew his artistic bounds. Though he did not talk much about poetry, we can glean the same from his poetry and letters. He said poetry is a therapy for man. Someone said Frost that his poem was like a talk. So Frost imbued 'sentence-sound' and 'vocal gesture'. Frost said since language only really exists in the mouths of men, the poet must write with his ear to the voice. He said, "Meter has to do with beat, and sound posture has a definite relation as an alternate tone between the beats. The two are one in creation but separate in analysis."[9] Frost says "poetry is never a put-up job.... It begins as a lump in the throat, a sense of wrong, a homesickness, a loneliness. It is never a thought to begin with. It is at its best when it is a tantalizing vagueness."[10] Frost said that a poem is an expression of an experience. Frost was a prosodist as Eliot and Yeats were. He was an experimentalist as that of Thomas Hardy.

NOTES

1. Norman Douglas, "Robert Frost", *Literary History of the United States*, ed. by Robert Spiller, p. 1189.
2. Robert Frost, *Encyclopedia of Literatures in English*, ed. Manmohan Bhatnagar, New Delhi: Atlantic Publishers, 2000, p. 672.
3. DC, *Who is Who in the 20th Century World Poetry*, ed. by Mark Willhardt, London: Routledge, 2003, p. 107.
4. Hyatt H. Waggoner, "Robert Frost", *Encyclopedia of America*, p. 128.
5. DC, *Who is Who in the 20th Century World Poetry*, p. 108.
6. *Literary History of the United States*, ed. by Robert Spiller, p. 1190.
7. *Ibid.*, p. 1191.
8. *Ibid.*, p. 1195.
9. *Ibid.*
10. *Ibid.*

Wallace Stevens's Poetry: A Note

14

Wallace Stevens was born on 2nd October 1879, in Reading, Pa., USA and he died on 2nd August 1955. He was a US poet. Stevens practiced law in New York City before joining an insurance firm in Hartford in 1916. He rose to Vice-President, a position he held until his death. His poems began appearing in literary magazines in 1914. In *Harmonium* (1923), his first and most verbally brilliant book, he introduced the theme that occupied his creative lifetime and unified his thoughts: the relationship between imagination and reality. His later poetry, in collections such as *Ideas of Order* (1936), *The Man with the Blue Guitar* (1937), *Transport to a Summer* (1947), *The Auroras of Autumn* (1950) and *The Rock* (1955) continued to explore this theme with greater depth and rigour. Not until his later years was he widely read or recognized as a major poet by more than a few. He received a Pulitzer Prize only with his *Collected Poems* in 1955. He is now often considered one of American's greatest 20th century poets.

Two 20th century critics Yvor Winters and Donald Davie think of Stevens as a major 20th century American poet. In Stevens' poetry we find a combination of calm and terror. His poetry is poetry of skepticism. Charles Tomlinson says, "He is indeed a poet to be mentioned in the same breath as Eliot and Yeats and Pound."[1] Like Yeats and Eliot Stevens was writing poetry at a time when the very idea of poetry was in crisis. Eliot and Pound were changing the concept of poetry. Yet, Stevens did not adhere to their new poetry. He continued to write poetry in the old mode. He used Victorian modes of poetic conventions and themes though he employed odd titles like 'Le Monocle de

Mon Oncle'. He used old conventions too much, in fact. The following poem has romantic access:

The dark shadows of the funeral magnolias
Are full of the songs of Jamanda and Carlotta
—The son and the daughter who come to the darkness
He for her burning breast, and she for his arms.

One finds the alliance of death and beauty in Stevens' poetry. For instance:

Beauty is momentary in the mind—
The fitful tracing of a portal;
But in the flesh it is immortal.
The body dies; the body's beauty lives.
So evenings die, in their green going,
A wave interminably flowing....
Susanna's music touched the bawdy strings
Of those white elder's; but, escaping,
Left only Death's ironic scraping.

Both Winters and Davie seize upon this section of the poem which results in Stevens' own. Intimations of freshness impinge through the nostalgia of another early sequence in 'Sunday Morning'. Here a woman is meditating on the fact of death:

She says, 'I am content when wakened birds
Before they fly', test the reality
Of misty fields by their sweet questionings;
But when the birds are gone, and their warm fields
Return no more, where, then is paradise?

Stevens' poetry expresses disbelief rather. Winters observes, "The language has the greatest possible dignity and subtlety, combined with a perfect precision. The imminence of absolute tragedy is felt and recorded, but the integrity of the feeling mind is maintained.... The calm clarity of tone would be impossible were the terror emphasized for a moment at any point...."[2] Stevens' poetry resembles the poetry of Keats, Hopkins and Emily Dickinson. Look at his poem "Thirteen ways of Looking at a Blackbird",

Icicles filled the long window
With barbaric glass.

The shadow of the blackbird
Crossed it, to and fro.
The mood
Traced in the shadow
An indecipherable cause.

It was evening all afternoon.
It was snowing
And it was going to snow.
The blackbird sat
In the cedar limbs.

The theme of loneliness is recurrent in the poem.

Another poem "The Anecdote of the Jar" speaks of art splendidly. Look at the poem:

I placed a jar in Tennessee,
And round it was, upon a hill.
It made the slovenly wilderness
Surround that hill.

The wilderness rose up to it,
And sprawled around, no longer wild,
The jar was round upon the ground
And tall and of a port in air.

It took dominion everywhere.
The jar was gray and bare.
It did not give of bird or bush,
Like nothing else in Tennessee.

The poem is a poem of art. Art helps man to realize the importance of life. It helps us to improve life. Just the presence of a jar on the hill makes the hill more important. Indeed, the poem has Keatsian signification.

If there is loneliness in Stevens' poetry it places him close to the European skepticism of Nietzsche—a disbelief that found its most lasting poetic embodiment in the *Duino Elegies* of Rainer Maria Rilke. His poem "American Sublime" suggests an American version of something of this kind. For example:

The spirit and space,
The empty spirit

In vacant space.
What wine does one drink?
What bread does one eat?

In such a universe, nature reflects back at man the order his imagination has projected on it:

Sad men made angels of the sun, and of
The moon they made their own attendant ghosts....

Stevens said he would write poetry of the earth. Keats wrote such poetry. His "Notes Towards a Supreme Fiction" speaks of poetry as supreme fiction. Once Stevens wrote: "Novelty must be inspired. But there must be novelty. This crisis is most evident in religion. The theologians whose thought it most astir today do make articulate a supreme need,...the need to infuse into the ages of enlightenment an awareness of reality adequate to their achievements and such as will not be attenuated by them. There is one most welcome and authentic note; it is the insistence on a reality that forces itself upon our consciousness and refuses to be managed and mastered."[3] Stevens said fiction must change life.

Stevens' poem "A Postcard from the Volcano?" is interesting. "The Idea of Order at Key West", another poem shows us once more the less wintry side of Stevens' imagination. The poem depicts a woman singing at sea:

It was her voice that made
The sky acutest at its vanishing.
She measured to the hour its solitude.
She was the single artificer of the world
In which she sang. And when she sang, the sea,
Whatever self it had, became the self
That was her song, for she was the maker. Then we
As we beheld her striding there alone,
Knew that there never was a world for her
Except the one she sang and singing, made.

The poem tells us much about one aspect of Stevens' imagination. Helen Vendler says "Stevens seems to have presented him with a world excessively interior, in which the senses, with the exception of the eye, are atrophied or impoverished...."

Stevens' "Of Modern Poetry" speaks of Eliot's concern for poetry. He writes:

The poem of the mind in the act of finding
What will suffice. It has not always had
To find: the scene was set; it repeated what
Was in the script.

Stevens once wrote what Eliot would himself say that: "In an age of disbelief, or what is the same thing, in a time that is largely humanistic, in one sense or the other, it is for the poet to supply the satisfaction of belief in his measure and in his style. I think of it as a role of the utmost seriousness. It is, for one thing, a spiritual role."[4] Another poem, "The Emperor of Ice-cream" is of similar tone. Stevens seems to say that life is a waste. His poem has the refrain 'The only Emperor is the Emperor of the Ice-cream'. That way Stevens' poem is unlike Eliot's *Waste Land* which ends in a positive note. Stevens does not speak of the use of past. His vision is not upward or onward. So his poetry is not of meditation.

Stevens' last collection *The Rock* has many good poems such as "Long and Sluggish Lines", "To an Old Philosopher in Rome", "Song of Fixed Accord", "The River of Rivers in Connecticut", "The World as Meditation". It is said the poems of the volume are more austere and free from gaudiness.

Kathryn Van Spanckeren observes, "Stevens' poetry dwells upon themes of the imagination, the necessity for aesthetic form and the belief that the order of art corresponds with the order in nature. His vocabulary is rich and various: He paints lush tropical scenes but also manages dry, humorous, and ironic vignettes."[5]

An Indian critic C.D. Narasimhaiahm observes, "Stevens feels strongly that the poems of heaven and hell have been written but the poems of the earth have yet to be written. He writes the poems of the earth: the sea itself flows in our veins, the sun gives comfort out of tenderness or grief; we are clothed with the blue of the sky and crowned with the glory of the stars. Thanks to him our perceptions are sharpened and our awareness of life's manifold beauty has increased and form from him, as from D.H. Lawrence, we learn that to deny life is evil. But in his abundant zest for life he has taken pitifully small notice of crises of the spirit in man, thus coming perilously close to the hedonistic doctrine. He may be the most finished poet of our age, but by no means a great poet. Despite his urbanity, grace and the shaping spirit of imagination he falls short of greatness; we miss in him Eliot's moral and spiritual centrality. But it is to Stevens' credit that he makes the quest, the inquiry, possible, for he does not shut the door on endeavor. As he posits in his famous poem "Sunday Morning":

> The river always seeks for the sea that is never found.
> A different thing from Eliot's
> Not fare well but fare forward, voyagers.

"...a realization which was Krishna's gift to Arjuna (in the Bhagavad Gita) which really underlines for us the essential difference between the two poets: with the one we are on an intellectual search; with the other, the search, for all its rigour, takes us to the still-centre and achieves a wholeness."[6]

NOTES

1. Charles Tomlinson, "Wallace Stevens and the Poetry of Scepticism", *The New Pelican Guide to English Literature*, ed. by Boris Ford, London: Penguin, 1991, p. 393.
2. Winters, qt. by Charles Tomlinson, "Wallace Stevens and the Poetry of Scepticism", p. 398.
3. Wallace Stevens, qt. by Charles Tomlinson, "Wallace Stevens and the Poetry of Scepticism", p. 405.
4. C.D. Narasimhaiahm, "Wallace Stevens", *Asian Response to American Poetry*, ed. by C.D. Narasimhaiahm, New Delhi: Viking Press, 1972, p. 111.
5. Kathryn Van Spanckeren, *American Literature,* United States Information Agency, p. 66.
6. C.D. Narasimhaiahm, "Wallace Stevens", *Asian Response to American Poetry*, p. 120.

Eugene O'Neill's *The Hairy Ape*: As a Critique of American Capitalism

15

Eugene O'Neill is America's first great playwright and he won the Nobel Prize in 1936. Yet he led a tragic life that provided the substance of his finest writings. He wrote nightmarish expressionistic works, costume dramas, bitter Strindbergian views of marriage, biblical fables, multiact, even multiplay mammoths and free adaptations of classical tragedy. In writing all this—nearly 30 long plays and a dozen short ones, he almost exhausted the stage's non-verbal resources through his use of masks, music, dance, pantomime, unusual scenic devices and novel sound effects.

Eugene Gladstone O'Neill was born in 1888, in New York City. His father, Tames O'Neill, was a noted 19th century actor. Eugene's mother, Ella was shy and devoutly Roman Catholic. O'Neill turned rebellious, rejecting all established authority. Yet like his hero he was at war with himself. His drug addict sharpened his own sense of guilt. O'Neill, in short, was an emotional hemophiliac. Under the tutelage of his brother, "O'Neill early took to drink, patronized brothels and as a disciple of Nietzsche, sought to establish a position beyond good and evil." In 1907 he dropped out of Princeton after a year. He later went to sea and once attempted suicide in a waterfront saloon. While working as a reporter in New London, Conn., where his family spent the summer, his health broke down and he was forced to spend six months in a TB sanatorium in 1912. O'Neill had literary ambitions. In 1916, after a year's study at Harvard with George Pierce Baker, his one-act play *Bound East for Cardiff* was produced on Cape Cod by the Provincetown Players.

O'Neill was married three times, to Kathleen Jenkins, to Agnes Boulton (a writer) and to Carlotta Monterey, an actress. O'Neill's last years were as tragic as any of his plays. He became estranged from his children. His third marriage became a Strindbergian nightmare. O'Neill died in a hotel in Boston in 1953, after crying out, "Born in a goddam hotel room and dying in a hotel room!"

O'Neill is a major American playwright. His notable plays include *The Iceman Cometh, The Emperor Jones* (1920), *The Hairy Ape* (1921), *Desire Under the Elms* (1924), *The Great God Brown* (1925), *Mourning Becomes Electro* (1929-31), *A Touch of the Poet* (1935-42) and *A Moon for the Misbegotten* (1941-43). O'Neill's checkered career was due to his subjective nature and he tried to write plays for confession and for salvation.

Louis Sheaffer says despite O'Neill's pre-eminent position, he had little direct or immediate influence on other playwrights, both because of his constant experimentation and because of the autobiographical nature of his writings. The chief effect of his writing was "to help lead the American theater, stale and long overdue for change, into the 20th century".

Eugene O'Neill, in his numerous plays, depicts the decline of values in modern times. He speaks of the evils of capitalism. His play *The Hairy Ape* (1921) that was first produced at the Princeton Playhouse, New York City, is a severe attack on moral devastation. It seems O'Neill also attacks upon racism so rampant in his times. He writes on social issues. In brief, the play *The Hairy Ape* portrays the evils of the capitalist system.

The Hairy Ape begins with a portrayal of the forecastle of a ship, that is about to voyage across the Atlantic Ocean. An impression of claustrophobia is created due to the crowded atmosphere of the firemen or stokers, many of whom are drunk. O'Neill tells us that the effect sought after is that of a cramped space in the bowels of a ship. All the men are "hairy chested, with long arms of tremendous power, and low, receding brows above their small fierce, resentful eyes". The stokers rhapsodize their adventures as seen below:

Voices Gif me trink dere, you!
'Ave a wer!
Salute!
Gesundheit!
Skoal!
Drunk as a lord, God stiffen you!
Heres how!
Luck!
Pass back that bottle, damn you!
Pouri' it down his neck!
Ho, Froggy! Where the devil have you been!
La Touraine.
I hit him smash in yaw, py Gott!
Jenkins—the First—he's a rotten swine—
And the coppers nabbed him—and I run—
I like peer better. It don't pig head gif you.
A slut, I'm sayin'! she robbed me aslape—
To hell with 'em all!
You're a bloody liar!
Say dot again![1] (p. 1192)

As J.M.J. Indra Mohan says, "Yank then expresses his sense of belonging when Paddy feels nostalgic about the past and says that the life of modern man is very much in contrast with that of the past when man was conjoined with his vocation."[2] This is one reason why the play is subtitled "A Comedy of Ancient and Modern Life in Eight Scenes".

The sea voyage begins: Two days are gone. It is a section of promenade deck. Mildred Douglas and her aunt, as passengers, appear there. The former is "a girl of twenty, slender, delicate, with a pale, pretty face marred by a self-conscious expression of disdainful superiority. She looks fretful, nervous and discontented". While the latter is "pompous and proud". Both represent the American capitalist society. They contrast each other even. The young niece is rather of modern make-up, and her aunt is vainglorious. Mildred Douglas is beautiful, rich and rational. She speaks of decline in good old life. She says, "Please do not mock at my attempts to discover how the other half lives. Give me credit for some sort of groping sincerity in that at least.

I would like to help them. I would like to be some use in the world. Is it my fault I don't know how? I would like to be sincere, to touch life somewhere (with weary bitterness). But I'm afraid I have neither the vitality nor integrity. All that was burnt out in our stock before I was born. Grandfather's blast furnaces, flaming to the sky, melting steel, making millions—then father keeping those home fires burning, making some millions—and little me at the tail-end of it all. I'm a waste product in the Bessemer process—like the millions. Or rather, I inherit the acquired trait of the by-product, wealth, but none of the energy, none of the strength of the steal" (p. 1196).

After a good deal of discussion about small matters with her aunt, Mildred Douglas with two engineers goes to have a look at the furnace.

When Mildred Douglas arrives at the forecastle the stokers are busy in supplying coal to the furnace of the ship. Yank, as their leader and main character, asks them to do as he guides them. Paddy complains of his backache. The scene is moving:

> YANK: (*In an exultant tone of command.*) Come on, youse guys! Into de game! She's gitten hungry! Pile some grub in her. Trow it into her belly! Come on now, all of youse! Open her up!

YANK: (*Chanting a count as he shovels without seeming effort.*) One—two—tree—(*His voice rising exultantly in the joy of the battle.*) Dat's de stuff! Let her have it! All together now! Sling it into her! Let her ride! Shoot de piece now! Call de toin on her! Drive her into it! Feel her move! Watch her smoke! Speed, dat's her middle name! Give her coal, youse guys! Coal, dat's her booze! Drink it up, baby! Let's see yuh sprint! Dig in and gain a lap! Dere she do-o-es.

PADDY: (*Groaning*) Me back is broke. I'm outbate—

YANK: (*Shaking his fist upward—contemptuously.*) Take it easy dere, you! Who d'yuh tinks runnin' dis game, me or you? When I git ready, we move. Now before! When I git ready, get me!

> Yank tal him, py golly!
> Yank ain't afeerd.

Goot poy, Yank!
Give him hell!
Tell 'im 'e's a bloody swine!
Bloody slave-driver! (pp. 1198-99)

Mildred looks at the furnace. It is ugly and fiery as the hell. Yank's hairy and clay-like look, frightens her. He looks like a 'hairy ape'. Now "she starts, turns paler, her pose is complaining, she shivers with fright in spite of the blazing heat, but forces herself to leave the engineers and take a few steps nearer the men. She is right behind Yank. All this happens quickly while the men have their backs turned" (p. 1199).

Mildred Douglas looks at Yank for long. She is disgusted, repulsed. Yet Yank does not care for her. When he looks at her, he imagines she is a white apparition. "He glares into her eyes, turned to stone. As for her, during his speech she has listened, paralyzed with horror, terror, her whole personality crushed, beaten in, collapsed, by the terrific impact of this unknown, abysmal brutalities, naked and shameless. As she looks at his gorilla face, as his eyes bore into hers, she utters a low, choking cry and shrinks away from him, putting both hands up before her eyes to shut out the sight of his face, to protect her own" (p. 1199). Shortly she cries "Take me away!" and the engineers take her away.

Scene IV reveals Yank's response to the insults that he experienced due to Mildred's visit to the forecastle. He now contemplates seriously and broods over the drastic confrontation. Once the act of fuelling was over, all stokers wash themselves, while Yank does not. He sits like Auguste Rodin's "The Thinker". Most of the others smoking pipes stare at Yank half-apprehensively. They feel there was a joke for them.

Yank, in response to their asking him to wash his body, says "Aw say, youse guys. Lemme aone. Can't youse see I'm tryin' to think?" The others just groan his words 'Think'. This infuriates them. Paddy, that jocular fellow, imagines the reason. He gueses Yank must be fallen in love with Mildred Douglas. Yank refuses it. Long expresses Yank's anguish:

LONG: (*Jumping on a bunch—hectically.*) Hinsultan' us! Hinsultan' us! The bloody cow! And them bloody engineers!

> What right 'as they got to be exhbitin' us 's if we was bleedin' monkeys in a menagerie? Did we sign for hinsults to our dignity as 'onest workers? Is that in the ship's articles? You kin bloody well bet it ain't. But I knows why they done it. I asked a deck steward 'o she was and 'e told me. 'Er old man's a bleedin' millionaire, a bloody Capitalist! 'E's got enuf bloody gold to sink this bleedin' ship! 'E makes arf the bloody steel in the world! 'E owns this bloody boat! And you and me, Comrades, we're 'is slaves! And the skipper and mates and engineers, they're 'is slaves! And she 'is bloody daughter and we're all 'er slaves, too! And she gives 'er orders as 'ow she wants to see the bloody animals below decks and down they takes 'er!" (p. 1200).

In the conversation that follows, we notice Yank hating American government, American social practices and capitalism. Mildred Douglas, to him, appears as representing American capitalist society. He abuses her. He says "she was white", looking like a ghost. He says:

> YANK: (*Grinning, horribly.*) Hairy ape, huh? Sure! Dat's de way she looked at me, aw right. Hairy ape! So dat's me, huh? Yuh skinny tart! Yuh whitefaced bum, yuh! I'll show you who's ape? (p. 1201)

Paddy asks Yank to calm down. He assures him that she will not visit them again. Yet Yank rushes to beat and kill her. All the stokers stop him. Their choking voices express the anguish in between:

> VOICES: Stop him!
> He'll get shot!
> He'll murder her!
> Trip him up!
> Hold him!
> He's gone crazy!
> Gott, he's strong!
> Hold him down!
> Look out for a kick!
> Pin his arms!

YANK: She done me doit! She done me doit, didn't she? I'll git square wit her! I'll get her some way! Git offen' me, youse guys! Lemme up! I'll show her who's ape! (p. 1202)

In the fifth scene, Yank and Long are at the Fifth Avenue, watching with annoyance to the very core, the capitalists and the affluent whom they detest vehemently. Yank who is now bereft of his sanity, behaves in a ludicrous manner in order to create a trifle with that of the capitalists.

But Long persuades Yank for a peaceful life. He tells him, "Easy goes, comrade. Keep yer bloomin' temper. Remember force defeats itself. It ain't our weapon. We must impress our proletarians of the bloody world!" (p. 1204).

Later Yank loses his temper. There is an emotional turmoil in him, haunting him. He notices some people selling monkey fur. He meditates of something. He comes across a construction site and looking at the labors at it, tells with bravado:

> See dat building goin' up dere?
> See de steel work? Steel, dat's me!
> Youse guys live on it and tink yuh're somep'n
> But I'm in it, see! I'm de hoistin' engine
> Dat makes it go up!
> I'm it—de inside and bottom of it!
> Sure! I'm steel and steam and smoke and de rest of it! (p. 1204)

Long finds it difficult to endure. He remains neutral. Shortly Yank disturbs a woman. Yet the lady neglects him. Then he disturbs a gentleman. The latter, due to that, misses his bus and asks Yank for the reason.

Shortly a team of police arrests Yank and puts him in a prison house. Critics observe: "The idea that man is an animal is presented throughout the play. He is presented as an animal in order to highlight the inhuman conditions in which he is placed. He is projected as an animal, caged by the world of machinery. He thus becomes a prisoner with respect to his vocation and his living. The proletariat lives in the machine world of steel and like steel it is hard, rigid and makes his life austere and unendurable."

O'Neill shows Yank in jail in scene sixth. Yank, partly due to his own inner conflict and pride and partly due to its encounter in the external world, lands into trouble. Mildred Douglas's words that 'he is a beast' hurt him. He turns mad. His madness works a frenzy of hysteria. He attacks a group of steel workers, some women and a good-looking gentleman. He then learns about the IWW and its methods of operation. He wants to take vengeance on the civilized world.

Yank is kept in a cell. He sits like Rodin's 'The Thinker'. His face has brushes and bondages. O'Neill describes him in jail thus:

> YANK: (*Suddenly starting as if awakening from a dream, reaches out and shakes the bars—aloud to himself, wonderingly.*) Steel. Dis 's the Zoo, huh? (*A burst of hard, barking laughter comes from the unseen occupants of the cells, runs back down the tier, and abruptly cease.*)
>
> VOICES: (*Mockingly*) The Zoo. That's a new name for this coop—a damn good name!
>
> Steel, eh? You said a mouthful. This is the old iron house.
>
> Who is that boob talkin'?
>
> He's the bloke they brung in out of his head. The bulls had beat him up fierce (p. 1205).

Yank in scene seventh in the cell speaks aloud about his mental agony caused by the feeling that he has been referred to 'an ape' by Mildred Douglas. Some prisoners ask him to join Industrial Workers of the World, IWW for short. One of them says it will not provide proletarians any justice. They say it is rather an Industrious Wreckers of the World. Yank knows Douglas's father is a millionaire, possessing steel plants and ships. So his wrath increases against the rich. It is his inner trauma. Later he breaks the cell bar, provoking jail guards.

In scene seventh Yank is released and he meets the Secretary of the Industrial Workers of the World, a guild for the welfare of the industrial workers. Yank is rendered the necessary formalities for joining in the organization and this exhilarates him, for it inculcates in him the feeling that he belongs somewhere.

But shortly Yank finds with the Secretary a lot of differences. Because Yank is not a man of modern world. The scene is interesting:

> SECRETARY: You mean change the unequal conditions of society by legitimate direct action—or with dynamite?
>
> YANK: Dynamite! Blow it often de oith—steel—all de cages—all de factories, steamers, buildings, jails—de Steel Trust and all dat makes it go.
>
> SECRETARY: So that's your idea, eh? And did you have any special job in that line you wanted to propose to us?
>
> YANK: (*Boldy*) Sure, I'll come out wit it. I'll show youse I'm one of de gang. Dere's dat millionaire guy, Douglas—
>
> SECRETARY: President of the Steel Trust, you mean? Do you want to assassinate him?
>
> YANK: Naw, dat don't get you nothin'. I mean blow up de factory, de woiks, where he makes de steel. Dat's what I'm after—to blow up de steel, knock all de steel in de woild up to de moon. Dat'll fix tings! I'll it by me lonesome! I'll show yuh! Tell where his woik is, how to git there, all de dope. Gimme de stuff, deold butter—and watch me do de rest! Wach de smoke and see it move! I'll soive life for it—and give 'em de laugh! And I'll write her a letter and tell her de hairy ape done it. Dat'll square tings. (p. 1209)

This situation reaches a crisis when Yank invites a bodily chastisement:

> SECRETARY: No. He isn't worth the trouble we'd get into, he's stupid. (*He comes closer and laughs mockingly at YANK'S face.*) Ho—ho! By God, this is the biggest joke they've put up on us yet. Hey, you Joke! Who sent you—Burns or Pinkerton? No, by God, you're such a bonehead I'll bet you're in the Secret Service! Well, you dirty spy, you rotten agent provocator, you can go back and tell whatever skunk is paying you blood money for betraying your brothers that he's wasting his coin. You couldn't catch a cold. And tell him that all he'll ever get on us, or ever has got, is just his own sneaking plots that he's framed up to put

> us in jail. We are what our manifesto says we are, neither more nor less—and we'll give him a copy of that any time he calls. And as for you—(*He glares scornfully at YANK, who is sunk in an oblivious stupor.*) Oh, hell, what's the use of talking? You're a brainless ape. (p. 1209)

True Yank is taken for a spy. He is compared to Black Hand, an Italian criminal society of the 19th century. He is finished, in fact. Yank gets insane. He loses his mind.

The police enquire Yank. This aggravates his agitated mental condition. He visits a zoo and gets enticed to go near a gorilla. He speaks he is an ape. He is a gorilla and as a gorilla he can revolt against the capitalists. In his insane state of mind, he releases the gorilla out of the cage and it crushes him.

Finally, he goes to the gorilla cell. He rises to speak to it. He says it is his brother. He says it and he should unite and kill the capitalists. He even befriends it bodily as if to kiss it. But the gorilla kills him:

> ...Yuh're reg'lar! You'll sick to de Me 'n' you huh?—bot' members of this club! We'll put up one last star bout dat'll knock 'em often deir seats. Dey'll have to make de cages stronger after we're trou!
>
> Christ, where do I get off at? Where do I fit in? (*Checking himself as suddenly.*) Aw, what de hell! No squawkin', see! No quittin', get me! Croak wit your boots on! (*He grabs hold of the bars of the cage and hauls himself painfully to his feet—looks around him bewilderingly—forces a mocking laugh.*) In de cage, huh? (*In the strident tones of a circus barker.*) Ladies and gents, step forward and take a slant at de one and only—(*His voice weakening.*)—one and original—Hairy Ape from de welds of—*He slips in a heap on the floor and dies. The monkeys set up a chattering, whimpering wail. And, perhaps, the Hairy Ape at last belongs*. (p. 1211)

The idea that man is an animal is presented here. At the same time, man's inborn or instinctual pride, stubbornness and animality mar his peaceful life as seen in Yank's life. Aristotle considered the pride of the tragic hero as a 'flaw and an-error or frailty' and it is the pride in man that binds him with self-deception as explicit in the case of Yank.

O'Neill's *The Hairy Ape* is a hilarious serious comedy. It is to speak more 'a single character play'. It is known for its expressionistic method which at intervals substitutes a fantastic kind of symbolism for external realism. The play deals with a psychological problem with social implications. O'Neill uses the techniques of asides, masks, symbolism and expressionism to convey his own understanding of life to his audience.

NOTES

1. All references are to O'Neill, *The Hairy Ape*.
2. J.M.J. Indra Mohan, "O'Neill's *The Hairy Ape* as a Reflection of Contemporary Society", *Studies in Literature in English,* ed. by Mohit Ray, New Delhi: Atlantic Publishers, 2001, pp. 88-89.

Arthur Miller's *Death of a Salesman*: A Critique of American Life

16

'America' means a 'dream' for many. In fact, all know what is an "American dream". America, as a great democracy stands for an ideal nation, a happy commonwealth. Many writers of America have represented their country faithfully.

Arthur Miller is one such great American playwright who, as an evolutionary meliorist, represented an ideal and secular way of American life. He was a great creative writer and humanist.

The son of a well-to-do clothing manufacturer, Arthur Miller was born in New York City on October 17, 1915. He grew up in Harlem, which then had a prosperous Jewish neighborhood and in Brooklyn. After high school he set his sight on becoming a playwright and studied dramatic arts at the University of Michigan, from which he graduated in 1938. While in college during the depths of Depression he wrote plays—none of which were produced—with radical anti-capitalist themes. Exempt from military service during World War II, because of a football injury, Miller worked in the early 1940's as a scriptwriter for network radio. In 1945 he published *Focus*, a novel about anti-Semitism. As with much of his fiction, this book was less than a success.

However, Miller was to shine in a different capacity. He was to become a world famous playwright. Miller's first Broadway play was *The Man Who Had All The Luck*, which closed after four performances when produced in 1914. His next play *All My Sons* (1947) that won him the New York Drama Critics Circle Award tells of a manufacturer who knowingly sells defective aircraft equipments during World War II and manages to transfer responsibility for the crime to his innocent partner. It is said 'sin recoils the sinner'. So the manufacturer loses his son in the war.

Miller's next play *Death of a Salesman* (1949), probably his greatest achievement, describes the disillusionment, ending in suicide of the character Willy Loman, a tragic figure who has lost the knack of selling himself—and the product—he represents. In a way, he reminds us Michael Henchard of Thomas Hardy's *The Mayor of Casterbridge*. With American indictment of commercialization and false values, *Death of a Salesman* ends with a plea by Willy's wife Linda that attention must be paid to those who fail in achieving the popular concept of success. Critics say the play is a universal success. Miller received the Pulitzer Prize for the play in 1949.

Miller's play *The Crucible* (1953) dealing with the Salem witchcraft trials had political overtones that were identified as a denunciation of the McCarthy senate hearings in regard to communist subversion in the federal government. We know, due to this, in 1956 the House of Un-American Activities Committee for refusing to identify left-wing associates, indicted Miller. But he was cleared of all charges. *The Crucible*, Miller's most characteristic play portrayed the 17th century Puritan America's infamous witchcraft trials. It very well reminds us Mrs Hester Prynne of Hawthorn's *The Scarlet Letters*.

Miller's later plays include *A View from the Bridge* (1955), *After the Fall* (1964), *Incident at Vichy* (1964) and *The Creation of the World and Other Business* (1972). *All My Sons, Death of a Salesman* and *A View from the Bridge* are made into motion pictures.

As for Miller's philosophy of life, he was an evolutionary meliorist. This is because of the reason that he suffered a lot in life. Why because, as a Hebrew, he had to face racial hatredness in America. Suffering made him strong, made him creative and made him humanistic. He hated racial wars, he hated America's policy of bossism over weaker nations and he hated cruelty in man. Miller, in his autobiography *Timebends* quotes the physicist Hans Bethe as saying, "Well, I come down in the morning and

I take up a pencil and I try to think." He did not like America go for wars in Vietnam and Iraq. He knew any sinister leadership would cause national disasters.

As a creative writer Miller thought that he has to reform society by his worthy writings. He says any individual has an abiding moral responsibility for the society's progress. He believed that an individual's, a writer's good conscience could keep a world from falling. Such of Miller's ideas and thoughts led to realism and humanism in literature.

As for Miller's personal life he lived happily. He married three times. His second wife was the famous American film star Marilyn Monroe, to whom he was married in 1956 and he lived with her upto 1961. For Miss Monroe he wrote the screenplay *The Misfits* (1961). *The Misfits* was the last of Miss Monroe's pictures.

The *Death of a Salesman* rightly described as a 'little man's tragedy' is about American life. The play has several characters such as Willy Loman, Linda, his wife, Biff and Happy, his sons, Ben, Charles and Bernard. Arthur Miller wrote the play in 1949 and it was first staged at Morosco Theatre in New York. *Death of a Salesman* was first staged by Kermit Bloomgarden and Walter Fried. The play takes place in Willy Loman's house and yard and in various places he visits in the New York and Boston of today. The play was an instant success. Brooks Atkinson in *The New York Times* wrote, "The play is one of the finest dramas in the whole range of the American theater" and John Mason Brown referred to its production as "One of the modern theatre's most overpowering evenings". It was a tremendously affecting work. The British drama critics called it a "skillful piece of stagecraft".

The play opens at Willy Loman's house in New York City. Arthur Miller gives a description of the Loman house. Willy Loman returns home rather exhausted. His wife Linda enquires about his business. The beginning is quite impressive:

> Linda: (hearing Willy outside the bedroom, calls with some trepidation). Willy!
>
> WILLY. It's all right. I came back.

LINDA. Why? What happened? (Slight pause) Did something happen, Willy?

WILLY. No, nothing happened.

LINDA. You didn't smash the car, did you?[1]

Linda thinks her husband has returned home quite in time as he did not do any business or something happened. Later, on enquiry, Willy tells he drove the car badly. She thinks he needs glass for his eyes. There is some misapprehension that Willy Loman could not meet with any success in his business. In fact, Willy Loman thinks of meeting his boss Howard for his transfer to New York City as he is ageing. He regrets that, unlike Wagner, Howard, his son, is not sympathetic enough. Still he wants to request Howard for his transfer to New York City. Willy Loman has a lot of dreams. He thinks of his sons Biff and Happy, Hap for short. He tells his wife that Biff, in spite of education and several years of service in many business firms, is not making much success. His pay is hardly thirty-eight dollars a week. He thinks he is lazy. Yet he contradicts it saying he is not lazy. Critics think Willy Loman has some false dreams for becoming a rich man. This is shown in his telling his children that he will take them to many cities and he knows many big people for help. Willy Loman, at the same time, worries of degeneration in American society. He thinks America has population explosion and mechanic life: "The street is lined with cars. There's not fresh air in the neighborhood. The grass doesn't grow any more, you can't raise a carrot in the backyard. They should've had a law against apartment houses. Remember those two beautiful elm trees out there? When Biff and I hung the swing between them?

There are more people! That's what's ruining this country! Population is getting out of control. The competition is maddening! Smell the stink from that apartment house! And another one on the other side..." (p. 6).

The children Biff and Happy who are presented to us when their father comes home with bad feelings about his business, speak ill of their father. Biff says his father cannot see things properly; and Happy says he is colour blind. Biff regrets for his failure for getting a right job. He says he served in many places like Nebraska, Dakota, Arizona and Texas. He wants to take Bill Oliver's help and buy a ranch in the west. He asks Happy to go with him. On the other hand, Happy who works somewhere now wants to be where he is. The boys talk of their love. It appears Loman asks Biff not to have an affair so young while Happy has one already. Willy Loman is in the kitchen all this time. He is eating.

Linda is a lady known for her concern for the whole family. She is not happy with her sons' behavior with their father. Besides, she knows Willy runs a rough weather with them. One day she regrets of Willy's bad life. She tells the sons that he is plus sixty and has opened unheard territories of business for the Wagner firm but the firm is not paying him much. This shocks the sons. She says the sons do not earn much. Her anguish is shown below:

> Are they any worse than his sons? When he brought them business, when he was young, they were glad to see him. But now his old friends, the old buyers that loved him so and always found some order to hand him in a pinch—they're all dead, retired. He used to be able to make six calls a day in Boston. Now he takes his valises out of the car and puts them back and takes them out again and he's exhausted. Instead of walking he talks now. He drives seven hundred miles, and when he gets there no one knows him any more, no one welcomes him. And what goes through a man's mind, driving seven hundred miles home without having earned a cent? Why shouldn't he talk to himself? Why? When he has to go to Charley and borrow fifty dollars a week and pretend to me that it's his pay? How long can that go on? How long? You see what I'm sitting here and waiting for? And not tell me he has no character? The man who never worked a day but for your benefit? When does he get the medal for that? Is this reward—to turn around at the age of sixty-three and find his son, who he loved better than his life, one a philandering bum.... (p. 20)

She tells Biff that his father's life is in the hands of him.

The parents advise Biff for better life. The latter says he will meet Bill Oliver and borrow some ten thousand dollars and buy a ranch in the west. He says that will help the family. The parents advise him to meet him in a right way. Willy tells him how he must dress and speak to Oliver. The next morning Biff goes to meet Oliver and Happy also goes off. When Willy is to go to see his boss Howard Linda receives his phone and she speaks to Biff the same thing—relating to his future and his goodness towards his father.

William Loman meets Howard and asks him for the transfer of his job to New York City. The reasons he cites for this are that he is aged and tired and he has a growing family. But Howard says he is helpless. Willy likes to have less pay but a sure transfer. Infact, their discourse takes a serious turn. Willy Loman says he was one of the first employees of the firm when Howard's father started it. He has been working there sincerely. He has served it for the last 34 years. Now he is aged and tired with a big family. Even he is ready to work for 65 dollars. When Howard does not consent to it, he agrees for 40 dollars. No use. Loman citing the example of old Dave Singleman says he became a salesman as Dave inspired him, or he would have been with his brother, like father before him, in Alaska or Africa. Loman's anger is uncontrollable. So he bursts: "In those days there was personality in it, Howard. There was respect, and comradeship, and gratitude in it. Today, it's all cut and dried, and there's no chance for bringing friendship to bear—or personality. You see what I mean? They don't know me any more" (p. 28).

When Howard goes off to see a customer for a trice, Willy gets annoyed and bangs the table and speaks harshly of him. Howard comes and he orders for his temporary termination from the job:

Howard: Willy look....

Willy: I'll go to Boston.

Howard: Willy, you can't go to Boston for us.

Willy: Why can't I go?

Howard: I don't want you to represent us. I've been meaning to tell you for a long time now.

Willy: Howard, are you firing me?

Howard: I think you need a good long rest, Willy.

Willy: Howard—

Howard: And when you feel better, come back, and we'll see if we can work something out.

Willy: But I gotta earn money, Howard. I'm in no position to—

Howard: Where are your sons? Why don't your sons give you a hand?

Willy: They're working on a very big deal.

Howard: This is no time for false pride, Willy. You go to your sons and tell them, that you're tired. You've got two great boys, haven't you? (p. 29)

Then the scene shifts to another locale. Ben comes to pay a short visit to his brother's family. Willy says he is in tension. He says he is in a bad position now. But his wife contradicts him. Linda opposes Willy's plan for going with Ben for work in Alaska. This is ununderstandable. Then Biff comes. Ben goes off. Willy goes to meet Charley for borrowing money. Now he hears about Bernard's prospectus, as he has become a lawyer and going to argue in the American Supreme Court. Charles, as usual a friend of Willy asks him to take a job with him. But the haughty Willy refuses it. Miller projects Willy's character as a false man. He is rather jealous of Charley and does not want to work under him though the other's conditions are quite good. There is Happy's brief episode with Stanley and a girl called Forsythe.

Willy shortly finds Biff waiting for him. There is a long and tense dialogue between the two over Biff's prospects. Biff tells him he met Bill Oliver with much difficulty and could not get any help from him. He says he snatched away Oliver's pen. It seems he did such things earlier. This establishes the fact that Biff is not a gentleman. However, Biff does not lie this time as Happy suggested him. There Bernard brings the news of Biff's failure in maths. The father decides to put a word to Birbaum for his son's passing graduation. At the same time, Biff finds his father in love with a woman in Boston. This fact enrages both—Willy and Biff. Biff devalues his father. Willy confesses he had an affair with her, as he was lonely. Critics point out that Willy is an adulterous man. When they go home, Happy speaks of his and Biff's meeting girls in a hotel. Linda calls them whores and scorns her boys. Linda dislikes them for their not inviting their father for dinner, which they had assured.

Willy Loman pays his insurance regularly as seen above. For he wants his family enjoy the benefit of it. Finally Willy cannot continue his sad life. One day the father and son Biff fight with each other. They turn violent. There is much blaming and mudslinging. Biff resolves to go off from home once for all. The very violence at home and his apparent frustration cause Willy to go out of his mind. So he boards his car and rides rashly. Miller's music effect shows the rashness in his drive and his meeting with death. Charley and Bernard join the funeral and all mourn his death.

Arthur Miller's *Death of a Salesman* is a great American tragedy. It is known as a psychological tragedy. The play was an instant success. It was staged in all the American cities and in several countries outside. Because *Death of a Salesman* has some kind of universal experience, values and arch-type myths. It is about American dream. Here Willy's initiative, hard work, family and relationships, son's upbringing, social fulfillment animate American cultural poetics. Walter Benjamin calls it a 'cultural treasure'. The play stages a nostalgic view of the plot of the universal masculine protagonist. The play is about a patriarchal world. Women like Linda are marginalized. The play is about an adulterous father, the marginalized mother and wayward children. It is about a family that battles to pay bills, that faces unemployment and that struggles to bring up children properly. There is spite, there is loss. There is guilt and shame. The watchers of the play or readers can feel themselves there. Critics say, "*Death of a Salesman* lays bare the private individual's sensibility, a sensibility neutralized by those very myths."[2] This a quintessential American play, making the audience weep and regret for man's guilt and shame.

Critics think that Miller has projected the tragedy on the basis of ancient Greek values—like personal flaws or hubris. False dignity is an added American value. Willy Loman is known for his false dignity. Miller, in his essay, "Tragedy and the common man", writes, "we are in the presence of a character who is ready to lay down his life, if need be, to secure one thing—his sense of personal dignity". Miller observes further, "Despite the deep irony of his life choices, Willy Loman represents, for many, the commonplace individual attempting to gain his 'rightful position in his society'; in 'his willingness to throw all he has into the contest, the battle to secure his 'rightful place in his world', Willy's struggle defines his Sisyphean heroism."[3]

NOTES

1. All the references to the text are from Arthur Miller, *Death of a Salesman.*
2. Matthew C. Roudane, "*Death of a Salesman* and the Poetics of Arthur Miller", *The Cambridge Companion to Arthur Miller*, ed. by Christopher Bigsby, London: CUP, 1997, p. 62.
3. Arthur Miller, "Tragedy and the Common Man", qt. by *ibid.*, p. 63.

Edward Albee's Two Absurd Plays

17

Edward Albee is one of the important 20th century American playwrights. His plays usually known as absurd plays focus upon man's tendency to torment others and destroy himself.

Edward Albee was born in Washington, D.C., in 1928. He was adopted by Reid Albee. He grew up in New York and Westchester County. He graduated from Choate in 1946. Yet he did not have any interest in formal education. He settled in New York City, doing various jobs.

Edward Albee's childhood dream was to become a writer. First he wrote poetry and a novel. Then he began to write drama. His first play *The Zoo Story* is a one-act play, about a psychopathic homosexual who induces an innocent stranger to kill him. This play won Albee the 1960 Vernon Rice Award. His next three one-actors are *The Death of Bessie Smith*, depicting the tensions between the races and the sexes in Memphis, Tenn., and *The Sandbox* and *The American Dream*, both ridiculing American middle-class values. Albee's first full length play—and his best known—is *Who's Afraid of Virginia Woolf?* (1962), a savage but witty dissection of two marriages in an academic setting. *A Delicate Balance* (1966), *Everything in the Garden* (1967), *Box and Quotations from Chairman Mao Tse-Tung* (1968), *All Over* (1971), *Seascape* (1975) and *The Lady from Dubuque* (1980) are his other works. *A Delicate Balance* and *Seascape* won Albee Pulitzer Prizes. Albee adapted a number of novels for the stage. Among these are *The Ballad of the Sad Café* (1963), from James Purdy; and *Lolita* (1981), from Vladimir Nabokov are significant.

Edward, as he was an orphan and later adopted by the family of the Albees, grew in an alien atmosphere. The sense of loneliness haunts him as can be seen in many of his plays. For example, this can be felt in *The American Dream* and *Who's Afraid of Virginia Woolf?* Martin Esslin says the latter which earned him an enormous success on Broadway, is undoubtedly one of the finest American plays since the heyday of Eugene O'Neill. He says, "It is a savage dance of death reminiscent of Strindberg, outwardly realistic in form, but in fact, as in the case of Pinter's best work, existing on at least two levels apart from the realistic one: an allegory of American society, a poetic image of its emptiness and sterility, and as a complex ritual on the pattern of Genet."[1]

Edward Albee's play *Who's Afraid of Virginia Woolf?* relates some absurd life. The play is about the couple George and Martha. George is an unsuccessful academician and his ambitious wife Martha entertains the young couple Nick and Honey and presents a perfect picture of realistic characters, their world, that of drunk sodden and frustrated university teachers. George and Martha have an imaginary child which they treat as real until in the cold dawn of that wild night they decide to kill it by abandoning their joint fantasy. There is a party with the guests and after that George in his wild mood relates his wife that the child died. Kalpana Purohit observes that, "The play's three-acts entitled 'Fun and Games', 'The Walpurgisnacht' and 'Exorcism' gives a neat sequential structure. 'Fun and Games' establishes the relationship between the two and introduces the outside couple who mirror the early George and Martha. 'The Walpurgisnacht', increases the complications to the point where the entire relationship George and Martha have built up is being subjected to assault. In conventional terms, the turning point is reached at the second-act when George resolves that the son, whom they have invented between them, is dead. The 'climax' is reached on 'Exorcism' when George actually reveals to Martha about the death of their son, and this is followed by a fight among both of them."[2] The play is a social satire. Albee's language is that of minimum. It is just words, imagery and symbolism. His humor is sharp.

Edward Albee's *The Zoo Story* was first performed in 1959 at the Schiller Theatre Werkstatt, Berlin. The play has just two characters. Peter is a man in his early forties, neither fat nor gaunt. He looks rather younger. Jerry is in his late thirties. He is careerless and weary. The play is just a one-acter. The two characters meet each other in a Central Park. Jerry arrives there and meets Peter sitting in the sun. He says

> Jerry. I've been to the zoo. I said, I've been to the zoo. MISTER, I'VE BEEN TO THE ZOO.
>
> Peter. Hm?...What?...I'm sorry, were you talking to me?
>
> Jerry. I went to the zoo, and then I walked until I came here. Have I been walking north?
>
> Peter. (*puzzled*) North? Why...I...I think so. Let me see."[3]

Jerry asks Peter as to where he lives and what he does. The other says he lives in Lexington and he works in a publishing firm. In fact, Peter has a fine business and he is a happy man. Jerry says he lives near Central Park West. He cannot answer Peter's question why he lives there. This is much absurdity in the play. Both chat thus for long. Jerry wants to tell Peter his zoo story and he never begins it. He tells him about the landlady of his flat and her dog, both having a lot of sexual interest. He says one day he poisoned the dog though it did not die. Jerry's long speeches are there expressing his frustration and angst. He says even, "A person has to have some way of dealing with SOMETHING" (p. 175). He asks the other whether he is interested in his zoo story. Jerry tells, "I went to the zoo to find out more about the way people exist with animals, and the way animals exist with each other, and with people too. It properly wasn't a fair test, what with everyone separated by bars from everyone else, the animals for the most part from each other, and always the people from the animals" (p. 179). Later they quarrel for a fine bench. Peter is asked by Jerry to vacate it for him. Peter does not. Jerry tries to kill him. This is out of sheer madness.

It is observed, "*The Zoo Story* is a parable. Its two characters are epitome of American experience. In fact, Jerry stands for sense of America which had become flaccid and lost its energy and vision. The play consists of an encounter between the two men—Peter sitting on a bench in Central Park, anxious at all costs to avoid human contact, and Jerry alarmingly irrational, apparently determined to provoke some response from the man he encounters. Peter is epitome of a successful businessman. Jerry has a wild-eyed intensity of a convert. The process of the play is the slow revelation of the nature of Jerry's convictions, the elaboration of a myth which he seems to understand through the process of narration. He taunts Peter, assaults him and finally in some kind of terrible blend of love and despair forces him to take a step, pulling him suddenly and into the world of casualty in which actions have consequences. He throws Peter a knife and kills him on it."[4] *The Zoo Story* is concerned with Jerry's attempts to convert Peter to his new religion of man. There is an urgent plea for human contact in the play. The play is an examination of American scene, an attack on the substitution of artificial for real values in our society, a condemnation of complacency and cruelty.

Martin Esslin adds that "*The Zoo Story*, one of Albee's earliest dramatic ventures, has a similar complexity: it is a clinically accurate study of schizophrenia, an image of man's loneliness and inability to make contact, and also, on the ritual and symbolic level, an act of ritual self-immolation that has curious parallels with Christ's atonement. (Note the names of Jerry—Jesus?—and Peter.)"[5]

It is said, "Albee dominated the American scene in 1960's. His brilliantly articulate calls for liberal humanism, a perfect control over language and its rhythms and nuances, unmatched the American theatre; he broke new ground with each play and his major concern had been the necessity to reconstruct a moral existence, to recuperate the liberal virtues of America which had betrayed its values."[6]

NOTES

1. Martin Esslin, Introduction, Absurd/Drama, London: Penguin, 1956, p. 22.
2. Kalpana Purohit, "Albee's *Who's Afraid of Virginia Woolf?* Studies in Literature in English", ed. by Mohit Ray, New Delhi: Atlantic Publishers, 2005, p. 113.

3. All the textual references are from Edward Albee, *The Zoo Story*, pt. in Absurd Drama, ed. by Martin Esslin, London: Penguin, 1956, p. 159.
4. Kalpana Purohit, op. cit., p. 110.
5. Martin Esslin, Introduction, Absurd/Drama, p. 22.
6. Kalpana Purohit, op. cit., p. 120.

E.E. Cummings's Poetry

18

E.E. Cummings is a fine modern American poet. It is said of him, "Beginning in the 1920s and 1930s, Edward Estlin Cummings built a reputation as author of a particularly agreeable kind of modernist poetry, distinguished by clever formal innovation, a tender lyricism, and the thematic celebration of individuals against mass society. These qualities were evident in his first literary success, a zesty prose account of his experience in a French prison camp during World War I, *The Enormous Room* (1922). He and a friend had joined the ambulance corps in France the day after the United States entered the war; their disdain for the bureaucracy, expressed in outspoken letters home, aroused antagonism among French officials and they imprisoned the two young men. It took intervention from Cummings's father and a letter to President Woodrow Wilson to get them out. To be made a prisoner of one's own side struck Cummings as outrageous and yet funny; from the experience Cummings produced an ironic, absurd celebration of the ordinary soldier and an attack on bureaucratic insensitivity".[1]

E.E. Cummings was born in Cambridge, Massachusetts. His father was a Congregationalist minister and teacher at Harvard; the family was cultured and Cummings, a much loved son. While a student at Harvard (he took M.A. in 1916) he began to write poetry based on the intricate stanza patterns of the Pre-Raphaelite and metaphysical writers. When he began to innovate as he did after discovering the poetry of Ezra Pound he was able to build from a firm apprenticeship in traditional techniques.

After the War, Cummings established a life that included a studio in Greenwich Village, travel and sojourns in France and summers at the family home in New Hampshire. He was a painter as well as a poet; simple living and careful management of a small allowance from his mother, along with prizes, royalties and commissions, enabled him to work full time as an artist. He was not in the least interested in wealth or celebrity. He published four volumes of well-received poetry in the 1920s and a book of collected poems toward the end of the 1930s. In the 1950s he visited and read at many college campuses, where students enjoyed his tricks of verse and vocabulary. He received a special citation by the National Book Award Committee in 1955 and the Bollingen Prize in 1957.

Cummings was less ambitious in his attempts to reshape poetry than were Eliot, Pound, Stevens or Williams, partly because he felt a greater continuity with the American past than they did. Standing up for the individual against society was, after all, the main theme of such 19th century writers as Emerson, Thoreau and Whitman, all three of whom, like Cummings, strove for flexible immediacy of style.

The special signature of Cummings's verse was its use of common speech and elements of popular culture in the diction, and its attention to the visual form of the poem, that is, the poem as it appears on the page as distinguished from its sound when read aloud. Experiments with capitalization or lack of it, punctuation, line breaks, hyphenation and verse shapes were all carried out for the reader's eyes rather than ears. Some critics took this as mere trickery, but Cummings can be credited with awareness that he lived in a culture where the poem was read rather than spoken. To express his sense that life was always in process, he wrote untitled poems without beginnings and endings, consisting of fragmentary lines. There is always much humor in his poetry, along with a willingness, even eagerness, to admit and express such traditional emotions as love and sadness. His love poems are often sexually explicit, celebrating the body of his beloved without guilt, free of the distrust of the physical that pervades the work of so many other modernists. If his poetry was simpler in thought and technique than the major modernists of his day, it compensated by a gusto and humor that they often lacked.

The present study of E.E. Cummings' poetry is based on his book of poems *Poems 1923-1954* (1954). Some of his unique poems are quoted below:

IN JUST

in Just
spring when the world is mud—
luscious the little
lame balloonman

whistles far and wee

and eddieandbill come
running from marbles and
piracies and it's
spring

when the world is puddle-wonderful

the queer
old balloonman whistles
far and wee
and bettyandisbel come dancing

from hop-scotch and jump-rope and

it's
spring
and
  the
      goat-footed

balloonman whistles
far
and
wee

BUFFALO BILL'S

Buffalo Bill's
defunct

who used to
ride a watersmooth-silver
stallion
and break onetwothreefourfive pigeonsjustlikethat
Jesus
he was a handsome man
and what i want to know is
how do you like your blueeyed boy
Mister Death

THE CAMBRIDGE LADIES WHO LIVE IN FURNISHED SOULS

the Cambridge ladies who live in furnished souls
are unbeautiful and have comfortable minds
(also with the church's protestant blessings
daughters, unscented shapeless spirited)
they believe in Christ and Longfellow, both dead,
are invariably interested in so many things
at the present writing one still finds
delighted fingers knitting for the is it Poles?
perhaps. While permanent faces coyly bandy
scandal of Mrs. N and Professor D
...the Cambridge ladies do not care, above
Cambridge if sometimes in its box of
sky lavender and cornerless, the
moon rattles like a fragment of angry candy

I SING OF OLAF GLAD AND BIG

i sing of Olaf glad and big
whose warmest heart recoiled at war:
a conscientious object-or

his well beloved colonel (trig
westpointer most succinctly bred)
took erring Olaf soon in hand;
but-though an host of overjoyed
noncoms (first knocking on the head
him) do through icy waters roll
that helplessness which others stroke
with brushes recently employed

anent this muddy toiletbowl,
while kindred intellects evoke
allegiance per blunt instruments-
Olaf (being to all intents
a corpse and wanting any rag
upon what God unto him gave)
responds without getting annoyed
"I will not kiss your f. ing flag"

IF THERE ARE ANY HEAVENS MY MOTHER WILL (ALL BY HERSELF) HAVE

If there are any heavens my mother will (all by herself) have
one. It will not be a pansy heaven nor
a fragile heaven of lilies-of-the-valley but
it will be a heaven of blackred roses.

NOTE

1. *Norton Anthology of American Literature*, p. 1956.

F. Scott Fitzgerald's *The Great Gatsby*

19

F. Scott Fitzgerald was an American writer. It is said of him, "In the century after the American Revolution, 'America' meant the land of freedom; after the Civil War, a different kind of 'American dream' came into being, the idea that in this country one might hope to satisfy every material desire and thereby achieve happiness". In the 1920s F. Scott Fitzgerald spoke complexly to and for this modern idea of the meaning of America. He believed it to be deceptive: proposing the satisfaction of all desire as an attainable goal and identifying desire with the material, it could only lead to dissatisfaction. Hence, the movement of all his work is toward disillusion.

Fitzgerald was born and raised in a middle-class neighborhood in St. Paul, Minnesota. On his mother's side he was descended from southern colonial landowners and legislators; but his father was a business failure. Fitzgerald retained a religious imagination. In 1911, when he was 15, he was sent to a Catholic boarding school in New Jersey; two years later he entered Princeton University. In both these schools he was in company with young men who were much better situated in life than he. Fitzgerald participated in extracurricular activities and thereby made lifelong friendships with campus intellectuals like Edmund Wilson.

After three years he left school and joined the army. He was stationed near Montgomery, Alabama. The war ended. There he fell in love with Zelda Sayre, a local belle, who broke their engagement when she became convinced that he could not support her. Crushed, Fitzgerald went to New York City in

1919, determined to make a fortune and win Zelda. He succeeded. He published a novel *This Side of Paradise*, which became an immediate bestseller, making its author a celebrity at the age of 24. He combined the traditional narrative and rhetorical gifts of a good fiction writer. His novel has a thoroughly modern sensibility. Now Scott and Zelda were married.

This is the point where fairy tales conclude with "and they lived happily ever after". The Fitzgeralds had to live the story out to a different ending. Neither of them could handle the pressures of life. They drank too much and spent too much. Though Fitzgerald quickly learned that a life of constant partying *was* incompatible with a serious literary career, he could not give up the fun. Living extravagantly in New York City and St. Paul and on Long Island, they more than spent the money Fitzgerald made from two collections of short stories—*Flappers and Philosophers* (1921) and *Tales of the Jazz Age* (1922)—and a second novel, *The Beautiful and Damned* (1922). They had a daughter in 1921.

In 1924, the Fitzgeralds moved to Europe where they hoped to live more cheaply. They made friends with the American expatriates—Hemingway, Stein and Pound among others—but were no more successful in managing their lives. During this time Fitzgerald published his masterpiece, *The Great Gatsby* (1925) and another book of short stories, *All the Sad Young Men* (1926). *The Great Gatsby* tells the story of a self-made young man whose dream of success, personified in a rich and beautiful young woman named Daisy, turns out to be a fantasy in every sense: Daisy belongs to a corrupt society, Gatsby corrupts himself in the quest for her and, above all, the rich have no intention of sharing their privileges. The novel is narrated from the point of view of Nick Carraway, an onlooker who is both moved and repelled by the tale he tells and whose responses form a sort of subplot: this experiment in narrative point of view was widely imitated. The structure of *The Great Gatsby* is compact, the style dazzling and its images of modern American life—automobiles, parties, garbage heaps—are unforgettable.

Fitzgerald wrote dozens of short stories during the twenties, some splendid and others tossed off for the quick money. In all he wrote 178 short stories. Scott became an alcoholic and Zelda became mentally unstable. Both were trapped. In 1930 she had a brokedown and had to live most of the rest of her life—she died in 1947—in mental institutions. In 1931 Fitzgerald re-established himself permanently in the United States, living at first near Baltimore. A second fine novel, *Tender is the Night,* appeared in 1934. The novel follows the moral decline of a young American psychiatrist whose personal energies are sapped and his professional career corroded, by his marriage to a beautiful and wealthy patient. The novel is a thematic indictment of American materialism.

By 1937 Fitzgerald was sick, alcoholic, unable to write and no longer earning royalties. To earn a living, he turned to Hollywood screenwriting; the money he made enabled him to pay for his wife's medical care and for the education of his daughter. Toward the end of the decade things were looking up for him. He had a confidence—renewing love affair with the gossip columnist Sheilah Graham, stopped drinking and planned to revive his career as a fiction writer. But it was too late; his health was ruined. He died of a heart attack in Hollywood at the age of 44, leaving an unfinished novel *The Last Tycoon*, which was published by Edmund Wilson in 1941. Fitzgerald was a fine social observer and skilled artist. Though he has written a few books his fame is secure.

The Great Gatsby looks like a confession story. Nick Carraway is the narrator. He is modest enough not to speak of others. Yet he cannot help telling James (here from Jay) Gatsby's life which haunted him. Jay Gatsby is the title character.

The action of the story begins when Nick comes East from a Midwestern city to join a brokerage firm and earn a living. He moves into a 'weather-beaten cardboard bungalow' just off the Long Island, south in West Egg. The house belongs to Jay Gatsby; although when Nick moves there he only knows the name, not the man.

Across a small bay lies the village of East Egg whose coast line is speckled with the 'white palaces' of the more blue-blooded wealthy. Nick's second cousin Daisy, lives there with her husband, Tom Bachanan. On the early summer evening Nick drives over to the Bachanan house to have dinner. The order of these two events—Nick investing the aura around Daisy with a fantastic quality and Tom's ability to deflate that romantic moment—presents a microcosm of the narrative as a whole. The rest of the evening at the Buchanan's conforms to this pattern. The novel is a travesty of domestic harmony. She asks Nick about people back home in the Midwest and she gushes forth patter about her childhood and how Nick looks like a perfect rose. Tom tells Nick that he has been reading racist literature which, he claims scientifically proves that white supremacy is best for whole order. At dinner Jordan, Daisy's friend, had asked if Nick lived near this man Gatsby, who has a reputation for throwing one lavish party after another. Nick remembers that Daisy appeared to recognize Gatsby's name but made little mention of it.

The opening of chapter II foregrounds the symbolic importance of geography in the novel. The village of West Egg and East Egg are separated by 'the valley of Ashes', an industrialized wasteland. By comparison, West Egg is the home of those who are longtime captains of industry. The rest of chapter II details Tom's life with his mistress Myrtle. On their way to Manhattan, Tom drags Nick off the train into the valley of ashes to meet 'his girl', Myrtle Wilson. Myrtle and her husband George Wilson live above a decrepit garage and car-repair shop. Tom stops briefly to tease George Wilson about his business and then arranges to meet his wife in New York. The scenes which follow record the sordid and brutal nature of their affair. Tom has an apartment on the Upper West Side where he and Myrtle entertain a small group of friends. Tom appears to derive perverse glee as he watches Myrtle and the people who seem to live a high life.

Chapter III consists two distinct sections. The first and longer section occurs at one of Gatsby's famous parties and presents a distinct lyrical composition with Tom and Myrtle's bitter soiree. Gatsby employs a corps of caterers and eight servants to feed the continued flow of guests. When Nick arrives she is daunted somewhat by the sheer number of anonymous merrymakers who have come to what Gatsby's chauffeur had called a 'little party'. Gatsby's absence is virtually the theme of the party. Wild rumors about his background and the mysterious source of his enormous wealth circulate like currency among the guests. One person heard that Gatsby killed a man, another that Gatsby was a German spy during the Great War. Whatever Gatsby is or was, it is clear that he will go to extraordinary lengths to avoid trouble, spending extravagant amounts of money to ensure goodwill. His house is impeccably decorated to suggest that he is a man of great accomplishment. Gatsby says, "I'm Gatsby". He calmly smiles at Nick. Gatsby is called to the phone on business and soon after sends his butler to ask Jordan to meet him when alone. Nick wanders around the flagging party which has begun to break up into jealous squabbles among husbands, wives, mistresses and paramours. Outside, a departing guest has crashed his car into a ditch. The shorter section of chapter III repeats the same theme of recklessness. Nick reports his growing excitement for life in the city and begins to develop an attraction, a 'tender curiosity', for Jordan. But he soon discovers that she is less than trustworthy.

Gatsby invites Nick to lunch with him in Manhattan. As they ride up together Gatsby tells his life story to Nick. He says that the rumors about his being a bootlegger or a murderer are false. He claims to be the sole inheritor of his family's fortune and that he has been educated, according to tradition, at Oxford. He builds a grandiose picture of himself in the years after college. He maintains that he lived like a 'young rajah' in the capitals of Europe—collecting rubles, hunting big game and painting. The outbreak of the Great War brought him relief from his life as a dilettante and he says that he 'tried very hard to die'. But fate seemed to be contrary. He claims that he fought too valiantly in the Argonne Forest and every Allied government awarded him a decoration. Gatsby's tale almost beguiles Nick, but the scene which immediately follows their drive to the city raises doubts about the truthfulness of his story. The reason for

Gatsby's odd exit and the key to the entire plot becomes evident in the final scene of chapter IV. Over afternoon tea, Jordan Baker tells Nick that Gatsby and Daisy had been in love before Daisy married Tom Bachanan.

Jordan's story clarifies the mysterious character of Gatsby for Nick. He realizes that the apparent 'purposeless splendor' of his neighbor's life is really all part of a glorious romantic quest for the dream-like love of his youth. He learns that Gatsby bought the house directly across the bay from Daisy's home just to be near her and that Gatsby throws his lavish parties with the sole hope of attracting her attention.

Chapter V records the reunion of Gatsby and Daisy. The rise of Jay Gatsby through the first five chapters begins to unravel in chapter VI. Nick exposes the truth about his neighbor. His real name is James Gatz and he is the son of shiftless and unsuccessful farm people. Fortune smiled on Gatz in the form of Dan Cody, a rough-and-tumble mining magnate, who had gone from rags to riches. Gatsby saw a drunken Cody anchor his yacht in the shallows of Lake Superior. Seizing the opportunity to warn Cody off the rocks, he rowed out to the boat and charmed his way on deck. Once aboard Gatz became Gatsby and he toured the seas with Cody for five years until Cody died. Nick reveals that Gatsby inherited no money from Cody, but rather he secured a much more valuable legacy—the indomitable spirit of a millionaire.

Things literally heat up in chapter VII. Such a grimy, summer swelter descends upon New York that Nick says he cannot imagine anyone caring about romance. But on an unbearable hot afternoon Tom and Daisy invite Nick and Jordan Baker over to their house for cocktails and dinner. Afterwards, they drive into Manhattan. Tom, who is driving Gatsby's yellow car, stops off at the Wilson's to buy gas and discovers that Mr. Wilson is ill. He has learned that Myrtle is having an affair and he has decided to move out West to tear her away from her lover. Nick notices Myrtle peering out from an upstairs window and surmises that she thinks Jordan is Tom's wife. Tom grows angry and speeds away to catch Gatsby and Daisy, who are riding together in Tom's blue coupe. Finally everyone agrees to go to the plaza for drinks and maybe to take cool baths. Nick notices that Tom is panicked by the fact that he appears to be losing both of the women in his life.

Once all five of them are alone in a hotel room, they hear the sounds of a wedding occurring in the ballroom below and conversation turns to the day of Daisy's own wedding. Tom becomes priggish and hypocritical and begins to argue with Gatsby. He complains that Gatsby is trying to break up his happy home and that he will not stand for it. Gatsby insists that Daisy tell Tom that she never loved him, that she has only ever loved Gatsby and that she wants a divorce. Daisy hesitantly complies until Tom exposes Gatsby for the uneducated, bootlegger that he is. She then admits that she loves both men, a fact which satisfies Tom but disappoints Gatsby. With tempers aflate, the party breaks up with Gatsby and Daisy driving back to Long Island in his car and the rest in Tom's car.

When Tom, Nick and Jordan pass back by the Wilson's garage they see that there has been an accident. Witnesses say that Myrtle Wilson came running out of the garage onto the road yelling and waving at a passing yellow car. The car hit her without stopping. Tom starts to cry and whimpers about how Gatsby is a coward to have left the scene of the accident. They arrive back at the Buchanan's to see Daisy's light on. Tom and Jordan enter the house, but Nick, disgusted by the whole affair, waits outside for a taxi. He finds Gatsby lurking in the bushes nearby. Gatsby asks about the accident and unwittingly divulges that Daisy had actually been the driver of the 'death car', as the newspapers called it the next day. He tells Nick that he is waiting to make sure that Tom does not try to brutalize Daisy because of 'that unpleasantness this afternoon'. To reassure Gatsby that nothing will happen to Daisy, Nick tiptoes up to the kitchen window and sees Tom and Daisy engaged in a calm, intense, intimate conversation. They are holding hands and Nick realizes that although they are not happy, they are not unhappy. But Gatsby refuses to leave the hide-out place. He persists to stand alone, 'a forlorn lover'.

The next day Nick finds Gatsby at home and suggests that he go away until things cool off. Shaken by the exposure of his lies and the previous day's accident, Gatsby confesses everything about his youth to Nick. He had been a war hero, but by the time he arrived back in the United States Daisy had married Tom. Meanwhile George Wilson makes his way to Gatsby's manor. Deranged by the loss of his wife, Wilson pursues the owner of the mysterious yellow car. Sure that this owner must be the man who killed Myrtle he goes to exact revenge. He finds Gatsby afloat on a pneumatic mattress in the swimming pool and he shoots him. Then he turns the gun upon himself. The last chapter records Gatsby's return to obscurity. Nick tries desperately to find people who will attend the funeral, but none comes. Tom and Daisy leave for safety. Only C. Gatz, Gatsby's father arrives to conduct his son's funeral. The father is proud of his son's rise and mistakenly sees him as one of the great builders of America. Nick realizes that his story had really been a story about the American West about the land of opportunity. He understands now that Gatsby had possessed that sense of manifest destiny, of unlimited promise which is at the heart of the myth of America. He decides to move back home to a place with perhaps enough room for a dreamy idealism. Maxwell Perkins thinks Fitzgerald's novel is "an extraordinary book suggestive of all thoughts and moods".[1] A.E. Dyson thinks "Gatsby is the apotheosis of his rootless society".[2]

NOTES

1. Maxwell Perkins, *Viva Bloom's Notes on Fitzgerald's The Great Gatsby*, New Delhi: Viva Books Pvt Ltd., 2007, p. 25.
2. A.E. Dyson, *ibid.*, p. 35.

20

William Faulkner's *The Sound and the Fury* as a Portrayal of Abnormal Psychology

William Faulkner was a great American novelist of the 20th century. He was a fine short story writer too. He is known for his intricate narrative technique. Faulkner has written works of fiction, which establish his vision of mankind and they speak of man's dignity and social position. Faulkner got many prizes like National Book Award, twice Pulitzer Awards and the Nobel Prize for Literature in 1949.

William Faulkner was born in New Albany in 1897. His great grandfather had moved from Tennessee to Mississippi where he was a plantation owner, colonel in the Confederate Army, railroad builder and author of a popular novel, *The White Rose of Memphis*. Faulkner's family moved from New Albany to Oxford in Mississippi when William was just five. William had his basic education there and then went to Canada and joined the Royal Air Force. On return, he became a postmaster. He made an effort to do education at University.

In the beginning Faulkner made an effort to write poetry. Phil Stone was his early mentor. Mr. Stone helped him publish his book of poems *The Marble Faun*. Later, Faulkner lived in New Orleans and befriended Sherwood Anderson. The latter encouraged him to write the novel *Soldier's Pay* (1926). Faulkner made a walking tour of Europe and wrote the novel *Mosquitoes*.

On return, Faulkner hit upon the idea of making Yoknapatawpha, a fictitious county for his later works. This town is based on his experience in the town of Lafayette, Oxford as its seat. He wrote *The Sound and the Fury* (1929), *As I Lay Dying* (1930), *These Thirteen* (1931) and *Absalom, Absalom*

(1936). His collections of short stories include *Sanctuary* (1931), *Light in August* (1932), *Doctor Martino and Other Stories* (1934), *Pylon* (1935), *The Unvanquished* (1938) and *Go Down Moses* (1942). His *Knight's Gambit* (1949) is a book of detective stories.

Some of Faulkner's novels of the later period are *The Wild Palms* (1939), *The Hamlet* (1940) and *Intruder in the Dust* (1948). Faulkner also wrote a play called *Requiem for a Nun* (1951), while *A Fable* (1954) is an allegory. His last work was *The Receivers* (1962), a nostalgic comedy of boyhood.

William Faulkner's novel *The Sound and the Fury* has its title from Shakespeare's play, *Macbeth* and has similar kind of despairing life. The concerned passage in *Macbeth* is as follows,

> To-morrow, and to-morrow, and to-morrow,
> Creeps in this petty pace from day to day,
> To the last syllable of recorded time,
> And all our yesterdays have lighted fools
> The way to dusty death. Out, out, brief candle!
> Life's but a walking shadow, a poor player
> That struts and frets his hour upon the stage.
> And then is heard no more. It is a tale
> Told by an idiot, full of sound and fury
> Signifying nothing.

The novel *The Sound and the Fury* is about the declining kind of life of an American Southern family. This is about decline of life in modern times between the two World Wars. It is said, unlike Cooper, Hawthorne, Melville and Poe and later Henry James, Hemingway, Passos and Fitzgerald Faulkner wrote of life realistically. Hemingway's *The Sun Also Rises* typifies the attitude of all these writers who are committed to the harsh realities of modern life. Faulkner shows us the decadent society haunted by ghosts of the past. The American fiction of the inert-war years is that of despair and pessimism. In form and style these novelists were experimental. Faulkner that way belongs to the elite of Henry James, James Joyce, Joseph Conrad, Marcel Proust and others. William Faulkner as a distinguished novelist has tried to depict the predicament of man in modern times. It is said:

> *The Sound and the Fury* is William Faulkner's favorite among his novels for he found it the most difficult, ambitious and challenging to write: "I must judge it on the basis that one which caused me the most grief and anguish, as the mother loves the child who became the thief or murderer more than the one who became the priest." In answer to a question asked by a group of students from Mississippi which of his novels he considered the best, Faulkner replies, "*The Sound and the Fury* still continues to move me." Obviously, it is the one that he feels the 'most tender toward', the one into which he says "I have written my guts".[1] Faulkner describes:

> I wrote it five separate times, trying to tell the story, to rid myself of the dream which would continue to anguish me until I did.... It began with a mental picture. I didn't realize at the time it was symbolical. The picture was of the muddy seat of a little girl's drawers in a pear tree, where she could see through a window where her grandmother's funeral was taking place.... I had already begun to tell the story through the eyes of the idiot child, since I felt that it would be more effective as told by someone capable of knowing what happened, but not why. I saw that I had not told the story that time. I tried to tell it again, the same story through the eyes of another brother. That was still not it. I tried to gather the pieces together and fill in the gaps by making myself the spokesman. It was still not complete,—not until fifteen years after the book was published, when I wrote as an appendix to another book the final effort to get the story told and off my mind, so that I myself could have some peace from it.[2]

The story of the novel is related to Caddy's loss of virginity as viewed by her three brothers, Benjamin (Benjy), Quentin and Jason. Each of them gives his own point of view. Faulkner shows extraordinary skill and virtuosity in getting the first three sections of the novel narrated by them. In section IV he takes the responsibility of filling the gap and rounding up the novel with a larger perspective. The genesis of the novel began as:

> That began as a short story; it was a story without a plot, of some children being sent away from the house during the grandmother's funeral. They were too young to be told what was going on and they saw things only incidentally to the childish games they were playing, which was the lugubrious matter of removing the corpse from the house...etc. And then the idea struck me to see how much more I could have got out of the idea of the blind self-centeredness of innocence, typified by children, if one of these children had been truly innocent, that is, an idiot. So the idiot was born and then I became interested in the relationship of the idiot to the world that he was in but would never be able to cope with and just where could he get the tenderness, the help, to shield him in his innocence.[3]

Faulkner's novel has a wonderful structure. As we know he was a great experimentalist. So he packs his novel not with events and incidents but with sense and nonsense. Actually very few events occur in the external world and they can be easily recounted as follows:

> The grandmother dies in 1898. The girl Candace (Caddy) has an affair with Dalton Ames by whom she is made pregnant. She is married to Herbert Head in April 1910. However, the birth of her illegitimate child Miss Quentin (named after brother Quentin) causes the annulment of the marriage. Her brother Quentin, who is at Harvard, commits suicide in June 1910. Mr. Compson, the father of the children—Benjy, Quentin, Jason and Caddy—dies in 1912. Caddy's daughter, who has been living at the Compson house, elopes with a 'carnival man', taking away with her the money that her uncle Jason had cheated her of. Subsequently Jason desperately tries to capture her but in vain. Even while this chase is going on the old Negro female servant of the Compsons attending the Easter Sunday service on 8 April 1928 is moved to ecstasy by a visiting preacher.

It is said the first three units form one unit of the story and the fourth one another. In the first three are recorded the impressions and reactions of the three brothers to certain incidents of the past and to what they are doing in the present. It is their private world that is revealed to us by the use of the stream of consciousness technique. The author is invisible in all this. Still each of the first three sections gives different impressions as different persons with different perspectives write them. For example, Benjy speaks just from sensations; Quentin, from an abstract mode; and Jason, from a kind of logic. Faulkner seems to tell us that truth cannot be easily got in life. Once he said, "There are thirteen ways of looking at a blackbird." Olga W. Vickery observes, "The theme of *Sound and the Fury*, as revealed by the structure, is the relation between the act and man's apprehension of the act, between the event and the interpretation.... Each man creates his own truth...truth is a matter of the heart's response as well as the mind's logic."[4] The novel makes use of interior monologue to reveal the personalities. The consciousness of Benjy, Quentin and Jason is well reflected in differing styles, images and syntax. The novel that way may be called a 'polyphonic composition'. Still each of the first three sections has some differences. For example, section I narrates the family story for the last thirty years. It gives clues for the next sections; section II gives special information about Quentin's joining Harvard, Caddace's marriage and Quentin's suicide; and section III is about Jason's affairs after Caddy's disappearance, in section IV, details are about Quentin's elopement and Jason's bankruptcy.

The gist of the story may be as follows. The Compson family had once been a good one, but the current generation had done everything to ruin the name of Compson. In the little Mississippi city in which the Compsons lived all laughed and made slighting remarks when the name Compson was mentioned.

Mrs. Compson has come from a gentile family but she married Mr. Compson of the degenerated family. She regrets of this for the last eighteen years. Her first son Benjamin is her great problem as he is an idiot. The second son Quentin is a reckless fellow known for his vulgarity. The third child Caddace is known for her wayward behavior. She is the only person to quieten Benjy. She did not allow the other members of the family including the Negro workers to tease Benjy. She loved the other people too.

Quentin is moody and he loved Caddace. It is said he loved her not as a sister but as a woman and she returned his love for him. Caddace loved Mr. Ames and got pregnant. She loved Sydney Herbert Head and married him with the condition that he should provide a job for Jason, her last brother. Quentin did not like Caddace marry Herbert Head, the banker. He said she couldn't marry him as he (Quentin) had an incest relation with his sister. He is quite wild. At last Quentin, when he is doing education at Harvard, commits suicide. The occasion is Caddace's marriage to Herbert Head. Mrs. Compson reigns herself to one more cross.

For some unknown reason, Head does not entertain his wife after she delivers her first girl child Quentin, named after her late brother. The Compson family does not shelter her. But they shelter her daughter. Jason believes that Caddace, the girl is born to Quentin though the others do not believe it. Caddace stays away from the little town for many years.

Quentin is as wild as her mother. She is just like her mother in manners. Caddace sends money for Quentin regularly. But Mrs. Compson burns her checks for she does not want Caddace's ill-gotten money. Mr. Compson dies soon in 1912. Jason becomes the head of the family. He blames Herbert Head refused to accept Caddace, for she has borne an illegitimate child. He feels sad as Head did not get him a job. Hating his sister, Jason gets checks from another bank and gives them to his mother for burning; while he forges her signature on the checks and gets cash. He plays the money in market.

Quentin hates Jason as much as he does her. They quarrel often. Mrs. Compson supports the girl's case. Once a show team comes to the town and Quentin takes up with one of the performers. One night she elopes with him. She elopes even with Jason's three thousand dollars. Jason feels sad and lodges a complaint against her. He tries to catch her in vain. Yet the money she has stolen is of her mother's, which Jason has manipulated for himself. Jason feels cheated and he gets enraged. He believes that everyone laughs at him because of his horrible family—because Bengy is an idiot, Candace, a lost woman, Quentin a suicide and the girl Quentin, a village harlot and a thief. He forgets that he too is a thief and has a mistress. He feels cursed. In a fit of rage he beats Benjamin. But he regains his composure and feels what the servant Dilsey says that she sees the beginning and end of life. The life of the family is at a sad end finally.

Critics feel that the novel is about abnormal psychology of the Southern family. It is about degeneration. It is too private, too mired in the psychic realm and too inarticulate about social forces that are more clearly revealed in Faulkner's later works. The novel is about filth and vulgarity. According to Cheryl Lester, the novel is about the black suffering. However, the most important facts about the success of the novel are that it is moving rather than enlightening upon an incident or situation. It is observed that, "The novel's stunning technical innovations partially account for its success."[5]

NOTES

1. William Faulkner, Introduction, *The Sound and the Fury*, Introduction by P.P. Sharma, Bombay: CUP, 1995, p. 12.
2. *Ibid.*, p. 14.
3. *Ibid.*, p. 15.
4. Olga W. Vickery, *ibid.*, p. 16.
5. Cheryl Lester, "Racial Awareness and Arrested Development: *The Sound and the Fury* and the Great Migration (1915-1928)", *A Cambridge Companion to William Faulkner*, ed. by Phillip M. Weinstein, Cambridge: CUP, 1995, p. 123.

21

Ernest Hemingway's *The Old Man and the Sea*: An Inspiration to the New Millennium

Only a few writers are timeless. Ernest Hemingway is one of them in the American chapter of world literature. This timeless Hemingway is the most illustrious member of the "lost generation", an independant Titan of the 20th century American literature. He was a sportsman, soldier, boxer, hunter, lover, journalist, author and the recepient of the Nobel Prize for Literature in 1954. In Michael Greenberg's view, "Ernest Hemingway is one of the leading characters in the story of the American century. From the cultural point of view, he may be the main character. He had a genius for presenting Americans as they wished to be seen, at a time when they were not sure how to see themselves."[1]

Ernest Miller Hemingway was born in 1899 in an upper middle class protestant family in Oak Park, Ill. With a view to escape the narrow minded people and parents' prescriptive behavior, he migrated to Michigan. Then, while his ambition becoming to roam about the world, he left for Europe. He failed to join the army due to his dim eyesight and he became a cab driver in the Red Cross during the First World War. No doubt, Hemingway's war experience was quite nauseating. Confronted with harsh and noxious realities of war Hemingway's personal life turned just a line of thread running in the web of American history. As the course of European history changed, he changed his wives (Hadley, Pauline and Martha) three times while in this private life, like James Joyce, he met with tragic incidents. His life never ran a smooth course as his autobiographical heroes Jake Barnes, Nick Adams and Frederic Henry. They are called the author's 'code heroes'. In his personal life his greater need for freedom as he no longer believed in the dictates of society, led him astray—coward, sad and bullying. Besides, he had a preoccupation with death, had no toleration toward his inferiors and he never liked those people who worked greater than him. For example, he did not like Dos Passos, F. Scott Fitzgerald and others. However, in spite of these pitfalls, Hemingway maintained "grace under pressure". Frank McConnell observes: "But I want to suggest, Hemingway managed to be all those absurd, laughable things, and also to be something else, something permanently valuable for American letters. He managed to be a hero of consciousness, a writer and a stylist who made his cowardice and his knowledge of his cowardice, the very stuff of his heroism and his endurance."[2] He was in James Salter's opinion, an intensely masculine writer criticizing the evils of social system. Herbie Butterfield is right when he elaborates: "The principal element, though, is Hemingway's imaginative world, the quality with which in some form or other virtually all his best writing is concerned is courage: simply courage. If life is intrinsically painful, and the prospect of death omnipresent, the act of living becomes by definition a test of courage. The courage required may be moral, or mental, or physical; it may be passive or active; it may be as ostensibly minimal as bearing it, with or without grinning, or it may be the stuff of awards for gallantry."[3]

Hemingway is one of the greatest writers of the twentieth century America. A master of prose, Hemingway wrote stories and novels. His output, during a writing career spanning four decades, includes fifty-five stories, two works of non-fiction, one novella and six novels. *The Sun Also Rises* (1926) is Hemingway's first novel, which like T.S. Eliot's *Waste Land* (1922) describes the deterioration of human life in modern times and at the same time, again as in Eliot's work, it brings in a hope to the ailing mankind. Hemingway's *Men Without Women* came in 1927, while his *A Farwell to Arms* (1929) was a phenomenal success. *The Old Man and the Sea* (1952) was again a hot cake selling 5,300,000 copies in only two days. This won him the Pulitzer Prize in 1953 and for his entire work, he was given the Nobel Prize in the following year. *The Green Hills of Africa* was based on a big game hunt he undertook. *For Whom The Bell Tolls* fictionalized the Spanish war he served as a correspondent in the thirties.

To Have and Have Not (1937), *Across the River and into the Trees* (1950), *Death in the Afternoon* (1932), *The Garden of Eden* (1986), *A Moveable Feast* (1964) and *The Dangerous Summer* (1985), are his other works of fiction and *In Our Time* is his well known book of fascinating stories.

The present study is a selective one—studying Hemingway by critically analyzing his novellette *The Old Man and the Sea*, his most important novel which displays his inspiration to the people of the next millennium. In the view of Charles Scribner, "the publication of *The Old Man and the Sea* is a curious fact of literary history that a story that describes the loss of a gigantic prize provided the author with the greatest prize of his career."[4] The reason is very clear. The novel though it describes loss, it shows the hero's dignified life in spite of his failures. It evinces Santiago, the hero's remaining hopeful despite of frustrations and striving towards perfection though ill, old and devastated mentally. Santiago, the protagonist says thus:

> Man is not made for death. A man can be destroyed but not defeated. Man should be like truth, may be made to brake but never to be broken. In Hardy's view, he must live as dignified even in the end as he does the same in the beginning. Hemingway describes, how, like his bullfighting hero Romero in *The Sun Also Rises*, Santiago struggles to capture a large fish, marlin. The hero fights the elements only to lose all but the fish's carcass to sharks. As is characteristic of Hemingway's fiction, the terse, almost journalistic prose, the compressed action and the subdued yet suggestive symbolism point to a deeper meaning appears on the surface. Hemingway stresses Santiago's heroism through subtle allusions to Christ and the simplicity of action serves to underscore Santiago's nobility and greater consciousness. Although Santiago is handicapped by age and misfortune, he persists with dignity, thereby gaining a moral victory and demonstrating Hemingway's lifelong interest in maintaining 'grace under pressure'.[5]

The novel *The Old Man and the Sea* is based upon an incident of a fisherman who one day went to catch a big fish, but in the fight, he lost his own life to the animal. Originally the novel was conceived in four parts under different titles such as "The Sea in Being", "Dignity of Man", etc. It is purely the tale of Santiago—standing an optimistic epilogue to all of Hemingway's works. The novel, in Carlos Baker's view, being a picture of the 'rhythms of nature and of human life', tells us the bitter fact of human life that "Winner Takes Nothing". Instead of being rescued at sea, Santiago returns alone and unaided to his native harbor and his home. The locale used for the story is the Spanish Main. The author's style of prose is marvelous tempting everyone to read it.

Santiago is an old man. One day as everyday, he goes on fishing. He comes back. He has a boy companion Manolina. This boy is both his servant and consolation. The old man is quite old, wrinkled, bent and fragile. But he is wonderfully strong, hale and hearty. His wants are few and far between; he is very resolute in his decision; and his nature is strikingly compromising. Hemingway says, "Everything about him was old except his eyes and they were the same colour as the sea and were cheerful and undefeated" (p. 2). He says he is always one with the nature—sea, fish, sky and Manolina. The latter brings the former food, drinks, water, what not, finally inspiration, encouragement, consolation, a benign warmth and the news about the world including the news about baseball which has a fascination for Santiago.

Santiago loved the sea and he always thinks of it as *la mar*, which is what people call her in Spanish when they love her. He thinks she is his mother and friend. On the sea he finds dolphin, sardines and sharks, etc. which at times are his only food. Besides, birds are his hearty companions. Once he makes a desperate attempt to talk to them. He consoles the tired birds as in the following: "Take a good rest, small bird", he said, "then go in and take your chance like any man or bird or fish" (p. 29).

Often the old man looks around for the birds for a company. So is his love for sea animals. One day, on finding no fish, the old man returns home only to be reassured of. His not finding a big fish, does not make him lose his heart. It is said, "But, he thought, I keep them with precision. Only I have no luck any more. But who knows? May be today. Everyday is a new day. It is better to be lucky. But I would rather be exact" (p. 15).

Santiago sleeps soundly. He dreams a dream in which he goes to the shores of Africa and hunts lions. In fact, in olden days he had gone there for hunting. What an image? Lion itself is an indication of heroism. Santiago says to Manolina, "I was before the mast on a square rigged ship that ran to Africa and I have seen lions on the beaches in the evening." Lions are the hero's benign obsessions. Besides, he thinks of DiMaggio who is a great baseball player, and he thinks of Cienfuegos, who is the strongest man on docks.

The next day on his 85th day of fishing on the seashore of Havana, Santiago is again on the deep sea, firm this time in his decision to catch a big fish.

So Santiago finally traces a marlin, supposed to be 800 pounds in weight—a good, tasty and precious marine food. His rope works. But the marlin is stronger than him, bigger than his boat and nobler. But Santiago admits that man can catch such an animal too as he is shrewder and crueler. He thanks God to have endowed man with reason. However, fishes are his brothers, they are to be caught for food. But the continuous jerks and dives of the marlin in spite of its suffering trouble him bringing pain to his palm. But he is not scarred of it. It is said, "And pain does not matter to a man" (p. 47).

Santiago is a true man in the sense he knows his limitations, which many do not. He blames his left hand to have been not deftly in handling the net. He tells, like the sea, the fish and the sky, his hands are his brothers. On being disturbed by the marlin, he sympathizes himself gathering all courage: "You better be fearless and confident yourself, Old Man", he said, "you're holding him again but you cannot get line. But soon he has to circle" (p. 46).

Incessant effort make Santiago exhausted. He needs human warmth. So he remembers the boy for getting his help and for teaching him bravery in the trade. Every time he gets a pain, a sad feeling, a disturbance, he consoles himself uttering. "I wish the boy was here...I wish I had the boy" (p. 27).... "I wish the boy were here and I had some salt" (p. 30). "If the boy were here he could rub it..." (p. 33).... "I wish I could show him what sort of man I am" (p. 34).

The first four wishes show the old man's expectation of Manolina for human companionship. He thinks had the boy been there, he would have learnt the old man's professional ethics.

So says Santiago, "No one should be alone in their old age." Nothing is more tragic to a man than his failure to secure his fellow beings' help in the hours of his difficulty. On having not the boy, the old man ultimately, prays the One who has created him: "God help me endur...I'll say a hundred Our Fathers and a hundred Hail Marys" (p. 48).

However, nothing comes to his avail except his innate strength. He tells to himself "Be calm and strong". He challenges the fish and he persists in his greater merit: "But man is not made for defeat, a man can be destroyed but not defeated."

However, unfortunate it is that two bigger and more dangerous sharks come there; dive beneath his skiff and they eat the marline leaving only its great spine and tail which later hang to Santiago's boat. This makes the hero repent, "Fish that you were. I am sorry that I went too far out" (p. 65).

Now Santiago wishes to kill the sharks: "Fight them", he said "I'll fight them until I die" (p. 65).

The old man fails to bring his big prize, but he does not lose his heart. He observes, "I must not think nonsense", he thought. "Luck is a thing that comes in many forms and who can recognize her" (p. 66).

This is in the line of Indian philosophy. So luck can come to us anytime.

The novel ends with Hemingway's characteristic note of optimism, "Up the road, in his shack, the old man was sleeping again. He was still sleeping on his face and the boy was sitting by him watching him. The old man was dreaming about the lions" (p. 72).

Santiago, like Nick Adams, is Hemingway's 'code hero', in the words of Cleanth Brooks and Robert Penn Warren, always working for perfection. To him, the only way to hold on to honour is to remain individual or to live by his code. In Carlos Baker's view this wave-like courage of Santiago is a rhythmic device through which Hemingway sustains the interest of his narrative. Philosophically speaking "the old man" in Archibald Henderson's remark of 1932: "demands for the incredible, the impossible and the superhuman". "Do or die" is Santiago's credo and always he adheres to it gladly.

Santiago resembles Marlow the narrator in Joseph Conrad's novella *Youth*. Marlow's words are equally applicable to Santiago of whom Hemingway remarks "everything about him was old except his eyes and they were the same colour as the sea and were cheerful and undefeated". In Conrad's memorable phrase, Santiago goes "beyond the boundaries of permitted aspiration" and wins truly Carnadian victory. Like the ancient mariner of Coleridge's poetry or Shelley's Prometheus or Abhimanyu in the Mahabharata, Santiago struggles for success, perfection and transcendental bliss. He remains dignified even in the face of a failure. As for work-ethics, he is no less industrious than Wordsworth's Leech Gatherer. The great nature poet writes,

> He told, that to these waters he had come
> To gather leeches, being old and poor:
> Employment hazardous and wearisome!
> And he had many hardships to endure:
> From pond to pond he roamed, from moor to moor;
> Housing with God's good help, by choice or chance;
> And in this way he gained an honest maintenance.[6]

This is how, one finds Santiago wrestling with the oddities of life just for his survival. Indeed, to the class of this kind of heroes, industry, courage, morality, honour and glory are the true barometers inspiring for perfection.

Hemingway is a great thinker. He is a great legend of his generation. Most of his works are translated into world languages. In fact, he is the most widely translated author.

Hemingway was a writer of a whole generation's despair and his birth centenary was celebrated in 1999. It is a great respect to a great man. Besides, how one can forget Norman Mailer's tribute to him: "It may be that the final judgment on his work may come to the notion that what he failed to do was tragic, but what he accomplished was heroic. For it is possible that he carried a weight of anxiety with him which would have suffocated any man."[7]

NOTES

1. Michael Greenberg, "Fearing Fear Itself", qt. by M.S. Nagarajan, *The Hindu*, August 1, 1999, p. 10.
2. Frank McConnell, "Ernest Hemingway", *Contemporary Literary Criticism*, Vol. 41, p. 199.
3. Herbie Butterfield, "Ernest Hemingway", *Contemporary Literary Criticism*, Vol. 41, p. 198.
4. Charles Scribner, "Timeless Hemingway", *The Hindu*, July 18, 1999, p. 3.
5. All the textual references are from Ernest Hemingway's novel *The Old Man and the Sea*.
6. Wordsworth, "Resolution and Independence", *The Works of William Wordsworth*, Herfordshire: Wordsworth Editions Ltd., 1994, p. 196.
7. Norman Miler, qt. by M.S. Nagarajan, "Timeless Hemingway", *The Hindu*, 18th July 1990, p. 3.

Langston Hughes's Poetry 22

Langston Hughes (1902-67) was a great African-American poet. He wrote of Negro's anguish making use of blues, spirituals and folktales. Hughes belongs to Harlem Renaissance. Active in social causes Hughes crusaded in the 1930s for the release of the 'Scottsboro boys'. Like many intellectuals of the time he was a leftist. He was not a man who swallowed any nostrum without questions and his writings defy easy categorization.

James Langston Hughes was born in Joplin, Mo., on February 1, 1902. He grew up in the Midwest and finished high school in Cleveland, Ohio. After spending his time in Mexico and Columbia he toured Africa and Western Europe. He graduated from Lincoln University in 1929. He was a class poet and edited the college magazine. He settled in Harlem in New York City. Later he worked in a hotel and one day he showed his poems to a client. The latter happened to be a great poet Vachel Lindsay who publicized Hughes's poetry.

It is said Hughes experimented with every form of literature. He wrote and edited alone or with others, poetry, drama, fiction, biography and even children literature. He and Countee Cullen were the bright young lyricists of the "Harlem Renaissance" of the 1920s. He was a spokesman for the group. This social protest had an impact upon his creative writing. For example, he created a break from the traditional American poetry. That is to say the Black poetry differed from the mainstream poetry. When he participated in Harlem Renaissance he was called 'O Henry of Harlem'.

Hughes described Harlem life poetically in *The Weary Blues* (1926), *Fine Clothes to the Jew* (1927) and *Montage of a Dream Deferred* (1951). He told about his own life in *The Big Sea* (1940) and *I Wonder as I Wonder* (1956). His Jesse B. Simple, a character originally created for a black newspaper audience revealed the uncensored thoughts of a naïve young urbanized black and became legendary in Black America. Byden Kackson says Hughes' novel *Not Without Laughter* (1930) provided one of American literature's finest *bildungsromans*.

In constant demand as a lecturer, Hughes traveled on speaking tours throughout the United States, to the West Indies and to parts of Europe and Africa. He received many awards and honors for his writings. His works have been translated into more than 25 languages.

Some of Langston Hughes' famous poems are "The Negro Speaks of Rivers", "Mother to Son" and "I, Too, Sing America". The first one speaks of Blackman's universal origin and importance:

I've known rivers:
I've known rivers ancient as the world and older than the
Flow of human blood in human veins.

My soul has grown deep like the rivers.

I bathed in the Euphrates when dawns were young.
I built my hut near the Congo and it lulled me to sleep
I looked upon the Nile and raised the pyramids above it.
I heard the singing of the Mississippi when Abe Lincoln
went down to New Orleans, and I've seen it's muddy
bosom turn all golden in the sunset.

I've known rivers:
Ancient, dusky rivers.

My soul has grown deep like the rivers.

The second poem "Mother to Son" explores Blackman's misery amidst universal racism:

Well, son, I'll tell you:
Life for me ain't been no crystal stair,

It's had tacks in it,
And splinters,
And boards torn up,
And places with no carpet on the floor—
Bare.
But all the time
I'se been a-climbin' on,
And reachin' landin's,
And turnin' corners,
And sometimes goin' in the dark
Where there ain't been no light,
So boy, don't you turn back.
Don't you set down on the steps
'Cause you finds it's kinder hard,
Don't you follow now—
For I'se still goin', honey,
I'se still climbin',
And life for me ain't been no crystal stair.

In the third poem "I, Too, Sing America", the poet sings as though a free citizen of America.

I am the darker brother,
They send me to eat in the kitchen
When company comes,
But I laugh,
And eat well,
And grow strong.

Tomorrow,
I'll sit at the table
When company comes.
Nobody'll dare
Say to me,
'Eat in the kitchen,'
Then.

Besides,
They'll see how beautiful I am
And be ashamed—

I, too, am America.

John Steinbeck's *The Grapes of Wrath* 23

John Steinbeck is a fine pastoral writer from the other side of Atlantic. He resembles Thomas Hardy whom he read widely. Most of his fiction concerns his native California and the Great Depression of the 1930's. Among influential novels from the period between the wars, his Pulitzer Prize-winning novel about "Okies" (Oklahoma sharecroppers who were forced off their land after the Dust Bowl storms of 1937), *The Grapes* of *Wrath* (1939), was one of the most important. It combined naturalist and symbolist techniques to depict his characters' plights and it expressed simple but strong responses to their sufferings: compassion, outrage and admiration.

John Steinbeck was born and raised in the rich Salinas Valley of California not far from San Francisco, a region producing wine and artichokes. His father was county treasurer, his mother a former school teacher. In the family library he found and read such standard authors as Milton, Dostoevsky, Flaubert, George Eliot and Thomas Hardy. In high school he was a good student, president of his graduating class and active in athletics and on the school newspaper. He began college at Stanford University as an English major but left school in 1925, and spent the next five years drifting, reading and writing.

In 1930 he married (the first of three times) and moved to Pacific Grove, California, where his father provided a house and small allowance to support him. His first success was his third novel, *Tortilla Flat*, which appeared in 1935. It was an episodic, warmly humorous treatment of the lives of paisanos—ethnically mixed Mexican-Indian-Caucasians—who lived in the Salinas Valley and whose earthy, uninhibited lives provided a colorful contrast to the valley's "respectable society". The subject of his second successful novel, *In Dubious Battle* (1936), was a fruit pickers' strike. The decency of the exploited workers is played off, on one side, against the cynical landowners and their vigilantes and, on the other, against the equally cynical Communist organizers who try to use the workers' grievances for their own purposes.

Steinbeck's sympathy for the underdog was shown again in *Mice and Men* (1937), about two drifting ranch-hands, one of whom is simpleminded; and in *The Grapes* of *Wrath*, about the Joad family, who, after losing their land, migrated westward to California on U.S. Highway 66 looking for, but not finding, a better life. Steinbeck meant to give these outcasts a tragic dignity and he succeeded, at least with Ma Joad, who tries to hold the family together throughout their sufferings.

It is observed, "After World War II Steinbeck's work became more sentimental and more heavily symbolic, even allegorical. Postwar prosperity led not to the simplicity he valued but to suburbia, television, and the explosion of a highly commercialized mass culture, from which Steinbeck could only turn in disgust. His short story *The Leader* of *the People* expresses his sense that America's best times are past and locates value in the story's socially insignificant characters—a child, an old man, and a farm hand. In a pre-war automobile with his poodle, named Charlie, he toured America; the title of his account, *Travels with Charlie in Search* of *America* (1962), again reveals this conviction that 'America' was now hard to find."[1] Throughout his career Steinbeck's writing brought certain modern literary techniques, in simple form, to a broad reading public, much as E.E. Cummings did for poetry. He was an accomplished craftsman, excelling especially in the creation of convincing dialogue. He won the Nobel Prize in 1963.

The plot of the novel *The Grapes of Wrath* runs thus:

Tom Joad was released from the Oklahoma state penitentiary where he had served a sentence for killing a man in self-defense. He traveled homeward through a region made barren by drought and dust storms. On the way he met Jim Casy, an ex-preacher; the pair went together to the home of Tom's people. They found the Joad place deserted. While Tom and Casy were wondering what had happened, Muley Graves, a hard tenant farmer, came by and disclosed that all of the family in the neighborhood had gone to California or were going. Tom's folks, Muley said, had gone to a relative's place preparatory to going west. Muley was the only sharecropper to stay behind.

All over the southern Midwest states, farmers, no longer able to make a living because of land banks, bad weather and machine farming, had sold or were forced out of the farms they had tenanted. Junk dealers and used-car salesmen profiteered on them. Thousands of families took to the roads leading to the promised land, California.

Tom and Casy found the Joads at Uncle John's place, all busy with preparations to leave for California. Assembled for the trip were Pa and Ma Joad; Noah, their mentally backward son; Al, the adolescent younger brother of Tom and Noah; Rose of Sharon, Tom's sister and her husband, Connie; the Joad children, Ruthie and Winfield; and Granma and Grampa Joad. They had bought an ancient truck to take them west. The family asked Jim Casy to go with them. The night before they started, they killed the pigs they had left and salted down the meat so that they would have food on the way.

Spurred by handbills which stated that agricultural workers were badly needed in California, the Joads, along with thousands of others, made their torturous way, in a worn-out vehicle, across the plains toward the mountains. Grampa died of a stroke during their first overnight stop. Later there was a long delay when the truck brokedown. Small business people along the way treated the migrants as enemies. And, to add to the general misery, returning migrants told the Joads that there was no work to be had in California, that conditions were even worse than they were in Oklahoma. But the dream of a bountiful West Coast urged the Joads onward. Close to the California line, where the group stopped to bathe in a river, Noah, feeling he was a hindrance to the others, wandered away. It was there that the Joads first heard themselves addressed as Okies, another word for tramps.

Granma died during the night trip, across the desert. After burying her, the group went into a Hooverville, as the migrants' camps were called. There they learned that work was all but impossible to find. A contractor came to the camp to sign up men to pick fruit in another county. When the Okies asked to see his license, the contractor turned the leaders over to the police deputy who had accompanied him to camp. Tom was involved in the fight which followed. He escaped and Casy gave himself up in Tom's place. Connie, the husband of the pregnant Rose of Sharon, suddenly disappeared from the group. The family was breaking up in the face of its hardships. Ma Joad did everything in her power to keep the group together.

Fearing recrimination after the fight, the Joads left Hooverville and went to a government camp maintained for transient agricultural workers. The camp had sanitary facilities, a local government made up of the transients themselves and simple organized entertainment. During the Joads' stay at the camp the Okies successfully defeated an attempt of the local citizens to give the camp a bad name and thus to have it closed to the migrants. For the first time since they had arrived in California, the Joads found themselves treated as human beings.

Circumstances eventually forced them to leave the camp, however, for there was no work in the district. They drove to a large farm where work was being offered. There they found agitators attempting to keep the migrants from taking the work because of unfair wages. But, the Joads, thinking only of food, were escorted by motorcycle police into the farm. The entire family picked peaches for five cents a box and earned in a day just enough money to buy food for one meal. Tom, remembering the pickets outside the camp, went out in night to investigate. He found Casy, who was the leader of the agitators. While Tom and Casy were talking, deputies, who had been searching for Casy, closed in on them. The pair fled, but were caught. Casy was killed. Tom received a cut on his head, but not before he had felled a deputy with an ax handle. The family concealed Tom in their shack. The rate for a box of peaches dropped, meanwhile; Tom's danger and the futility of picking peaches drove the Joads on their way. They hid the injured Tom under the mattresses in the back of the truck and told the suspicious guard at the entrance to the farm that the extra man they had had with them when they came was a hitchhiker who had stayed on to pick.

The family found at last a migrant crowd encamped in abandoned boxcars along a stream. They joined the camp and soon found temporary jobs. Tom, meanwhile, hid in a culvert near the camp. Ruthie innocently disclosed Tom's presence to another little girl. Ma, realizing that Tom was no longer safe, sent him away. Tom promised to carry on Casy's work in trying to improve the lot of the downtrodden everywhere.

The autumn rains began. Soon the stream which ran beside the camp overflowed and water entered the boxcars. Under these all but impossible conditions, Rose of Sharon gave birth to a dead baby.

It is said, "In *The Grapes of Wrath* Steinbeck has achieved an interesting contrapuntal effect by breaking the narrative at intervals with short, impressionistic passages recorded as though by a motion picture camera moving quickly from one scene to another and from one focus to another. The novel is a powerful indictment of our capitalistic economy and a sharp criticism of the southwestern farmer for his imprudence in the care of his land. The outstanding feature of *The Grapes of Wrath* is its photographically detailed, if occasionally sentimentalized description of the American farmers of the Dust Bowl in the mid-thirties of the twentieth century."[2]

NOTES

1. *Norton Anthology of American Literature*, p. 2101.
2. *Masterplots*, p. 1377.

Ralph Ellison's *Invisible Man* as a Depiction of Identity Crisis

24

Ralph Ellison (1914-94) is a great American novelist. His *Invisible Man* (1952) became a classic of American fiction. Blydon Jackson observes, "The novel which deals with a Blackman's negligibility in a white man's world, shows Ellison to be a virtuoso craftsman and dedicated thinker. Exploration of issues of race and identity remained his abiding concern."[1]

Ralph Ellison was born in Oklahoma City, Okla., in 1914. He was born the second son of three children of Lewis Ellison and Ida Ellison. His father was a restaurant operator. His mother was a sort of social reformer, who organized protests against segregating conditions in Dayton, Ohio. The boy was named by his father after the well-known 19th century thinker-writer Ralph Waldo Emerson. In fact, the writer Ellison represented Emerson in most ways. Ellison was raised in whites' atmosphere of learning and intellectual curiosity. Music was his first interest. He liked jazz. Later he had training even in sculpture. Oklahoma City's lively life provided him interest in social life. The boy read many great writers like Emerson, Hardy, the Brontes and Eliot. He, once said, "*Wuthering Heights* had caused me an agony of inexpressible emotion, and the same seized my mind. I was intrigued by its power to move me while eluding my understanding somehow its rhythm was often closer to jazz than those of the Negro poets, and even though I could not understand them, its range of allusion was as mixed and as varied as that of Louis Armstrong."[2] Later Ralph Ellison came in contact with black American leaders Langston Hughes and Richard Wright—both great writers. Wright's novel

Native Son and collection of short stories *Uncle Tom's Children* impressed him.

In 1933 Ellison entered Tuskegee Institute meant for the black people. Later he went to the north for stay and work. He did not get back either to the south or to Tuskegee Institute. He did some research for the federal writer's project from 1938 to 1942. He served in the US Merchant Marine during the World War II. From 1939 he contributed many articles and stories to magazines. His novel *Invisible Man* published in 1952 won him National Book Award and Pulitzer Prize. Ralph Ellison was in Rome from 1955 to 1957 on a fellowship from American Academy of Arts and Letters. He settled in New York City and lectured on Afro-American culture. He taught at many universities including New York University where he was Albert Schweitzer Professor of Humanities from 1870. Ralph Ellison died in New York City in 1994.

Ralph Ellison took seven years to prepare for the novel *Invisible Man.* His second book *Shadow and Act* (1964) and *Going to the Territory* (1986) are collections of essays and criticism. He began to work on another novel in the late 1950s but he did not complete it.

Ralph Ellison wanted to write about his experience, his people and Afro-American racial problems and prejudices. His short story "Flying Home" (1944) tells a black pilot who crashes into an Alabama cotton field and finds in a lengthy dialogue with a black peasant that he remains rooted in folk life despite his aspirations to rise above it. Yet Ellison thought of Negro leadership and thought of antiheroic conception of Negro invisibility. "Here is his discovery of the meaning of his experience as an individual and as an Afro-American. Each choice of incident and each decision about technique has been tailored to communicate simultaneously a sense of the protagonist's character and personality and a sense of the typically black aspects of his experience."[3] Ellison's readings of the black novels like Wright's *Native Son* and Ann Petry's *The Street* might have encouraged him to write it. Many black American writers, speakers and thinkers, particularly Booker T. Washington, have inspired him. For example, W.E.B. DuBois's words ring true in the context: "It is a peculiar sensation, this double-consciousness, this seen of always looking at one's self through the eyes of others, of measuring one's soul by the tape of world that looks on in amused contempt and pity. One ever feels his twoness—an American, a Negro; two souls, two body, whose dogged strength alone keeps it from two asunder."[4] Both the prologue and epilogue speak of Ellison's viewpoints of the theme and structure. The presentation is rather surreal.

Ralph Ellison's only great novel *Invisible Man* received a mixed response. The *Daily Worker* wrote negative reviews. John Oliver Killens said the novel is a 'vicious distortion'. But Saul Bellow gave a thudding appreciation for the new writing. He felt that Ellison has expressed the absurdity and the pain of black life in America; he has also transcended the usual stereotypes and self-imposed limitations of black writers and of ethnic writers in general, to create a powerful work whose themes and implications were universal in scope. Bellow conceded that the book was "not by any means faultless...but it is an immensely moving novel and it has greatness".[5] The novel got the writer innumerable opportunities, in fact. In the novel "Ellison combined great imaginative gifts with a profound intelligence, a style of exceptional grace and strength, and an unswerving respect for all of the mystery and complexity of human life. Our culture is immeasurably the richer for his short stories and especially his essays, but even if he had published nothing but *Invisible Man*, that novel alone would guarantee him a permanent place among the great American writers."[6]

Yet to Ellison's contemporaries *Invisible Man* appeared to be a book of his times. They viewed it as a depiction of black life. Something of the sort of identity issue.

Invisible Man opens brilliantly: "I am an invisible man.... Simply because people refuse to see me." The unnamed protagonist whom we can simply call as the 'Invisible Man' says, "That invisibility to which I refer occurs because of a peculiar disposition of the eyes of those with whom I come in contact.... I am not complaining nor am I protesting either."[7] He narrates his life, events and situations in it, his difficulties and agonies.

He says one night he accidentally bumped into a man and even spoke badly of him. Yet he is disgusted of the event. He is in a state of hibernation, for he lives in a subterranean way, in a hole. His life is rather disenchanting. He is aware of his poor, oppressed black life. He chants Louis Armstrong's words:

> What did I do?
> To be so black
> And blue. (p. 10)

The *Invisible Man* speaks that man must be responsible. He introspects: "Responsibility rests upon recognition and recognition is a form of agreement" (p. 11). The protagonist is at school where one day he makes a fine speech. So he is offered a prize—a kind of fellowship for his college education. The master who awards it to him says, "Gentleman, you see that I did not overpraise this boy. He makes a good speech and some day he'll lead his people in the proper paths. And I don't have to tell you that that is important in these days and times. This is a good, smart boy, and so to encourage him in the right direction, in the name of the Board of Education I wish to present him a prize in the form of this..." (p. 25). But his college life is not so comfortable though it is a black college. Its president is Mr. Bledsoe, and Norton is one of the trustees. One day the 'Invisible Man' drives Norton's car and Norton speaks, on the way with a farmer called Jim Trueblood. Then the car moves to a place called The Golden Day which is a black men's hub. The 'Invisible Man' wants some whisky for Norton as the latter falls sick. But the people will not offer it easily. So Norton is taken there personally. Here a colored physician ridicules the protagonist: "You see", he said turning to Mr. Norton, "he has eyes and ears and a good distended African nose, but he fails to understand the simple facts of life. *Understand*. Understand? It's worse than that. He registers with his senses but short-circuits his brain. Nothing has meaning. He takes it in but he doesn't digest it...the mechanical man" (p. 72).

The 'Invisible Man' gets the feeling that 'white is right'. Soon they reach home. The president is uneasy and unhappy about the 'Invisible Man'. He asks him as to why he took the trustee in a car ride. Though the other tries his best to convince him, Bledsoe does not believe him. So uneasiness lingers between the two.

There is some programme in the college and during which many guests speak. One guest Homer Barbee of Chicago speaks on equality of man: "...this barren land after emancipation, this land of darkness and sorrow, of ignorance and degradation, where the hand of brother had been turned against brother, father against brother, father against son, and son against father; where master had turned against slave and slave against master; where all was strife and darkness, and aching land" (p. 92). This is about black despair. Bledsoe's words ring in the mind of him. "Power is confident, self-assuring, self-starting, and self-stopping, self-warming and self-justifying. When you have it, you know it. Let the Negroes snicker and the crackers laugh: are the facts, son. The only ones I even pretend to please are big white folk, and even those I control more than they control me. This is a power set up, son, and I'm at the controls. You think about that. When you buck against me, you're bucking against power, rich white folk's power, and the nation's power—which means government power" (p. 110). After that Bledsoe asks the 'Invisible Man' to leave the college almost incomplete. Even he gives him some letters of introduction to his business people in New York City.

The 'Invisible Man' goes to New York City and stays in a lady called Mary's flat. He tries for a job in many places of familiarity. Yet he cannot get a situation at Mr. Bates' office. When he reaches Emerson's office, the officer opens Bledsoe's letter and to his surmise notes that Bledsoe has written that the 'Invisible Man' should not be given any assignment. It is read: "This case represents, my dear Mr. Emerson, one of the rare, delicate instances in which one for whom we held great expectations has gone grievously astray, and who in his fall threatens individuals and the school. Thus, while the bearer is no longer a member of our scholastic family, it is highly important that his severance with the college be executed as painlessly as possible. I beg of you, sir, to help him continue in the direction of that promise, which likes the horizon, recedes ever brightly and distantly beyond the hopeful traveler" (p. 145). The protagonist feels that he could hardly sleep.

Later the 'Invisible Man' joins some factory and he cannot work well. After this brief stint in the firm, he takes interest in Harlem renaissance. He meets black leaders like Jack, Clifton, Ras and others. The black organize Brotherhood Association. They speak in the line of Booker T. Washington. They go violent when wealthy whites ask black dwellers to vacate their houses in Harlem.

The 'Invisible Man' speaks of the crisis: "Yes, we're the uncommon people—and I'll tell you why. They call us dumb and they treat us dumb. And what do they do with dumb ones? Think about it, look around!" (p. 259).

The slogans "Sisters! Brothers! We are the true patriots! The citizens of tomorrow's world. We'll be dispossessed no More!" are uttered.

Black leaders Jack, the 'Invisible Man' and Ras have many differences between them. The man called Ras is violent and separatist. Ras speaks with gusto: "You my brother, mahn. Brothers are the same color; how the hell you call these white men brother? Shit, mahn. That's shit! Brothers the same color. We sons of Mama Africa, you done forgot? You black. BLACK! You—goddahm, mahn!" (p. 280). Clifton, however, does not like separatism and violence with Ras. Unfortunately he is murdered by some whites. There is his elaborate funeral. A newspaper mentions of his death thus: "Here are the fats. He was standing and he fell. He fell. He fell and he kneeled. He kneeled and he bled" (p. 344). Somebody says was he a white man he would not be killed.

M.K. Singleton observes, "Tod Clifton's apostasy features more deliberate, and thus more troubling acquiescence in a negro stereotype. Clifton is defined as an outstanding political activity, but so deep is his disillusionment with the brotherhood movement that he not only abandons his leadership role, but he also takes to huckstering on street corners."[8]

Shortly after this the 'Invisible Man' finds a leaflet:

Behold the invisible
Thy will be done O Lord!

I see all, Know all, Tell all, Cure all.
You shall see the unknown wonders.
Rev. B.P. Rinehart, *Spiritual Technologist.* (p. 374)

The 'Invisible Man' intones the words. "And I could tell Harlem to have hope where was no hope" (p. 383). He says it again at the end of the novel: "Let me be honest with you—a feat which, by the way, I find of the utmost difficulty. When one is invisible he finds such problems as good and evil, honesty and dishonesty, of such shifting shapes that he confuses one with the other, depending upon who happens to be looking through him at the time. Well, now I've been trying to look through myself, and there's a risk in it. I was never more hated than when I tried to be honest" (p. 432).

The novel is a book about a universal indemnity crisis, told by means of a black protagonist. After the hero the secondary characters like Mary Rambo and Peter Wheatstraw, Lucius Brockway and Rinehart and Ras—come from the primary reality—black life. And so the narrative style of Trueblood, the discourse at the Golden Day and Bledsoe's rationalization. John Reilly observes the narrator is a responsible man. He says man must be responsible in society. His various attitudes towards a white society—from early accommodations to eventual repudiation—have counterparts in the collective history of Afro-American as well as in the personal lives of the citizens. He says, "The absurdity, ambiguity and irrationality of caste experience that so many authors have documented coalesce in an existentially self-aware figure who serves as archetype of the black experience in America."[9]

Today Ralph Ellison's *Invisible Man* is considered as a classic. When a white magazine conducted a poll it found that the novel is a hit for the last twenty years. It is about American reality, about man's identify crisis.

NOTES

1. Blydon Jackson, "Ralph Ellison", *American Encyclopedia*, Vol. 10, p. 255.
2. "Ralph Ellison", qt. in *Encyclopedia of Literature*, ed. by M.K. Bhatnagar, New Delhi: Atlantic Publishers, 2001, p. 576.

3. John Reilly, "Introduction" to *Invisible Man: Twentieth Century Interpretations*, Englewood Cliffs, N.J., Prentice Hall Inc., 1970, p. 3.
4. W.E.B. DuBois, qt. by Reillp. John Reilly, "Introduction" to *Invisible Man: Twentieth Century Interpretations*, Englewood Cliffs, N.J., Prentice Hall Inc., 1970, p. 5.
5. *Encyclopedia of Literature*, ed. by M.K. Bhatnagar, New Delhi: Atlantic Publishers, 2001, p. 65.
6. *Ibid.*, p. 579.
7. All the textual references are from Ralph Ellison's *Invisible Man*, New York: The Modern Library, 1952.
8. M.K. Singleton, *Leadership as Antagonists in "Invisible Man"*, p. 18.
9. John Reilly, "Introduction" to *Invisible Man: Twentieth Century Interpretations*, p. 8.

Saul Bellow's *Henderson the Rain King* as Fantasy

25

Saul Bellow was born in Lachine, Montréal, Canada in 1915. He was the youngest of four children of Russian emigrants, Abraham and Liza Bellow. The Bellow-ancestors were from Russia who immigrated to Canada from St Petersburg. Saul Bellow grew up in a polyglot environment where English, French, Russian and Yiddish were spoken. Abraham Bellow failed in many of his businesses and in 1924 he and his family emmigrated to Chicago, the USA. This Saul Bellow describes in his novel *The Adventures of Augie March*. His father's business failures are alluded to in his great work *Herzog*.

Saul Bellow had his high school education in Chicago; he graduated from the University of Chicago and in 1937 he obtained a degree in Anthropology from Northwestern University. His knowledge of Anthropology can be seen in *Herzog*. Saul Bellow married four times. Saul Bellow, when young, had started the Russian Literary Society. Later he taught at Pestolozzi Froebel Teachers' college in Chicago.

Saul Bellow has written many important novels. *Dangling Man* (1944) was his first novel. *The Adventures of Augie March* (1953) and *The Victim* (1947) are his next works of fiction. His *Augie March* received National Book Award for fiction. *Seize the Day* (1956), *Henderson the Rain King* (1959) and *Herzog* (1964) are quite good. The last one was an instant bestseller. Saul Bellow wrote plays too. *Mosby's Memoir* (1960) is his collection of short stories. *Humboldt's Gift* (1975) is his last work of importance. Saul Bellow got Pulitzer Award and the Nobel Prize for Literature in 1976.

Saul Bellow's *Henderson the Rain King* is a great fantasy, a burlesque and a comic extravaganza on modern times. It is also a travel book; and an adventureous story. Some critics call it an allegory.

Henderson the Rain King is an interesting novel. As it is a mixed narrative it is also an attack on American dream. It depicts the 1950's American depression. As well as it attacks the American affluence and degeneration. What more it is a portrayal of the degenerated American's quest for happiness and peace?

The story of the novel is as follows:

> Eugene Henderson, as a millionaire, lives in a town of America. He has married twice. He has got five children—Edward, Ricey, Alice and twin-boys. He has even a richer ancestry. He has had his education in a University affiliated to Ive League Universities. He has served in World War II. Physically he is a giant—six feet four inches tall, weighing 230 pounds. He behaves like a bun, getting drunk, fighting in country saloons, being arrested by the police, swearing and crying out in public. He is crazy, moody, roach and tyrannical. He plays upon violin and he has the hobby of rearing pigs. Yet this enormous Henderson is not happy. He says 'I want I want'.

Henderson is unhappy with his first wife. So he married Miss Lily for a second time. He does not find peace with her, for he has not found it with himself first. One day his daughter Ricey brings a foundling Negro and he quarrels with her to avoid the Negro and he kills Miss Lenox in the connection. So he is in mental crisis. Then he decides to go to Africa with Charlie Albert who is just married and decides for his honeymoon. The latter is interested in photography. They alight at Cairo airport. First they spend their time near a lake. After some days Henderson feels bored and he wants to go interior with a local guide Romileyu. Both go to a tribal village called Arnewi. There Henderson fights a customary battle with the reigning prince-king Itelo. The queen of the kingdom Willatale and her sister Mtalba are attracted by him. All of them—the royal people speak English. In fact, they have studied in Europe. Yet the fun is that they live like Africans. No change. The western education has not helped them much. Or maybe they have to live like the natives and guide them as their rulers. This is Henderson's spiritual African safari. Critics say Henderson is in quest of peace and for the sake of it, he discards the trapping of modern civilization—America and even the company of Albert.

Henderson lives like the natives. He tries to adopt their ritualism and barbaric practices. He appreciates their 'primitive' culture though he gives it up later. In consequences, the queen's sister Mtalba likes to marry him. The sisters present him rich gifts. He asks the queen about himself. She says, "He is a strong and large personality, a mind full of thought, in love with sensations, a sore heart, full of grief, fierceness and frenzy; a man who looks like a suffering monument of flesh, who is not at home in life." Henderson is grateful to the queen for sympathizing with his troubles and starts singing from Handle's *Messiah*, whereupon the queen remarks: "'Grun-tu-molani. Man wants to live.' The queen's remark makes Henderson feel quite elated. To show his gratitude, he is more determined than ever to rid the Arnewi of their plague of frogs."[1]

The Arnewi people have a strange problem shortly. They have a big cistern and it is full of frogs. So they are unable to enable their cows drink the water. They worry about it. Henderson plans something in the western manner. He prepares a bomb and explodes it in the tank. Unfortunately the whole cistern is destroyed. Consequently, the cattle die due to lack of water. The Arnewi people are enraged. Henderson thinks they may kill him. This is treated as an evil omen to the natives. Saul Bellow thinks the western means of life are a threat to the African natives. It is how he attacks upon the western technology. Yet he with his guide runs away to another tribal village called Wariri. Saul Bellow suggests an ironic contrast between the hero of *A Connecticut Yankee in King Arthur's Court* (1889) by Mark Twain, who works wonders with a pocket electrical battery and other 'gadgets' and Henderson whose application of technical know-how results in a disaster. It is said, "Henderson knows that he has not yet found what he has been looking for in

Africa. Still, he is quite aware of the distinction between the reality outside the self and the 'reality' created by the self and of which the self often becomes a prisoner" (p. 20).

The tribe Wariri is in sharp contract to the Arnewi tribe. If the Arnewi people are innocent, kind and cow-worshippers, the Wariri people are clever and cruel. Their mark of greatness is lion. Be it as it may, Wariris do not welcome Henderson. Once he lands there they arrest him. He is asked to stay with a dead body in a hut. Henderson removes the corpse and sleeps with his guide. Surprisingly the dead body is placed beside him at the time of dawn. They are enquired by the police. Henderson thinks it is a kind of disgrace to him. He remembers his episode with Mrs. Clara Spohr the painter's wife: "One winter afternoon Clara Spohr and Henderson met in New York and had a few drinks together. Then Henderson took her home and Clara Spohr, an ageing former beauty, started kissing Henderson, who kissed back instead of pushing her away in full view of Lily and of Clara's husband.... Henderson feels something distorts his inner self so that, when telling Romilayu the story of his life, he 'came out still more exotic and fantastic'. Furthermore, we are reminded that Henderson's journey into primitive Africa is also a journey into 'the heart of darkness', for the Wariri are explicitly referred to as the 'chillen darkness'. The Arnewis had been clearly associated with light, so that they can be regarded as the children of light. In Christian terms the Wariri are like fallen angels. Indeed, Henderson will compare the Wariri herdsman who sends him into an ambush with the biblical figure who directed Joseph toward Dothan, and who Henderson thinks 'must have been an angel'. The Wariri territory is described as a hostile, forbidding, dangerous landscape, a fallen world. The warlike, fierce attitude of the Wariri buildings, reinforce this impression of a hellish world" (p. 21). This is, in fact, Henderson's awareness about himself. Henderson is more and more troubled in mind. One day he meets the king Dahfu, who happens to be a friend of Itelo. The king himself is as gigantic as Henderson. Saul Bellow writes, "The king is a kind of physical alter ego of Henderson: six feet or even taller. But the resemblance stops there. Indeed, unlike Henderson, whose tenseness increases every hour, Dahfu is reclining 'sumptuously at rest' with his twenty or thirty naked wives attending to his every need. This first interview with the king in his palace is carried out with a maximum of elegance and courtesy on the king's part. The whole tribe then proceeds to an arena in the village where the rain ceremony begins amid incredible noise and excitement. The first ritual takes place between Dahfu and a young woman who 'play' at catching human skulls, they throw high up into air, a ritual whose meaning Henderson does not quite understand, except that it is a contest whose outcome could be deadly if either of the two contestants missed a skull" (p. 24). The American is now on being and becoming process.

As in Arnewi, here are some events like rain rites. The Wariris celebrate a rain rite called the worship of Mummah on an appointed day. They worship the deity removing her a few feet away in a public place. According to the custom, the strong men are to lift the statue to a fixed place. But they fail. Then the king asks Henderson to lift it to the place. Henderson does so and is appreciated by all. The king says he will be his successor if he does not get any male issue. It is said, "Henderson's involvement with the affairs of the tribe increases, but whereas the moving of Mummah in the preceding chapter came out of his own initiative, everything that occurs now is forced upon him. As rain king, he has no choice but to submit to the various duties inherent in his new status: he is stepped naked, forced to run through the town while being whipped by the amazons, plunged into a pond of dirty water and finally has to whip the stone gods along with the rest of the villagers. He fully realizes the irony of the situation he has got himself into. But he is also dimly aware that his orders may make him discover the truth in some way. Finally the rain comes in a sudden deluge." Dahfu concludes this chapter with these words: "You have lost the wager" (p. 27). Another close event is the king's playing with a lioness. One day the king takes Henderson to the din where his lioness stays. He asks the foreigner to play with the animal. Dahfu's conviction is that if one behaves like a lion, one can indeed become a lion. His lion is named Atti. What more the king finds a male lion outside and he thinks it should be Atti's kin. So he wants to capture it.

He tries to capture it and when he shortly does so the lion wounds him. He does it so even when Henderson warns him against it. The king dies. According to the custom, the rain king has to succeed the king. In fact, Henderson reigns as the king of Wariri people for a few months. Now the thoughts of living like the African and satisfying the former king's sixty wives oppress him. It is said, "He ran away from western civilization and came to Africa, we remember, in search of peace. He has not been able to find calm or rest, for his experiences with the two tribes have been marked by a certain amount of violence, especially his 'lion-training'. 'Maybe', as he says, 'every guy has his own Africa..., by which I meant that as I was a turbulent individual, I was having a turbulent Africa'. But he has changed enough for him to realize that he has come to a turning point in his life and he takes two decisive steps. Firstly he sends Romilayu away to avoid getting him involved in the trouble that he senses is just about to occur between Dahfu and his tribe, and in which Henderson will be caught. Secondly he writes a long letter to his wife Lily, in which he unburdens his heart and makes plans for the future. The letter is frequently interrupted by passages in which Henderson recalls significant events of his life" (p. 31).

So one day Henderson runs away with his guide. Henderson runs away to the airport of Khartoum and then via Athens, Rome, Paris and London, he reaches Newfoundland. On the way, he meets an American orphan who cannot speak English. By the by he has taken away a lion cub. When the novel ends we see him with the cub and the boy, as a jolly man in America. "Some critics have charged that the novel is incomplete. Henderson left America and never quite returns to it. He has changed, but the ending does not really indicate how effective his change could be in the midst of western, materialistic civilization. This charge will be answered elsewhere, but it is clear at this point that, because of his recollection of the bear Smolak and the tender care he takes of the orphan, Henderson has acquired a knowledge of nature and of life—and an understanding of love—that had been denied him before he went to Africa" (p. 34).

The novel *Henderson*...reminds us Ernest Hemingway's novel *The Short Happy Life of Francis Macomber* based on African experience. But Hemingway's hero lives and dies in Africa and Hemingway's novel is realistic. On the other hand, Saul Bellow's novel is of 'wasteland outlook'. It is a condemnation of western society which is seen as dehumanizing. Henderson's hero is 'anti-hero' and he is meant for potential vitality for regeneration. The hero of Bellow's earlier novel *The Adventure of Augie March* states that "I know I longed very much, but I didn't understand for what. This yearning is taken over by Henderson in an even more intense way. He mentions several times the voice within him that says 'I want, I want. I want'" (p. 37).

Saul Bellow's hero of *Dangling Man* says, "The quest, I am beginning to think, whether it be for money, for notoriety, reputation, increase of pride, whether it leads us to thievery, slaughter, sacrifice, the quest is one in the same. All striving is for the one end. I do not entirely understand this impulse. But it seems to me that its final end is the desire for pure freedom. We are all drawn toward the same craters of the spirit—to know what we are and what we are for, to know our purpose, to seek grace. And, if the quest is the same, the differences in our personal histories, which hitherto meant so much to us, become of minor importance."[2]

NOTES

1. All the textual references are taken from the York Notes on Saul Bellow's *Henderson the Rain King*, ed. by Edmond Schraepa and Pierre Michel, Beirut: Immeuble Esseily, 1981, p. 18.
2. *Masterplot*, Vol. 17.

Flannery O' Conner's Short Stories

26

Flannery O' Conner (1925-64), a native of Georgia lived a short life. She wrote bleak, uncompromising yet humorous stories. The illiterate southern characters appear there with their violence and ruggedness. *Wise Blood* (1952) is about a religious fanatic who establishes his own church. It is said, "The Black humor of O' Conner links her with Nathaniel West and Joseph Heller." Her works include short story collections *A Good Man is Hard to Find* (1955) and *Everything That Rises Must Converge* (1965); the novel *The Violent Bear It Away* (1960); and a volume of letters, *The Habit of Being* (1979). Her *Complete Stories* came out in 1971.

Flannery O' Conner is an American short story writer. She has written many short stories like *Wise Blood, A Good Man is Hard to Find, The Violent Bear It Away, The River, The Artificial Nigger, Good Country People, You can't be any Poorer than the Dead, The Comfortable Home, A View of the Woods, Revelation* and many more. What is so important about her is that she writes of things violently. She writes about whites as much as blacks. She writes of comedy and tragedy. Her depiction is rather of the Gothic mode. It is said, "Flannery O' Conner's strategy is just this: as the threat of violence and the irrational increases, our cold judgment turns to human understanding and caricatures turn into characters. The moment of our deepest understanding coincides with the moment of the most irrational destruction—and the characters are turned back into caricatures, human beings frozen into comic-strip outline by an objective and irrelevant observer. Because of the double point of view, the culminating destruction contains elements of senseless terror and slapstick comedy. The effect is the same as the outrageous mixture of terror and jest in the medieval miracle plays: a sense of apocalypse. Not only are all the clichés destroyed but our very foundations for rational and moral judgment are annihilated. And, most unexpectedly, in the harshest light from the most detached viewpoint, we realize the fullest sympathy."[1] It is said Conner's judgment of human beings is severe. O! she deals with people where there is no God.

Some of Conner's short stories are studied here. One of her important short stories is *A Good Man is Hard to Find*. Here a grandmother is depicted. She has her family of kith and kin. One of her sons is Bailey. The family wants to go to Florida for outing. But the grandmother hears that there is a gangster called Misfit. So she decides to go to Tennessee. She wants to meet some of her connections. The family goes in a car with others like a woman and her two children—John Wesley and June Star. So they leave their own Atlanta at 8.45 am. She asks Bailey to drive the car not so speedily. On the way, the people watch the fine countryside. It is said, "The grandmother points out interesting details of the scenery." While the other two children—Wesley and Star—read children's classics. They eat some launch. The story grows interestingly. Flannery O' Conner writes,

> The grandmother said she would tell them a story if they would keep quiet. When she told a story, she rolled her eyes and waved her head and was very dramatic. She said once when she was a maiden lady she had been courted by a Mr. Edger Atkins Teagarden from Jasper, Georgia. She said he was a very good-looking man and a gentleman and that he brought her a watermelon every Saturday afternoon with his initials cut in it, EAT. Well, one Saturday, she said, Mr. Teagarden brought the watermelon and there was nobody at home and he left it on the front porch and returned in his buggy to Jasper, but she never got the watermelon, she said, because a nigger boy ate it when he saw the initials, EAT![2]

They stopped at The Tower for barbecued sandwiches. A fat man Red Sammy Butts ran it. There were some monkeys. It is said, "Inside The Tower was a long dark room with a counter at one end and tables at the other and dancing space in the middle" (p. 121). There is a talk of disbelief. Grandmother says, "People are certainly not nice like they used to be." She alludes to Misfit, the criminal. The innkeeper and the grandmother speak of better times. They drove into the hot afternoon once again. Outside of Tombsboro she recalls of some old plantation. She likes to pay a visit there. "Hey!" said John Wesley, "Let's visit it." But Bailey said no. The children began to yell and scream that they wanted to see the house with the secret panel. The grandmother argued: "It would be very educational for them." They drove a dirty road which was hilly too. Conner says "The road looked as if no one had traveled on it in months." Shortly their car falls down into a pit. Soon another car arrives there. The people of the car are Mr. Misfit and two of his rascals—Bobby Lee and Hiram. The rowdy Misfit asks his two men to catch hold of all except the grandmother with the help of a pistol and dispatch them to hell. They do it. The grandmother prays him not to harm them. He speaks of his anguish thus: "I was a gospel singer for a while. I been most everything. Been in the arm service, both land and sea, at home and abroad, been twict married, been in a tornado, seen a man burnt alive oncet, and looked up at the children" (p. 129). Finally he murders her by shooting. When the two of his servants return they see her dead body in a puddle of blood. The fanatic man says, "It's no real pleasure in life" (p. 133).

In the next story *The River* we find Conner's depiction of a family that goes to a river for healing. The family of Mrs. Connin has an orphan with it. They go to a river to meet a preacher called Bevel Simmers. Accidentally the orphan's name appears to be Bevel. The following passage speaks of her children: "That's Bevel", Mrs. Connin said, taking off her coat, "it's a coincident he's named the same as the preacher. These boys are J.C. Spivey, and Sinclair, and that's Sarah Mildred on the porch. Take off the coat and hang it on the bed post, Bevel" (p. 160). The three children and Bevel talk of pigs which they have not seen elsewhere. All walk to the river—Mrs. Connin in front with him and the three boys string out behind and Sarah Mildred, the tall girl at the end to holler if one of them runs out on the road. When they go to the river, they find the preacher in the water. He says, "If you won't come for Jesus, you can't come for me." Somebody says him, "I have seen you cure a patient." He sings: "Listen I read in Mark about an unclean man, I read in Luke about a lame man, I read in John about a dead man. Oh you people hear! The same blood that makes this River red, made that leper clean, made that blind man stare, made that dead man leap! You people with trouble", he says, "lay it in that River of Blood, lay it in that river of Pain, and watch it move away toward the kingdom of Christ" (p. 165). He tells them they can lay their pain in the river. A woman says this preacher can heal. Mrs. Connin makes use of the chance. She says, "Listen here, preacher, I got a boy from town today that I'm keeping. His mamma's sick and he wants you to pray for her." The preacher asks Connin whether Bevel is baptized. She says no. Then he asks the boy his name. The boy says, "My name is Bevvvuuuuuuul." He says he will baptize him. Connin adds that the preacher must pray for Bevel's mother's health. Later the boy's mother arrives there saying that the boy's name is not Bevel. The story is of religious nature and there is some irony in it.

The Artificial Niggers is another fine short story. The story begins: "Mr. Head awakened to discover that the room was full of moonlight." He thinks man matures with age. He sat up and the hour was two in the morning. Conner writes of Head's peculiar position: "He might have been Virgil summoned in the middle of the night to go to Dante, or better, Raphael, awakened by a blast of god's light to fly to the side of Tobias" (p. 250). The man has a grandson and the latter, a boy is irked when the elder gets up first. One day both plan to go to Atlanta where the boy had been born. The genesis is that: "Mr Head had once had a wife and daughter and when the wife died, the daughter ran away and returned after an interval with Nelson. Then one morning, without getting out of bed, she died and left Mr. Head with sole care of the little child. He had made the mistake of telling Nelson that he had been born in Atlanta. If he hadn't told him that, Nelson couldn't have insisted that this was going to be his second trip" (p. 251). The fun is that the grandfather says the child that he was born in Atlanta. The child on that basis argues that 'yes'. Then this trip is my second trip to the town. 'How' the elder asks. Thus, the funny argument goes on. When the old man asks whether he had seen a nigger, the latter asks him: "How you know I never saw a nigger when I lived there before?" He says, "I probably saw a lot of niggers." So both the elder and the boy look as if they waited for an apparition. Both board a bus for Atlanta. They notice a nigger on the way. Yet the boy cannot see him as a nigger. There are more of niggers...negroes everywhere. It is a strange place. There is some rush when they get down a train car. The train stops. The two alight leaving their launch pack on their seats. They see their weight. Head's ticket bears the funny details: that he's 120 pounds and he is upright and brave and all his friends admire him. But his actual weight is 110 pounds. The boy's weight is shown as 98 pounds while he is 68 pounds. It is said the boy must be beware of black women. They go to a black area and Head says Nelson was born there to his disgust. The elder joks again: "This is where you were born—right here with all these niggers." They want some information about a location or right way for their destination. They enquire a negro woman. She confuses the boy. In a noisy place the boy hurts the ankle of a black woman and the latter demands money for it. But the two whites disown each other and escape the niggers. After hearing the elder's satire about his birth in a black area the younger says with despair: "I never said I was nothing but born here", the boy said in a shaky voice. "I never said I would or wouldn't like it. I never said I wanted to come. I only said I was born here and I never had anything to do with that. It was all your big idea. How you know you ain't following the tracks in the wrong direction" (p. 263). The humour of the two as in a Laurel and Hardy's film is explicit: "Mr. Head looked like an ancient child and Nelson like a miniature old man. They stood gazing at the artificial Negro as if they were faced with some great mystery, some monument to another's victory that brought them together in their common defeat. They could feel it dissolving their difference like an action of mercy. Mr. Head had never known before what mercy felt like because he had been too good to deserve any, but he felt he knew now. He looked at Nelson and understood that he must say something to the child to show that he was still wise and in the look the boy returned he saw a hungry need for that assurance. Nelson's eyes seemed to implore him to explain once and for all the mystery of existence.

Mr. Head opened his lips to make a lofty statement and heard himself say, "They ain't got enough real ones here. They got to have an artificial one."

After a second, the boy nodded with a strange shivering about his mouth and said, "Let's go home before we get ourselves lost again" (p. 269).

Finally the grandfather and the boy go home peacefully. The story is comical.

Flannery O' Conner's other stories too depict a similar kind of predicament. There are a kind of cardboard characters in the story *The Comforts of Home*. In *A View of the Woods* Mr. Fortune tries to save his granddaughter from her cruel and stupid father.

NOTES

1. *Master Plots*, p. 4550.
2. All textual references are from Flannery O' Conner's Short Stories, p. 120.

An Understanding of Allen Ginsberg's Poetry

27

One of the modern America's popular poets is Allen Ginsberg. The new poet was born on 3 June 1926 (he died on 6 April 1997), in Newark, New Jersey, as the younger son of Louis Ginsberg, a high school English teacher and poet and Naomi Levy Ginsberg, also a teacher. Ginsberg grew up with his older brother Eugene in a household shadowed by his mother's mental illness for long. She suffered from recurrent epileptic seizures and paranoia. An active member of the Communist Party, USA, Naomi Ginsberg took her sons to meetings of the radical left dedicated to the cause of international communism during the Great Depression of the 1930s.

In the winter of 1941, when Allen was a junior in high school, his mother insisted that he took her to a therapist at Lakewood, New Jersey. Rest home, a disruptive bus journey he described in his long autobiographical poem "Kaddish". Naomi Ginsberg spent most of the next fifteen years in mental hospitals, enduring the effects of electroshock treatments and a lobotomy before her death at Pilgrim State Hospital in 1956. It is said witnessing his mother's mental illness had a traumatic effect on Ginsberg's mind and he wrote poetry about her unstable condition for the rest of his life.

Allen Ginsberg graduated from Newark's East Side High School in 1943. He later recalled that his most memorable school day was the afternoon his English teacher Frances Durbin read aloud from Walt Whitman's "Song of Myself" in a voice "so enthusiastic and joyous...so confident and lifted with laughter" that he never forgot the image of "her black-dressed bulk seated squat behind an English class desk, her embroidered collar, her voice powerful and high" (quoted in Schumacher, p. 17). Despite his passionate response to Whitman's poetry, Ginsberg listed government or legal work as his choice of future occupation. But he changed his avocation to poetry later.

Allen Ginsberg attended Columbia University on a scholarship. He attended a seminar taught by Lionel Trilling. Later Ginsberg cited the renowned literary critics and biographers Mark Van Doren and Raymond Weaver as influential professors at Columbia. But Ginsberg's friends at Columbia were an even greater influence than his professors on his decision to become a poet. As a freshman he met undergraduates Lucien Carr, William S. Burroughs and Jack Kerouac, part of a diverse (and now legendary) circle of friends that grew to include the Times Square heroin addict Herbert Huncke, the young novelist John Clellon Holmes and a handsome young drifter and car thief from Denver named Neal Cassady, with whom Ginsberg fell in love. Kerouac described the intense encounter between Ginsberg and Cassady in the opening chapter of his novel *On the Road* (1957). Ann Charters says "These friends became the nucleus of a group that named themselves the 'Beat Generation' writers. The term was coined by Kerouac in 1948 during a conversation with Holmes in New York City. The word 'beat' referred loosely to their shared sense of spiritual exhaustion and diffuse feelings of rebellion against what they experienced as the general conformity, hypocrisy, and materialism of the larger society around them caught up in the unprecedented prosperity of postwar America."

As I said Ginsberg decided to become a poet. He said he underwent a vison in which William Blake, a visionary poet came to him as if inspiring him to write poetry. The poet is said to have heard William Blake reciting the poem "Ah! Sunflower". Experimenting with drugs like marijuana and nitrous oxide to induce further visions, or what Ginsberg later described as "an exalted state of mind", he felt that the poet's duty was to bring: "a visionary consciousness of reality to his readers. He was dissatisfied with the poetry he was writing at this time, traditional work modeled on English poets like Sir Thomas Wyatt or Andrew Marvell whom he had studied at Columbia".

In June 1949 Ginsberg was arrested due to a friend's act of stealing. Soon Ginsberg's professors Van Doren and Trilling arranged with the Columbia dean for a plea of psychological disability, on condition that Ginsberg was admitted to the Columbia Presbyterian Psychiatric Institute. The poet spent eight months there befriending the young writer Carl Solomon, who was treated there for depression with insulin shock.

In 1953 Ginsberg left New York City on a trip to Mexico to explore Indian ruins in Yucatan and experiment with various drugs. He settled in San Francisco, where he fell in love with a young artist Peter Orlovsky; he took a job in market research. In 1955, inspired by the manuscript of Korouac's long jazz poem titled "Mexico City Blues" Ginsberg found the courage to begin to type what he called his most personal "imaginative sympathies" in the long poem "Howl for Carl Solomon". In this poem the poet seems to have admitted his homosexuality and he stopped trying to become 'straight'.

In 1955 Ginsberg read the first part of his new poem in public for the first time to tumultuous applause at the Six Gallery reading in San Francisco with the local poets Kenneth Rexroth, Gary Snyder, Michael McClure, Philip Whalen and Philip LaMantia. Journalists were quick to herald the reading as a landmark event in American poetry, the birth of what they labeled the San Francisco Poetry Renaissance. Lawrence Ferlinghetti, who ran the City Lights Book Store and the City Lights publishing house in North Beach, sent Ginsberg a telegram echoing Ralph Waldo Emerson's response to Walt Whitman's Leaves of Grass: "I greet you at the beginning of a great career. When do I get the manuscript?" A part of the first stanza of the poem is as follows:

> I saw the best minds of my generation destroyed by madness, starving hysterical naked,
>
> dragging themselves through the negro streets at dawn looking for an angry fix, angelheaded hipsters burning for the ancient heavenly connection to the starry dynamo in the machinery of night,
>
> who poverty and tatters and hollow-eyed and high sat up

smoking in the supernatural darkness of cold-water flats
floating across the tops of cities contemplating jazz,
who bared their brains to Heaven under the El and saw Mohammedan angels staggering on tene-ment roofs illuminated,
who passed through universities with radiant cool eyes hallucinating
Arkansas and Blake-light tragedy among the
scholars of war,
who were expelled from the academies for crazy & publishing obscene odes on the windows of the skull,
who cowered in unshaven rooms in underwear, burning their money in wastebaskets and listening to the Terror
through the wall,
who got busted in their pubic beards returning through Laredo with a belt of marijuana for New York,
who ate fire in paint hotels or drank turpentine in Paradise Alley, death, or purgatoried their torsos night after night
with dreams, with drugs, with waking nightmares, alcohol and cock and endless balls,
incomparable blind; streets of shuddering cloud and lightning in the mind leaping toward poles of Canada &
Paterson, illuminating all the motionless world of Time between,
Peyote solidities of halls, backyard green tree cemetery dawns, wine
drunkenness over the rooftops, storefront
boroughs of teahead joyride neon blinking traffic light, sun and moon and tree vibrations in the roaring winter dusks
of Brooklyn, ashcan rantings and kind king light of mind,
who chained themselves to subways for the endless ride from Battery to holy Bronx on benzedrine until the noise of
wheels and children brought them down shuddering mouth-wracked and
battered bleak of brain all drained of
brilliance in the drear light of Zoo,

who sank all night in submarine light of Bickford's floated out and sat
through the stale beer after noon in desolate
Fugazzi's, listening to the crack of doom on the hydrogen jukebox,
who talked continuously seventy hours from park to pad to bar to Bellevue to museum to the Brooklyn Bridge,
lost battalion of platonic conversationalists jumping down the stoops off fire escapes off windowsills off Empire State out of the moon,
yacketayakking screaming vomiting whispering facts and memories and anecdotes and eyeball kicks and shocks of hospitals and jails and wars,
whole intellects disgorged in total recall for seven days and nights with brilliant eyes, meat for the Synagogue cast on the pavement,
who vanished into nowhere Zen New Jersey leaving a trail of ambiguous picture postcards of Atlantic City Hall,
suffering Eastern sweats and Tangerian bone-grindings and migraines of China under junk-with drawal in
Newark's bleak furnished room,
who wandered around and around at midnight in the railroad yard wondering where to go, and went, leaving no broken hearts.

Michael McClure writes of 'Howl' thus: "Allen began in a small and intensely lucid voice. At some point Jack Kerouac began shouting 'GO' in cadence as Allen read it. In all of our memories no one had been so outspoken in poetry before—we had gone beyond a point of no return—and we were ready for it, for a point of no return. None of us wanted to go back to the gray, chill, militaristic silence, to the intellective void—to the land without poetry—to the spiritual drabness. We wanted to make it new and we wanted to invent it. We wanted voice and we wanted vision....

Ginsberg read on to the end of the poem, which left us standing in wonder, or cheering and wondering, but knowing at the deepest level that a barrier had been broken, that a human voice and body had been hurled against the harsh wall of America and its supporting armies and navies and academies and institutions and ownership systems and power-support bases.

A week or so later I told Allen that 'Howl' was like Queen Mab—Shelley's first long poem. Howl was Allen's metamorphosis from quiet, brilliant, burning bohemian scholar trapped by his flames and repressions to epic vocal bard. Shelley had made the same transformation."

Ginsberg's great friend-poet William Carlos Williams writes of 'Howl' thus: "It is a howl of defeat. Not defeat at all for he has gone through defeat as if it were an ordinary experience, a trivial experience. Everyone in this life is defeated but a man, if he be a man, is not defeated.... Poets are damned but they are not blind, they see with the eyes of the angels. This poet sees through and all around the horrors he partakes of in the very intimate details of his poem."

Mark Doty writes "The publication of Allen Ginsberg's Howl sounded a cry of rage, and in turn other cries of rage—or downright dismissals—were raised against it." Ginsberg announces himself, in the opening of the volume's title poem, as speaking for his compatriots, naming their collective condition of disaffection: "I saw the best minds of my generation, starving, hysterical, naked". The title poem explicitly identifies itself as a lamentation for those most promising and most excluded from the "American ideal". In a long descriptive catalogue Ginsberg makes clear his contention that the finest have been driven, by what a critic called "the overwhelming pressures of conformity, competition, prestige and respectability", toward madness, dissipation and the outraged enactments of the denied. Not only is he exiled from the tranquilized suburbs by virtue of ethnicity, sexuality, political philosophy and intellectual energy; he also cannot locate in the codified possibilities of American society a tenable way of living. Thus, the speaker inhabits a sort of psychic inferno, a territory of the lost which underlies the flawless, bourgeois vision of American life. "He avoids nothing", William Carlos Williams wrote in his introduction to the volume, "but experiences it to the hilt.... Hold back the edges of your gowns, Ladies, we are going through hell." M.L. Rosenthal offered a more balanced appraisal: "Despite the danger that he will screech himself mute any moment now, he has brought a terrible psychological reality to the surface with enough originality to blast American verse a hair's breadth forward in the process."

"'Howl' lies", as Kenneth Rexroth observed, "in one of the oldest traditions, that of Hosea or the other, angry Minor Prophets of the Bible." The fault for the condition of Ginsberg's generation—and his own violated psychic state—thus lies with "Moloch", the embodiment of the State as evil, the demon of this world. But even in the "belly of Moloch" lies the possibility of transcendence. This tension between existential despair at the political and social conditions of the world and the prophetic optimism of vision would continue to inform all of Ginsberg's work. Transcendence is always possible, even in the shattered universe of Howl—through visionary experience, sex, or chemical transformation of the psyche through drugs: "flower of industry,/ tough spiky ugly flower,/flower nonetheless,/with the form of the great yellow/Rose in your brain." This excerpt from the concluding stanza of the final poem in the volume exemplifies Ginsberg's vision of the possibility of transcendence, a Neoplatonism in the tradition of Blake. The form of the poems in Howl is likewise Blakean and biblical; Ginsberg relied on parallel constructions and long incantatory lines which, like those of Whitman before him, take the form of the King James Bible as their model. Ginsberg fuses his Whitmanic apostrophes and catalogues with verbal play influenced by the prose of Jack Kerouac.

Allen Ginsberg's other poems include his whitmanesque like poem "Sleepers". Here we find much obscenity. For example:

> The married couple sleep calmly in their beds, he with his palm on the hip of the wife, and she with her palm on the hip of the husband,
> The sisters sleep lovingly side by side in their bed,
> The men sleep side by side in theirs,
> Another mother sleeps with her little child carefully wrapt

...
I go from bedside to bedside, I sleep close with the other sleepers
each in turn
...
I roll myself upon you as upon a bed, I resign myself to the dusk

It is said the poem celebrates the theme of homosexuality. Thomas Merrill observes, "Clothes are not only a hindrance to lovemaking; they are the garment of illusion with which men shamefully hide their humanity. Mind, too often, is the grim tailor, which appears to be one of the underlying themes of "Love Poem on a Theme by Whitman". In this poem, the poet shares the nuptial bed of "the bridegroom and the bride" of humanity whose "bodies fallen from heaven stretched out waiting naked and restless" are open to his physical visitation. As he buries his face "in their shoulders and breasts, breathing their skin...bodies locked shuddering naked, hot lips and buttocks screwed into each other", he hears the "bride cry for forgiveness" and the groom "covered with tears of passion and compassion". What is described so sensually is an orgasm of community—a nude coming together of primal human hearts from which the poet rises "up from the bed replenished with last intimate gestures and kisses of farewell".

The other of Ginsberg's poems are 'America', 'A Supermarket in California', 'In Back of the Real', 'Song', 'Sunflower Sutra' and others. 'America' celebrates again a whitmanesque democracy for mankind.

The poem 'Song' is an experimental one. This is about the common thread that binds us all:

The weight of the world
is love.
Under the burden
of solitude,
under the burden
of dissatisfaction
the weight,

the weight we carry
is love.
...
for the burden of life
is love,
but we carry the weight
wearily,
and so must rest
in the arms of love
at last,
must rest in the arms
of love.
No rest
without love,
no sleep
without dreams
of love—

Lydia Howell's poem about Allen Ginsberg is of immense importance for understanding Ginsberg's popularity:

I'm listening for your finger-cymbals,
worn like wedding rings
for your unrecognized husband.
We still need you, Allen Ginsberg,
son of Blake & Walt Whitman.

You shouted your illegal love
from Golden Gate bridge.
Sang love across the Grand Canyon.
Proclaimed love at the Washington Monument.
Prayed love outside the Pentagon.
Danced love over the rooftops of Manhatten.

In this new Plague-time,
when love has married death.
When a shopping mall stands on a sweatshop.
Now, they want our hearts
behind barbed wire and the militarized border.
Padlocked shut.

Oh! playful wanderer & rebel,
we need you now!

They're making new wars.
They're misquoting God.
You would hail all the lovers
to monkey-wrench the killing machine.
Tell us to writhe blissfully
until all the deadly parts stop.
Inspire a strike in every weapons factory.
Disarm the gun of every cop
with a poem, making him remember
he's one of us.

Oh! great chant-sayer!
Summon all the lovers
to finally Ban the Bomb once and for all.
We'd caress the men at the controls
until they abandon their posts.
We could rust all the triggers
with our tears & spit & sweat.

Bearded Puck! dear Allen,
we need you now.
Lead us in shedding our clothes
& skipping thrugh the halls of government.
So they see men, women & children.
Not collateral damage statistics.
Not profit margin.

Read HOWL to the Supreme Court.
Sprinkle love-dust in the Attorney General's eyes.
Take a rose in your teeth
& tango with generals.
Lead us in singing torch songs
that echo every extinct bird,
every murdered man of color,
until they make a shrine
of every death chamber.
Say your poems until CEOs

& their hired torturers
can weep once more.
Embrace the soldiers
until they refuse to go to war
& scribble love-letter on their duty-notice.

We need you now, Allen.
Give us the courage to stand & resist
until the guns & the greed
are transformed into a bad dream
we finally wake from.
The TVs are blasting so loud.
They're banning your poems again.
In the streets, no dancing is allowed.
I'm carrying your book like a secret passport
to the America that we dream is possible.

Now, in our great trouble,
we need you, Allen Ginsberg.
Great sunflower,
grown tall out of the rubble.

Later Ginsberg wrote that "in publishing 'Howl', I was curious to leave behind after my generation an emotional time bomb that would continue exploding in U.S. consciousness in case our military-industrial-nationalist complex solidified into a repressive police bureaucracy".

Early in the following year Howl and Other Poems was published with an introduction by William Carlos Williams. In May 1956 copies of the small black-and-white stapled paperback were seized by the San Francisco police, who arrested Ferlinghetti, the publisher and Shigeyoshi Murao, his shop manager and charged them with publishing and selling an obscene and indecent book. The American Civil Liberties Union took up the defense of Ginsberg's poem in a highly publicized obscenity trial in San Francisco, which concluded in 1957 when Judge Clayton Horn ruled that Howl had redeeming social value. So Allen Ginsberg was read more widely and he became almost a national poet over the night.

During the furor of the trial, Ginsberg left California and settled in Paris with Orlovsky. Then the two went for a world tour. They traveled to Tangier to stay with Burroughs and help him assemble the manuscript later published as his novel *Naked Lunch* (1959). In 1958 Ginsberg returned to New York City, still troubled by his mother's death. Then Ginsberg wrote his greatest poem, "Kaddish for Naomi Ginsberg", modeling his elegy on the traditional Jewish memorial service for the dead.

Ginsberg wanted to experiment for visionary experience. He went to South America, Europe, Morocco and India with Orlovsky in 1962. It was the most important trip of his life. Staying in India for nearly two years, he met many holy men in an effort to find someone who could teach him a method of meditation that would help him deal with his egotism and serve as a vehicle for heightened spiritual awareness. On a train in Japan, Ginsberg recorded in his poem "The Change" his realization that meditation, not drugs, could assist his enlightenment. He returned to North America in 1963 to attend the Vancouver Poetry Conference with Charles Olson, Robert Duncan, Robert Creeley, Denise Levertov and many other poets who felt that they formed a community of non-academic experimental writers.

In 1968 Ginsberg received wide coverage on television during the Democratic National Convention when he and the members of the National Mobilization Committee opposed America's war in Vietnam. Even they confronted the police tear gas and he chanted the Hindu mantra "OM" in an attempt to calm the crowds being brutally attacked. It is said, "Ginsberg's courage, his humanitarian political views and support of homosexuality, his engagement in Eastern meditation practices, and his charismatic personality made him one of the favorite spokesmen chosen by a younger generation of radicalized Americans known as "hippies" during the end of this turbulent decade."

In 1960's, Ginsberg appeared in some of the most famous experimental films of the decade, including the well known Pull My Daisy. His longtime interest in the visual arts—especially photography, a practice encouraged by his longtime friend

Robert Frank—have now been collected in two books, *Photographs* (1991) and *Snapshot Poetics* (1993). Ginsberg's photographs were also represented in a groundbreaking exhibit organized by the Whitney Museum of Art, "Beat Culture and the New America: 1950-1965".

Since 1974, Ginsberg has been a member of the American Institute of Arts and Letters—the highest official recognition. Ginsberg has also been named a Guggenheim fellow and is currently a Distinguished Professor at Brooklyn College. To date, "Howl" has been translated into some 23 languages, including Chinese, Japanese, Czech, Hebrew, Macedonian, Norwegian and Polish. The just published Selected Poems, 1947-1995, chosen by Ginsberg from throughout his long career, collects many of the poet's well known works—and in the words of Ginsberg, "isolates & points attention to work less known, more subtle, rhetorically wild, beyond 'Beat Generation' literary stereotypes".

In 1971 Ginsberg met Chogyam Trungpa Rinpoche, who became his meditation teacher at the Naropa Institute, a Buddhist college in Boulder, Colorado. Three years later, Ginsberg, founded a creative writing program called the Jack Kerouac School of Disembodied Poetics at Naropa. Ginsberg taught summer poetry workshops there and lectured during the academic year at Brooklyn College as a tenured professor until the end of his life.

In the rest of his life Ginsberg traveled widely and gave readings in Russia, China, Europe and the South Pacific. In the bardic tradition of William Blake, who played a pump organ when he read his poetry, Ginsberg often used a portable harmonium bought in Benares (India) for fifty dollars. He was the archetypal Beat Generation writer to countless poetry audiences and to the general public. Unlike Kerouac, who died in 1969, Ginsberg remained a radical poet, the embodiment of the ideals of personal freedom, non-conformity and the search for enlightenment. As a member of the American Academy and Institute of Arts and Letters, he unabashedly used his prestige to champion the work of his friends. Two months short of his seventy-first birthday, he died in 1997, of liver cancer at his home in the East Village, New York City.

Ginsberg's major works include *Reality Sandwiches, 1953-1960* (1963); *Planet News, 1961-1967* (1968); *Indian Journals: March 1962-May 1963* (1970); *The Fall of America: Poems of These States, 1965-1971* (1972), which won the National Book Award; *Mind Breaths: Poems, 1972-1977* (1978); *Plutonium Ode: Poems, 1977-1980* (1982); *Collected Poems: 1947-1980* (1985); *White Shroud: Poems, 1980-85* (1986); *Cosmopolitan Greetings: Poems, 1986-1992* (1994); *Selected Poems, 1947-1995* (1996) and *Death and Fame: Last Poems, 1993-1997* (1999). Bill Morgan compiled the 456-page descriptive Ginsberg bibliography, *The Works of Allen Ginsberg, 1941-1994* (1995). J.W. Ehrlich edited Howl of the Censor (1961), an account of the 1957 San Francisco trial investigating obcenity in Ginsberg's poem. Jane Kramer's *Allen Ginsberg in America*, was an early biography, followed by two full-length biographies: Barry Miles's *Ginsberg* (1989) and Michael Schumacher's *A Critical Biography of Allen Ginsberg* (1992).

Morris Dickinson writes, "Along with Robert Lowell, Ginsberg was the writer most responsible for a great shift in American poetry in the late 1950s. Poetry in the forties and fifties was dominated by formal, metrical, often rhymed verse, densely impacted with wit, irony, and allusion, as in Lowell's early poems. By the mid-fifties, however, both Ginsberg and Lowell had come under the spell of William Carlos Williams, who had worked for decades to bring his poems closer to the supple rhythms of prose and the transparency of spoken language. Ginsberg was also influenced by the jazzlike flow and immediacy of his friend Jack Kerouac's as-yet unpublished fiction."

REFERENCES

Morris Dickstein, *Gates of Eden: American Culture in the Sixties* (1989); Internet material.

Source: http://www.anb.org/articles/16/16-03394.html; American National Biography Online June 2000 Update. Access Date: Sun Mar 18 11:32:26 2001 Copyright (c) 2000 American Council of Learned Societies. Published by Oxford University Press.

Sylvia Plath's Poetry and Fiction

28

Sylvia Plath (1932-63) was a famous American poet and novelist. She is known for her confessional poems as appeared in collections like *Crossing the Water* (1971), *Winter Trees* (1971), *Ariel* (1965) and *Colossus* (1960). Her best known work is *The Bell Jar* (1963), a novel published posthumously in 1963. She has published many short stories, *Johnny Panic and the Bible of Dreams* (1978), letters *Letters Home* (1975) and *Journals of Sylvia Plath* (1983).

Sylvia Plath was born in Boston, Mass., on October 27, 1932 to well educated parents. She lost her father Otto Emil Plat, a Polish when she was just eight years old. Her mother Aurelia Schober, an Austrian, was a staff in a college to support the family. Sylvia attended Smith College and even experienced a nervous breakdown. She graduated in 1955. In the following year, she married a great English poet Ted Hughes when she was doing her education at Cambridge on Fulbright Fellowship. Yet the couple did not live happily and for long. Bored of social constrictions and husband's rigidity in matters of woman's conduct she committed suicide in 1963 in London. Her last days are described in A. Alvarez's book on suicide *The Savage God* (1972).

As is mentioned above Sylvia Plath has written four collections of poems like *Crossing the Water* (1971), *Winter Trees* (1971), *Ariel* (1965) and *Colossus* (1960). Her first book *The Colossus* is known for her themes of pains and losses. She writes about her life's throes. One of her poems, "Spinster" refers to her personal experiences,

And round her house she set

Such a barricade of barb and check
Against mutinous weathers no mere
insurgent man could hope to break
With curse, fist, threat,
Of love, either.[1]

'All the Dead Dears' shows of a kind of experience of kinship with the dead. 'Departure' deals with her specific emotional reactions to a specific situation. 'Hardcastle Crags' shows her reactions to her husband's native land Yorkshire. 'Show' is a distinct and more powerful poem revealing her freshness. 'Two Sisters of Persephone' is a study of two girls with two different attitudes and temperaments. 'Loreler' is a description of a river at night time. 'Snakecharmer' is a beautiful presentation of word picture and imagery. About these poems her husband-poet Ted Hughes writes, "It was a difficult time for her, a life times training and fierce a highly successful effort to prepare herself to teach in a university, with many of her deep compulsions to the same end, where not surrounded so easily. From this year there was not much poetry but it was a decisive time."[2]

In the poem "Aftermath", she tries to recount her painful experiences,

They! loiter and stare as if the house
Burnt—out were theirs, or as if they thought
Some scandal might any minute ooze
From a smoke—choked closet into light;
No deaths, no prodigious injuries
Glut these hunters after an old meat,
Blood spoor of the austere tragedies.[3]

There are many poems like 'The Colossus', 'A Winter Ship', 'The Manor Garden' and 'Who'. In the last poem she talks of her pregnancy and hospital memories. Most of the poems of the collections are nature poems. *The Colossus* and *The Other Poems* are about women's problems.

The second collection *Crossing the Water* consists of thirty-four poems and the poems are full of perfectly realised works. "Wuthering Heights" expresses her feeling of personal isolation.

"Rock Lake Canada" is about her feelings about America in general. "Surgeon at 2 a.m." reveals a fascination with various aspects of surgery and disease. "Small House" is a contrast between expectation and actuality. "Three Women" and that of "Magi" read like Yeats' "Prayer to my Daughter". In "Event" quiet restrained sorrow can be felt. "Stillborn" shows her dissatisfaction with her own work. "Mirror" is another fine poem,

> I am silver and exact. I have no preconceptions.
> Whatever I see I swallow immediately
> Just as it is, unmisted by love or dislike.
> I am not cruel, only truthful.[4]

Crossing the Water constantly confronts the known and the normal with the unknown and the terrible world.

The next book *Winter Trees* has many poems of note. It has two sections. "Three Women" shows the fusion of the public and private. "Mary's Song" displays religious persecution and sacrifice. For example,

> Their thick palls float
> Over the cicatrix of Poland, burnt-out
> Germany.
> They do not die.
> Grey birds obsess my heart,
> Mouth-ash, ash of eye.[5]

"Lesbos" gives an account of a fusion of external and internal landscapes. For example,

> Viciousness in the kitchen!
> The potatoes hiss.
> It is all Hollywood, windowless...
> Stage curtains, a window's frizz[6]

"Rabbit Catcher" presents the dilemmas of Plath's visions and tensions. The theme of oppression is seen in "Purdah".

Ariel, the book of poems, is her posthumous volume published in 1965. Despair and grotesque dominate the poems here. "Elm" begins thus,

> I am inhabited by a cry.

Nightly it flaps out
Looking with its hooks, for something to love

I am terrified by this dark thing
That sleeps in me.[7]

The "Rival" is a poem which focuses on man-woman relationship. "Berck-Plage" celebrates the notion of death. So is the poem "The Arrival of the Bee Box". "Cu" is a sensational poem. "Lady Lazarus" is about the world of pain and suffering. For example,

Dying
Is an art, like everything else.
I do it exceptionally well.[8]

In "A Birthday Present" she talks of rebirth and release. "Kindness" deals with Plath's separation from Ted Hughes. It is said, *Ariel* connects up the themes of female subjectivity, suffering and negativity to the Holocaust and questions of racial identity. "Plath's own consistent and unique challenge, to the way we think about women's identity, writing and madness demands that we read her work beyond the stereotype of self-obsessed and indulgent 'mad-woman-writer' which so often accompanies readings of her life and work."[9]

Sylvia Plath's novel *The Bell Jar* is about an artist. It was originally published under the pseudonym Victoria Lucas as the Victorian women novelists did for attracting male attention and achieving a note of public seriousness. This sardonically comic, autobiographical novel has suffered from uncritical readings of it as solely confessional and a direct reflection of Plath's private life. Here the narrator Esther Greenwood is an aspiring writer and attempts suicide after visiting her father's grave. The novel examines the position of women in the 1950s. It is said, Plath exposes the way in which the stereotype of women's roles limits the talented, ambitious woman's options through Esther's agonized experiments with different types of female identity.

The Bell Jar is about a woman plunged into a crisis so severe that she attempted suicide as the author herself did it. So the novel is autobiographical. It recounts its heroine's rebellion against the constricting forces of society and her psychological conflicts largely resulting from family tensions. Her extraordinary novel *The Bell Jar* reveals however how her identity as a woman writer had a darker subtext in the form of her nervous breakdown.

Sylvia Plath's book of short stores *Johnny Panic and The Bible of Dreams* is a record of her personal life. Plath's short stories display her development as a creative writer. Her stories as well as her novel have the structure of confessional poetry. One such story is "Ocean 1212-W", about her calling upon her grandmother in the sea town where they lived for long until the death of her father. The story was broadcast on the BBC in 1962 and it appeared in *The Listener* in 1963. Actually the title is her grandma's telephone number.

Sylvia Plath's work of letters *Letters Home* forms a kind of autobiography. The letters speak of how she grew up, had her education, particularly at Cambridge, had her love marriage and life with the English poet Ted Hughes. They speak of her complex life, in fact. The family matters are deeply mentioned. The book is a picture of Plath's wax image of herself.

It is said, "Sylvia Plath's *Journals* serves as a background, a supplementary work to understand her emotional undercurrents. Usually her *Journals* began with the description of nature and her mood. It is the description of experiences with peoples and places. Really her mood was always varying. She was always unsatisfied and striving to do some thing concrete in her writing."[10]

NOTES

1. Sylvia Plath, *The Colosus*, London: Faber and Faber, 1960, p. 69.
2. Ted Hughes, Charles Newman, *The Art of Sylvia Plath*, London: Indiana University Press, 1971, p. 190.
3. Sylvia Plath, *The Colosus*, p. 29.
4. *Crossing Waters*, London: Faber and Faber, 1971, p. 52.
5. *Winter Tress,* London: Faber and Faber, 1971, p. 39.
6. *Ibid.,* p. 34.
7. *Ariel,* London: Faber and Faber, 1965, p. 16.
8. *Winter Tress*, p. 7.

9. *Guide to Women's Literature*, ed. by Claire Buck, London: Bloomsbury, 1992, p. 673.
10. N.B. Masal, PhD Thesis "Sylvia Plath: A Critical Study", Shivaji University, Kolhapur, 2006.

Amy Tan's *The Joy Luck Club* as a Work of Magic Realism

29

Amy Tan is a Chinese-American living in America. She has had a kind of international footing in her education and creative writing. Amy Tan was born in Oakland, California in 1952 and grew up in the San Francisco Bay area. She graduated from high school in Montreux, Switzerland and received her master degree in linguistics from San Jose State University. Tan is the author of *The Joy Luck Club, The Kitchen God's Wife, The Hundred Secret Senses* and two books for children, *The Moon Lady* and *The Chinese Siamese Cat.* Her work has been translated into twenty languages. She has been married for the past twenty-two years to Lou DeMattei. They live in San Francisco and New York with their cat, Sagwa and their dog Mr. Zo.

Amy Tan's present book is a kind of new writing. It is part memoir and part children's stories. More so the latter. The book has four sections—Feathers from a Thousand Li Away, The Twenty-Six Malignant Gates, American Translation and Queen Mother of the Western Skies. Each section has as many as four pieces of entertainments, being retold by some fictitious characters. The main characters who narrate the Chinese tales are mothers and daughters. Mothers include Suyuan Woo, An-mei Jong, Lindo Jong and Ying-ying St. Clair and daughters include Jing-mei "June" Woo, Rose Hsu Jordan and Waverly St. Clair. The first section "Feathers from a Thousand Li Away" for example, begins with Jino-mei Woo's "The Joy Luck Club". As a preliminary there are details about some old woman having a swan. She goes to America with it. But the immigration officers do not allow her bird go with her. So she takes a feather of it. Later she gives it to her daughter over there. The title tale *The*

Joy Luck Club is about some Chinese families in America. There are several Chinese with their white kindred and with their American names and customs. They remember their ancestral history. Some of them still follow Chinese culture and practices. Such of them found their Joy Luck Club in 1949 in San Francisco before the author was really born. In fact, the fictitious heroine Jino-mei Woo's mother started it. Their Joy Luck Club does not mean they are happy ever. They have their own miseries. The chief character says, "It's not that we had no heart or eyes for pain. We were all afraid. We all had our miseries." Woo seems to gather at Joy Luck Club in the house of Hsus' house. The leader of the club Uncle George speaks of the Club's programs. He says, "Our capital account is 24,825 dollars. We sold Subaru for a loss at six and three quarters. We bought a hundred shares of Smith international at seven."[1] The Club invests in Canada gold fields. There is reference to Hsu girls—Rose, Ruth and Janice, about the difference between Jewish and Chinese. Mah Jong, the reference to a girl whose mother's swan is mentioned in the preliminary is a sort of heroine here. All people speak of her, her late mother and their Chinese Kwelin story. The story ends with a note of joy.

In the second story "Scar" narrated by An-mei Hsu, we find how a girl, An-mei Hsu, is raised by her mother and grandmother. The two latter ones hated each other. The grandmother (Popo) called the mother as ghost. An-mei Hsu has a brother. The elders are strict with children's morals. References to Chinese polygamy are common. For example, Popo says An-mei Hsu's mother had married a man who had already married one and two concubines. As said above, Popo used to say An-mei Hsu's mother was a ghost. Still An-mei Hsu thinks of knowing about her mother as to why she was called a 'ghost'.

In the third story "The Red Candle", the family of the girl Lindo Jong lives in a valley. The girl Jong lives happily. Once she watches an American movie in which an American soldier falls in love with a girl and tells her to sleep with him promising that he will marry her. So they enjoy a night. He goes back and falls in love with another girl and he maries her. Jong's parents live in the plains of Fen River. Once the river overfloods and drains the whole area where her family lived. So the family vacates their house. Already they have, through a matchmaker, made marriage alliance with Tyan, a young man in the same neighborhood. The girl's family gives its furniture as dowry to the groom's family. They migrate to safer land Wushi, near Shanghai. The girl speaks of her predicament: "This is how I became betrothed to Huang Taitai's son, who I later discovered was just a baby, one year younger than I. His name was Tyan-yu—*tyan* for 'sky', because he was so important, and *yu*, meaning 'leftovers', because when he was born his father was very sick and his family thought he might die. Tyan-yu would be the leftover of his father's spirit. But his father lived and his grandmother was scared the ghosts would turn their attention to this baby boy and take him instead. So they watched him carefully, made all his decisions, and he became very spoiled" (p. 44). The girl is made to follow the family traditions. She says, "Can you see how the Huangs almost washed their thinking into my skin? I came to think of Tyan-yu as a god, someone whose opinions were worth much more than my own life. I came to think of Huang Taitai as my real mother, someone I wanted to please, someone I should follow and obey without question" (p. 51). The wife learns to love her husband, Tyan-yu. Yet he does not have love-feelings. The mother-in-law forces her to sleep with him. She does so. Yet no use. There is a fine servant girl in the family. One day, finally on the festival of Pure Brightness Lindo Jong dreams and she either pretends or tells the reality that she dreamt thus, that the servant girl is really of some royal origin and her husband can marry her for children. The mother-in-law believes this and marries her son to the servant girl. The newlyweds get many issues later. Soon after, Lindo Jong takes a leave of the family and goes to America.

In the next story of the *Joy Luck Club* "The Moon Lady", Ying-ying St. Clair with her sisters, brothers and parents goes to see the Moon Lady on a Moon Festival. Ying-ying St. Clair's father is a history scholar. The fun is at a lake called Tai Lake, the biggest lake in China. The scene is fine with much festivity and mystery. There appears a moon goddess and her husband. The lady sings songs of despair. The lady asks Ying-ying

St. Clair whether she has any wishes. The latter tells she has some, yet she does not reveal them as it is formal. The passage reveals thus: "'I have a wish', I said in a whisper, and still she did not hear me. So I walked closer yet, until I could see the face of the Moon Lady: shrunken cheeks, a broad oily nose, large glaring teeth, and red-stained eyes. A face so tired that she wearily pulled of her hair, her long gown fell from her shoulders. And as the secret wish fell from my lips, the Moon Lady looked at me and became a man."

Part Two is "The Twenty-Six Malignant Gates". The first story is "Rules of the Game" and its heroine is Waverly Jong. The preliminary is interesting. Here a mother asks her daughter not to ride a bicycle in corners. If she does she might fall down. The girl argues against it. She asks the mother about its authenticity. The latter says it is in the book *Twenty-Six Malignant Gates*. The girl argues against it and as soon as she rides she falls down. This serves for a parable. The girl Waverly Jong is six when the story opens. Her brothers and she learn the secrets of chess. She wins it all. Later she plays with a man called Lau Po and he defeats her every time, of course, teaching her the secrets of the game. Later she goes on playing in all rounds, even upto the national level. She wins everywhere in America. On the other hand, she becomes lonely as her mother does not cooperate with her station and dignity. The story ends thus, "I closed my eyes and pondered my next move" (p. 103).

In the story "The Voice from the Wall", we find the main character Lena St. Clair enacting her predicament. The story begins thus: "When I was little, my mother told me my great-grandfather had sentenced a beggar to die in the worst possible way, and that later the dead man came back and killed my great-grandfather. Either that, or he died of influenza one week later" (p. 104). She says she used to think the role of the beggar's ghost. She says "she saw devils dancing feverishly beneath a hole I had dug in the sandbox"(p. 106). The girl's father is an English-Irish. She says she also stayed in China. It is said, the girl's mother was scared of often. She spoke in moods and silences. The family of Lena St. Clair moves from their home in Oakland to San Francisco. Lena St. Clair remembers of her school education.

She remembers of her mother's second delivery with pain and the death of the baby. She says her mother looked like a 'living ghost'. At the end of the story a reference to Lena St. Clair's two neighbors—Teresa and Mrs Sorci is mentioned. The story is a sort of magic realism.

In the next story, Rose Hsu Jordan's "Half and Half" we find Rose Jordan's family story. Rose has a mother and four brothers—Matthew, Mark, Luke and Bing. She has three sisters. The mother, who was once a theist, does not believe god or the Bible. The story proceeds. One day Rose Jordan marries a man called Ted, a doctor. Rose Jordan tells why she married Ted: "I have to admit that what I initially found attractive in Ted were precisely the things that made him different from my brothers and the Chinese boys I had dated: his brashness; the assuredness in which he asked for things and expected to get them; his opinionated manner; his angular face and lanky body; the thickness of his arms; the fact that his parents immigrated from Tarrytown, New York, not Tientsin, China" (p. 123). One day Ted invited the girl for picnic and there his mother liked Rose Jordan. The two married and their life was one. They were like yin and yang as the Chinese say. Later the doctor lost a malpractice against one of his patients. Then he got some disillusionment in life. He depended upon his wife for everything for some time. One day he went to Los Angeles and said her on phone that he wanted a divorce. What he did is he followed some prostitute girl and lived with her some time. Even he loved a concubine daughter later. In fact, the latter belonged to Rose Jordan's clan. And he died.

Rose Jordan suffered much. This makes Rose's mother lose her faith in god. But one day when the brothers and sisters go to a beach for picnic, they lose their brother Bing in the sea tides. The mother suddenly turns theistic. She takes the Bible in one hand and rides her car to the beach for the recovery of the boy. But no use. The mother is superstitious as most Chinese are. She believed in the 'twenty-six malignant gates'. Rose Jordan remarks ironically, "I know now that I never expected to find Bing, just as I know now I will never find a way to save my marriage. My mother tells me, though, that I should still try" (p. 139).

The section "American Translation" has another four stories. The first story is Lena St. Clair's "Rice Husband". The story begins thus: "To this day, I believe my mother has the mysterious ability to see things before they happen.... I remembered this ability of my mother's, because now she is visiting my husband and me in the house we just bought in Woodside. And I wonder what she will see" (p. 162).

Lena St. Clair and her husband Herald work in some architectural firm. Herald is a concept man, the chief architect and designer. There are details about Lena's romance with Herald as a special man. Details about their life based upon the figure "fifty-fifty" is mentioned. The following passage talks of their American life for standardization: "During dinner, Harold keeps the conversation going. He talks about the plans for the house: the skylights, expanding the deck, planting flower beds of tulips and crocuses, clearing the poison oak, adding another wing, building a Japanese-style tile bathroom. And then he clears the table and starts stacking the plates in the dishwater" (p. 177).

Lena St. Clair tells that she and her husband develop some sort of difference gradually. As she says, "And now I don't know what to think. What am I saying? What's he saying? We sit in the room, not saying anything" (p. 180).

The last section "Queen Mother of the Western Skies", has another four stories—"An-mei Hsu: Magpies", "Ying-Ying St. Clair: Waiting Between", "Lindo Jong: Double Face" and "Jing-mei Woo: A Pair of Tickets". The second one is of interest. Here Ying-ying St. Clair writes of her existential crisis. The girl writes, "When I was a young girl in Wushi, I was *lihai*. Wild and stubborn. I wore a smirk on my face. Too good to listen. That is why her mother named her 'Ying-ying'. When she was 16 her aunt married and went off. Later a man came there and her kins asked her to marry him. Lena St. Clair says there are many women in her house. She is her father's wife's only daughter while many others, his concubines' daughters—her half sisters.

She marries the man and he is a businessman. Lena St. Clair gets a baby. But afterwards, her husband does not love her. He stays out of the station. So the young woman writes of her despair: "What I did not know is that the north wind is the coldest. It penetrates the heart and takes the warmth away. The wind gathered such a force that it blew my husband past my bedroom and out the back door. I found out from my youngest aunt that he had left me to live with an opera singer" (p. 281). Lena St. Clair is unhappy. So she suffers from despair. Even she kills her baby out of hatredness for her husband. It is conjectured that he has eloped with one of her half-sisters. Even she goes out from her mother-in-law's house. After ten years she turns out to be a strange woman. She serves in a shop in China. She lives in China for many years. She hears the death of her husband. Then suddenly she finds a chance to fall in love with a Chinese-American Mr. Saint. He marries her and she goes back to America. This is something like a family reunion. She writes about the return of her joys: "Saint took me to America where I lived in houses smaller than the one in the country. I wore large American clothes. I did servant's tasks. I learned the western ways. I tried to speak with a thick tongue. I raised a daughter, watching her from another shore. I accepted her American ways" (p. 286).

NOTE

1. All the textual references are to Amy Tan's *The Joy Luck Club*, New York: Ivy Books, 1995, p. 12.

The "Ghost of the Past" in Toni Morrison's *Beloved*

30

Toni Morrison is a great American novelist. She is a Black writer. More than that, she is a feminist. Toni Morrison was born in Lorain, Ohio in 1931. She received an undergraduate degree in English from Howard University and completed a master's program at Cornell. When many of her classmates had difficulty pronouncing her uncommon name, Chloe she changed it to Toni, a derivative of her middle name. In 1958 she married Harold Morrison, an architect from Jamaica and the couple had two sons. They divorced six years later. After pursuing an academic career teaching English at Howard, Morrison became an editor at Random House, where she specialized in Black fiction. She now divides her time between Rockland County, New York and Princeton, New Jersey. She is Robert S. Goheen Professor, Council of Humanities, at Princeton University. She is the author of seven novels so far: *The Bluest Eye, Sula, Song of Solomon,* which won her the 1978 National Book Critics' Circle Award for fiction; *Tar Baby, Beloved* which won her the 1998 Pulitzer Prize for fiction, *Jazz* and most recently *Paradise.* Toni Morrison was awarded the Nobel Prize for Literature in 1993.

The theme of Toni Morrison's *Beloved* is: "It is the mid-1800's. At Sweet Home in Kentucky, an era is ending as slavery comes under attack from the abolitionists. The worlds of Halle and Paul D. are to be destroyed in a cataclysm of torment and agony. The world of Sethe, however, is to turn from one of love to one of violence and death—the death of Sethe's baby daughter Beloved, whose name is the single world on the tombstone, who died at her mother's hands, and who will return to claim retribution."

Toni Morrison's *Beloved* that fetched her Pulitzer Award is thematically a masterpiece. The novel is set during the Reconstruction era in 1873. The novel centers on the powers of memory and history. The former slaves think that their past is a burden and they try to forget it. Yet for Sethe, the protagonist of the novel, memories of slavery are inescapable. They continue to haunt her, literally in the spirit of her diseased daughter. Eighteen years earlier, Sethe had murdered this daughter in order to save her from a life of slavery. Morrison borrowed the event from the real story of Margaret Garner, who, like Sethe, escaped from slavery in Kentucky and murdered her child when slave catchers caught up with her in Ohio. *Beloved* straddles the line between fiction and history; from the experience of a single family, Morrison creates a powerful commentary on the psychological and historical legacy of slavery. The Spart Notes records that, "Part of Morrison's project in *Beloved* is to recuperate a history that had been lost to the ravages of forced silences and willed forgetfulness. Morrison writes Sethe's story with the voices of a people who historically have been denied the power of language. Beloved also contains a didactic element. From Sethe's experience we learn that before a stable future can be created, we must confront and understand the 'ghosts' of the past. Morrison suggests that, like Sethe, contemporary American readers must confront the history of slavery in order to address its legacy, which manifests itself in ongoing racial discrimination and discord. Many readers believe Morrison's novels go a long way toward the establishment of her envisioned tradition. The poetic elegant style of her writing in *Beloved* panders to no one. Morrison challenges and requires the reader to accept her on her terms."[1]

The novel is divided into three parts and each part has similar sections which we may take as chapters going upto 26. *Beloved* begins thus: "124 (Bluestone Road, Cincinnati, Ohio. The time is that of 1873) was spiteful. Full of a baby's venom."[2] The novel has two parts thematically. It is knit around part past and part present. The two are interdependent. *Beloved* is like a half sunken ice in water. The first part narrates, partly through memory and partly through history, making use of myths, symbols and the supernatural, the story of former slaves of Kentucky. The novel starts in 1873 in the protagonist's house 124 Bluestone Road, Cincinnati, Ohio. The landlady Sethe and her 18 years old daughter Denver have been living in Baby Sugg's house haunted by the ghost of Sethe's firstborn daughter whom she murdered years ago just to avoid her suffer in the hands of white masters' oppression. Now the two are living in the house which is haunted by the old daughter's spirit to such an extent that Sethe's two sons—Howard and Bugler—each ran away from there following an encounter with their sister's ghost. Most of Sethe's painful memories involve Sweet Home, a plantation in Kentucky where she lived as a slave until her escape 18 years ago. The novel opens with Paul D's visit to Sethe. Paul D was one of the many slaves at Mr. Garner's estate. The other slaves were Paul D's two brothers Paul A and Paul F, Sethe's husband Halle and Sixo. Paul D finds Sethe's life in a pool of red light and feels grief. Sethe explains that the presence of the sad specter of her dead baby whose throat was cut before it was two years old. Sethe had named her "Beloved" just because she has heard a sermon with that expression then. She slept with an engraver for ten minutes just because he carved "Beloved" on the tombstone of that girl. Baby Suggs left her son Halle as he bought her freedom by extra-working weekends for five years. She settled down in Cincinnati, in house gifted to her by a white abolitionist. She passed away eight years ago as she was depressed due to her son Halle's mysterious end and also due to the ghost. One must remember the fact that Suggs had eight sons from six men and except Halle all were taken away and sold. After all, she had with him, lost all her sons. When in Kentucky Sethe and Halle had a girl and two boys and she was pregnant when she escaped white man's hunt for slaves. Neither Paul D nor Sethe knows what happened to Halle. Once Paul D stays with Sethe he notices the Sethe family in dread and isolation. This is more so with Denver. Paul D fights the ghost and annoys Denver as she loved the ghost.

One needs to remember the old story in flashback. When Sethe arrived at Kentucky after Suggs was liberated by her son Halle, she was liked by all. The Paul brothers and Sixo pined after her. Halle too. Finally she married Halle because she loved his idea of freedom. Now Paul D remembers all that and loves Sethe.

The third chapter has many memories of the past as Paul D revives them. First of all, Sethe speaks to the ghost of her dead baby; secondly she remembers to Denver that she was pregnant when she escaped from the Sweet Home, from the clutches of the schoolteacher (after the death of Mr. Garner, Mrs. Garner asked her brother-in-law, the so-called 'Schoolteacher' to help her run the estate. The man came there with two of his nephews who were crueler than him. He was a schoolteacher or called so). Sethe ran into a forest and fell exhausted. A white sympathetic girl Amy Denver, who was going to Boston, nursed her back to life and even helped her deliver a baby whom Sethe named Denver in honor of that love. There Sethe lied to Denver her name as 'Lu' as, in case she was found out she would be taken back to Sweet Home. Sethe tells Denver, her daughter that she was thinking about 'time, memory and the past'. In Sethe's philosophy, "nothing ever dies". The past re-lives in the present, in the real world. Paul D remembers how the schoolteacher finished Sixo and made Paul D suffer at Alfred, Georgia. After that Paul D tried to forget his past. "Walk, eat, sleep and sing" were the bywords for him. Now Sethe thinks he is a hope for her future.

When Denver feels isolated and Sethe unhappy, Paul D comes to them as a hope. The three participate in the town's carnival. Paul D promises Sethe that she can safely re-enter her past because he will be there to catch her if she falls. He helps reintegrate Sethe and Denver into the community. The symbol of their shadows in 'togetherness' is optimistic for the 'ruined maid'.

When the three return home, they notice a strange phenomenon that a fully dressed woman has arrived and sleeping there. They pick the young lady whose name is 'Beloved'. Beloved does not remember anything of her past. She drinks lots of water and sleeps for long. As soon as Beloved is come there, the dog 'Boy' disappears mysteriously. Denver cares for Beloved. Sethe is happy about Beloved. They think that

Beloved is their resurrected daughter or daughter-incarnate. Only Paul D is uneasy.

Beloved develops a strange attachment with Sethe. Denver likes her as well. Sethe, though disliked her past, pours her past to her. Beloved asks her about her mother. Sethe says she did not see her mother properly. She remembers her mother and her friend Nan came from Africa. A white crew raped them several times. Sethe's mother had many babies from the white fathers and she threw them to sea. She did not throw Sethe because she was born to a Black man and Sethe was named after him. She mentions that her mother was hanged.

Beloved is grown tall and beautiful and she attracts Paul D. He interrogates her about her past which, however, Sethe dislikes. Paul D remembers how Halle suffered the agony of insult when Sethe was harassed sexually by schoolteacher's nephews. This annoys Sethe. Not to speak of Paul D has his own agony of shame and pain. So he has kept it secret calling it as 'Tobacco tin' of his heart. There is a fine discourse between the mother and two daughters and between Denver and Beloved. The latter asks how Denver was born and all that. Denver interrogates Beloved as to how she came from the 'dark'.

Sethe remembers how she was rescued by the white lady Amy Denver and with her help, she delivered her babe in her boat journey. Afterwards, she was rescued by Stamp Paid. Ella also helped her. Ella asked Sethe not to love anything too much as life is ephemeral. Stamp Paid and Ella worked at the Underground Railroad, a Black association. Sethe got to her mother-in-law's house 124 in Bluestone Road. Baby Suggs produced her girl child and two sons—Howard and Buglar. Sethe nursed her last girl child Denver. In those days Baby Suggs preached the Black at Clearing in Cincinnati. She would instruct them to love their hands that had been bound, their mouths that had been silenced and, most of all, their hearts.

Sethe lived 28 days as a free person. One day the schoolteacher came to claim her back. Then she killed 'Beloved' just to avoid her children get tortured by the whites. Now she wanted to kill the rest of the children. But Stamp Paid and Baby Suggs saved them. Now she preferred to get jailed with Denver who had helped her. She was released later. The schoolteacher, in disgust, went off.

In the tenth chapter Paul D recounts his experience. He knows how he was sold to Brandywine from the 'Sweet Home'. The new master took him to Alfred in Georgia State. There, the Blacks were asked to work in chained gangs. One day when there was a rainstorm, Paul D escaped. Somebody told him to go northward following the bloom of some flowers. In Delaware he met a weaver woman and lived with her for the next 18 months.

Paul D feels inexplicably restless and uncomfortable in Sethe's house. So he sleeps outside even when it is cold. But Beloved tempts him for sex.

Denver's attachment to Beloved intensifies. In fact, she surrenders herself, loses herself. This is also bad for her. She cannot lose her identity and cannot go on listening to Sethe and Beloved's past. Denver wants to live in the present. One day Denver and Beloved go to a cold house where Beloved disappears in the dark and when she returns she defines her as "This the place I am".

Sethe and Paul D continue their affairs in a doubtful manner. He feels to have children from her which she refuses. She thinks Beloved like Ella may be an 'escape' from some captivity.

Chapter 15 is a reflection of Baby Suggs' past that she was given of her freedom. She was called Jenny, the name on the bill of her sale. She was offered the house 124 from the Bodwins, the white abolitionists.

It is said "White people believed that...under every dark skin was a jungle.... In a way, Stamp Paid thought they were right.... But it wasn't the jungle blacks brought with them.... It was the jungle white folks planted in them. And it grew until it invaded the whites" (p. 26).

One day Paul D goes off without a notice. Sethe and Denver go to ice-skating for pleasure. Sethe thinks Beloved is virtually her 'resurrected daughter'. Stamp Paid who pays a visit to the family meditates upon Beloved's mystery. He too has his own mystery. He, when a slave, was forced to ask his wife to sleep with his white master and his son. Thus, he paid back his wife, Vashti. Therefore, he (Joshua) is called 'Stamp Paid'. Sethe now worked in a restaurant and she brought her food home. Sometimes, she stole a part of it. She felt bad too. She remembered how Sixo once stole his master's small pig. When the schoolteacher blamed him of it, Sixo said after all he was his servant. This hurt the master and he treated the Blacks cruelly. He said: "Definitions belonged to the definers—not to the defined." He treated slaves like farm stock. The schoolteacher even disallowed Halle to work outside on holidays to earn his freedom at the earliest. When the slaves tried to escape he oppressed them. For example, Halle went insane; Paul A was hanged, Sixo was burned and Paul D ended up with a bit of iron in his mouth. The chapter ends with Stamp's thought about how slavery dehumanizes everyone involved, including whites. By defining the blacks as 'jungle-like' the whites 'plant' resentment among the blacks that burgeons into a real, 'jungle' anger. The whites, in turn, become so frightened of their own creation that they too, begin to behave brutally, like animals. The jungle, Stamp thinks, touches everyone, but it is normally hidden.

Chapter 20 is about Sethe, 21 about Denver and 22 about Beloved. There is a series of stream of consciousness monologues. In chapter 20 Sethe tells Beloved that she is her daughter-incarnate. She killed her just to die herself and be buried with her. She knew how her own mother was hanged. In the next chapter, Denver speaks emotionally. She thinks, like Beloved, her father Halle may come to them one day. In chapter 22 Beloved tells Sethe not to leave her. Beloved's speech is fragmented and complex. She speaks of thirst and hunger, of death and sickness and of men without skin. She says 'she is alone'. There are many poetic passages. Beloved says Sethe that she lost her mother and she gained her again. She asks Sethe that she should not lose her again.

Paul D who is resting in the local church basement is filled with despair. He remembers his two brothers and he does not know anything about his parents. Paul D feels alienated. He remembers how Mr. Garner called him 'no man'.

Gradually Beloved becomes a source of trouble to everyone. She eats all the food and behaves badly even with Sethe. Sethe, as a result, wastes away. Denver leaves the house for her future. One day, Stamp Paid, Ella and all others visit 124 and scold Beloved. Sethe mistakes the Bodwins for schoolteacher and tries to kill him. Sethe's fear is unfounded. The novel ends with Beloved's disappearance.

NOTES

1. Spart Notes, Google Internet, p. 1.
2. All the textual references are from Toni Morrison's *Beloved*, London: Vintage, 2005.